C-4766   CAREER EXAMINATION SERIES

This is your
PASSBOOK for...

Supervisory Test Battery (STB)

Test Preparation Study Guide
Questions & Answers

NATIONAL LEARNING CORPORATION®

COPYRIGHT NOTICE

This book is SOLELY intended for, is sold ONLY to, and its use is RESTRICTED to individual, bona fide applicants or candidates who qualify by virtue of having seriously filed applications for appropriate license, certificate, professional and/or promotional advancement, higher school matriculation, scholarship, or other legitimate requirements of education and/or governmental authorities.

This book is NOT intended for use, class instruction, tutoring, training, duplication, copying, reprinting, excerption, or adaptation, etc., by:

1) Other publishers
2) Proprietors and/or Instructors of "Coaching" and/or Preparatory Courses
3) Personnel and/or Training Divisions of commercial, industrial, and governmental organizations
4) Schools, colleges, or universities and/or their departments and staffs, including teachers and other personnel
5) Testing Agencies or Bureaus
6) Study groups which seek by the purchase of a single volume to copy and/or duplicate and/or adapt this material for use by the group as a whole without having purchased individual volumes for each of the members of the group
7) Et al.

Such persons would be in violation of appropriate Federal and State statutes.

PROVISION OF LICENSING AGREEMENTS – Recognized educational, commercial, industrial, and governmental institutions and organizations, and others legitimately engaged in educational pursuits, including training, testing, and measurement activities, may address request for a licensing agreement to the copyright owners, who will determine whether, and under what conditions, including fees and charges, the materials in this book may be used them. In other words, a licensing facility exists for the legitimate use of the material in this book on other than an individual basis. However, it is asseverated and affirmed here that the material in this book CANNOT be used without the receipt of the express permission of such a licensing agreement from the Publishers. Inquiries re licensing should be addressed to the company, attention rights and permissions department.

All rights reserved, including the right of reproduction in whole or in part, in any form or by any means, electronic or mechanical, including photocopying, recording, or by any information storage and retrieval system, without permission in writing from the Publisher.

Copyright © 2024 by
National Learning Corporation

212 Michael Drive, Syosset, NY 11791
(516) 921-8888 • www.passbooks.com
E-mail: info@passbooks.com

PUBLISHED IN THE UNITED STATES OF AMERICA

PASSBOOK® SERIES

THE *PASSBOOK® SERIES* has been created to prepare applicants and candidates for the ultimate academic battlefield – the examination room.

At some time in our lives, each and every one of us may be required to take an examination – for validation, matriculation, admission, qualification, registration, certification, or licensure.

Based on the assumption that every applicant or candidate has met the basic formal educational standards, has taken the required number of courses, and read the necessary texts, the *PASSBOOK® SERIES* furnishes the one special preparation which may assure passing with confidence, instead of failing with insecurity. Examination questions – together with answers – are furnished as the basic vehicle for study so that the mysteries of the examination and its compounding difficulties may be eliminated or diminished by a sure method.

This book is meant to help you pass your examination provided that you qualify and are serious in your objective.

The entire field is reviewed through the huge store of content information which is succinctly presented through a provocative and challenging approach – the question-and-answer method.

A climate of success is established by furnishing the correct answers at the end of each test.

You soon learn to recognize types of questions, forms of questions, and patterns of questioning. You may even begin to anticipate expected outcomes.

You perceive that many questions are repeated or adapted so that you can gain acute insights, which may enable you to score many sure points.

You learn how to confront new questions, or types of questions, and to attack them confidently and work out the correct answers.

You note objectives and emphases, and recognize pitfalls and dangers, so that you may make positive educational adjustments.

Moreover, you are kept fully informed in relation to new concepts, methods, practices, and directions in the field.

You discover that you are actually taking the examination all the time: you are preparing for the examination by "taking" an examination, not by reading extraneous and/or supererogatory textbooks.

In short, this PASSBOOK®, used directedly, should be an important factor in helping you to pass your test.

SUPERVISORY TEST BATTERY

The Supervisory Test Battery (STB) measures a candidate's ability to effectively handle a variety of situations which a supervisor would likely face. Typically, the STB is the only evaluation instrument administered for supervisory level titles that are included in this program. However, if candidates for a particular job announcement have not been adequately assessed in prior positions with respect to their technical, non-supervisory knowledge and abilities, a second test component covering these technical areas may also be administered.

The STB is a work simulation. Candidates are asked to assume the role of a supervisor in a fictitious organization. No special knowledge regarding the work of this fictitious organization is required in advance. Candidates are provided with a booklet of background information about the organization, along with a booklet containing in-basket items, such as memos and letters. Candidates are given a total of 3 hours and 15 minutes to answer the 89 questions on this test. Additional time has been built into this total time to allow candidates an opportunity to review the background information and in-basket item booklets. Candidates are encouraged to spend at least 30 minutes reviewing this material prior to answering any questions. After this review, candidates may then begin answering multiple-choice test questions on a computer. Test questions deal with issues, tasks, situations, decisions, etc., that the candidate will need to handle as a supervisor in the fictitious organization. The candidate may keep the background information and booklet of memos and letters throughout the examination and may refer to them at any point during the test.

This test is administered via computer. Candidates do not use the computer keyboard when they take the test. The computer's mouse is used to point and click on their selected answers. Please be aware that candidates may not "skip" over questions presented on the computer. They must choose an answer to each question before they can move forward to answer the next question. Since the STB attempts to simulate real life situations, successive questions may contain information not available earlier. For this reason, candidates are not permitted to go backwards to change their answers on any questions they have already completed. A countdown clock is displayed on the computer screen which shows candidates how much time is remaining to finish the test. Candidates receive their test scores when they finish the test and will know immediately whether they passed or failed the STB. A copy of their test results will also be emailed to candidates at the address provided during their initial login to the examination.

Since this exam simulates actual situations that may occur on the job, it's possible that a question may contain more than one acceptable response. That is, as in life, there may be more than one way to appropriately address a situation, but some ways may be better than others. To represent this in a testing situation, we use differentially weighted options for each question. Each option presented for a given question will carry a test weight from 0.0 to 0.8 depending on how well it addresses the situation posed in the question. The score, received immediately after completing the test, will be a raw score which is equal to the sum of scores across all questions. When candidates are notified of their test results by mail, they will receive their rank on the eligible list and their final scores. Final scores on test result notices will be shown in terms of a percentage score that may include seniority and PAR points in the case of state promotional announcements. Therefore, in every case, the percentage scores which appear on candidate notices will differ from the raw scores received at the test center.

Any eligible list that is generated as a result of the STB has a list duration of two years. A candidate's test score is typically banked for five years for possible future use. That is, should a candidate apply to a future STB announcement within this five year period, his STB score will be applied to that new announcement. Candidates, however, may retake the STB after one year in response to a future announcement for which they are eligible. Since this test will be used repeatedly in the future, candidates will not be permitted to review its content (i.e., the test questions and answers).

The five year period for which a candidate's STB score is valid may be reduced if a new version of the test is scheduled for release. In this situation, candidates will be notified that the STB score they attain will be banked and usable only until the date on which the new test version is released.

The Supervisory Test Battery has been extensively reviewed by supervisors and managers from various occupations and agencies. They have served as subject matter experts to determine that the test content accurately represents competencies that are required in supervisory positions. Also, through research and job analyses conducted throughout the state, these competency areas have been found to be important for a supervisor to possess to perform well in a wide variety of public sector positions.

Below is a list of some of the major competency areas associated with the STB.

- **PROBLEM SOLVING** — Identifies and analyzes problems; uses sound reasoning to arrive at conclusions; finds alternative solutions to complex problems; distinguishes between relevant and irrelevant information to make logical judgments.
- **LEADERSHIP** - Inspires, motivates, guides and directs others toward goal accomplishment; coaches, supports, mentors, and challenges subordinates. Adapts leadership styles to a variety of situations. Inspires others by modeling high standards of behavior (e.g. courage, honesty, trust, openness, and respect for others, etc.) and by applying these values to daily behaviors.
- **DECISION-MAKING** - Makes sound and well-informed decisions; perceives the impact and implications of decisions; commits to action and causes change, even in uncertain situations, in order to accomplish organizational goals.
- **INTERPERSONAL SKILL** - Considers and responds appropriately to the needs, feelings, and capabilities of others; adjusts approaches to suit different people and situations. Develops and maintains collaborative and effective working relationships with others.
- **HUMAN RESOURCE MANAGEMENT** - Empowers people by sharing power and authority; develops lower levels of leadership by pushing authority downward and outward throughout the organization; shares rewards for achievement with employees; ensures that staff are appropriately selected, utilized, appraised, and developed and that they are treated in a fair and equitable manner.
- **COMMUNICATION** - Expresses facts and ideas both orally and in writing in a succinct, clear, accurate, thorough, organized and effective manner. Reviews, proofreads and edits written work constructively. Presents facts to individuals or groups effectively; makes clear convincing oral presentations; listens to others; facilitates an open exchange of ideas.
- **TEAM BUILDING** - Manages group processes; encourages and facilitates cooperation, pride, trust, and group identity; fosters commitment and team spirit; works with others to achieve goals.
- **CONFLICT MANAGEMENT** - Manages and resolves conflicts, confrontations, and disagreements in a positive and constructive manner to minimize negative personal impact.

HOW TO TAKE A TEST

I. YOU MUST PASS AN EXAMINATION

A. WHAT EVERY CANDIDATE SHOULD KNOW

Examination applicants often ask us for help in preparing for the written test. What can I study in advance? What kinds of questions will be asked? How will the test be given? How will the papers be graded?

As an applicant for a civil service examination, you may be wondering about some of these things. Our purpose here is to suggest effective methods of advance study and to describe civil service examinations.

Your chances for success on this examination can be increased if you know how to prepare. Those "pre-examination jitters" can be reduced if you know what to expect. You can even experience an adventure in good citizenship if you know why civil service exams are given.

B. WHY ARE CIVIL SERVICE EXAMINATIONS GIVEN?

Civil service examinations are important to you in two ways. As a citizen, you want public jobs filled by employees who know how to do their work. As a job seeker, you want a fair chance to compete for that job on an equal footing with other candidates. The best-known means of accomplishing this two-fold goal is the competitive examination.

Exams are widely publicized throughout the nation. They may be administered for jobs in federal, state, city, municipal, town or village governments or agencies.

Any citizen may apply, with some limitations, such as the age or residence of applicants. Your experience and education may be reviewed to see whether you meet the requirements for the particular examination. When these requirements exist, they are reasonable and applied consistently to all applicants. Thus, a competitive examination may cause you some uneasiness now, but it is your privilege and safeguard.

C. HOW ARE CIVIL SERVICE EXAMS DEVELOPED?

Examinations are carefully written by trained technicians who are specialists in the field known as "psychological measurement," in consultation with recognized authorities in the field of work that the test will cover. These experts recommend the subject matter areas or skills to be tested; only those knowledges or skills important to your success on the job are included. The most reliable books and source materials available are used as references. Together, the experts and technicians judge the difficulty level of the questions.

Test technicians know how to phrase questions so that the problem is clearly stated. Their ethics do not permit "trick" or "catch" questions. Questions may have been tried out on sample groups, or subjected to statistical analysis, to determine their usefulness.

Written tests are often used in combination with performance tests, ratings of training and experience, and oral interviews. All of these measures combine to form the best-known means of finding the right person for the right job.

II. HOW TO PASS THE WRITTEN TEST

A. NATURE OF THE EXAMINATION

To prepare intelligently for civil service examinations, you should know how they differ from school examinations you have taken. In school you were assigned certain definite pages to read or subjects to cover. The examination questions were quite detailed and usually emphasized memory. Civil service exams, on the other hand, try to discover your present ability to perform the duties of a position, plus your potentiality to learn these duties. In other words, a civil service exam attempts to predict how successful you will be. Questions cover such a broad area that they cannot be as minute and detailed as school exam questions.

In the public service similar kinds of work, or positions, are grouped together in one "class." This process is known as *position-classification*. All the positions in a class are paid according to the salary range for that class. One class title covers all of these positions, and they are all tested by the same examination.

B. FOUR BASIC STEPS

1) Study the announcement

How, then, can you know what subjects to study? Our best answer is: "Learn as much as possible about the class of positions for which you've applied." The exam will test the knowledge, skills and abilities needed to do the work.

Your most valuable source of information about the position you want is the official exam announcement. This announcement lists the training and experience qualifications. Check these standards and apply only if you come reasonably close to meeting them.

The brief description of the position in the examination announcement offers some clues to the subjects which will be tested. Think about the job itself. Review the duties in your mind. Can you perform them, or are there some in which you are rusty? Fill in the blank spots in your preparation.

Many jurisdictions preview the written test in the exam announcement by including a section called "Knowledge and Abilities Required," "Scope of the Examination," or some similar heading. Here you will find out specifically what fields will be tested.

2) Review your own background

Once you learn in general what the position is all about, and what you need to know to do the work, ask yourself which subjects you already know fairly well and which need improvement. You may wonder whether to concentrate on improving your strong areas or on building some background in your fields of weakness. When the announcement has specified "some knowledge" or "considerable knowledge," or has used adjectives like "beginning principles of..." or "advanced ... methods," you can get a clue as to the number and difficulty of questions to be asked in any given field. More questions, and hence broader coverage, would be included for those subjects which are more important in the work. Now weigh your strengths and weaknesses against the job requirements and prepare accordingly.

3) Determine the level of the position

Another way to tell how intensively you should prepare is to understand the level of the job for which you are applying. Is it the entering level? In other words, is this the position in which beginners in a field of work are hired? Or is it an intermediate or advanced level? Sometimes this is indicated by such words as "Junior" or "Senior" in the class title. Other jurisdictions use Roman numerals to designate the level – Clerk I, Clerk II, for example. The word "Supervisor" sometimes appears in the title. If the level is not indicated by the title, check the description of duties. Will you be working under very close supervision, or will you have responsibility for independent decisions in this work?

4) Choose appropriate study materials

Now that you know the subjects to be examined and the relative amount of each subject to be covered, you can choose suitable study materials. For beginning level jobs, or even advanced ones, if you have a pronounced weakness in some aspect of your training, read a modern, standard textbook in that field. Be sure it is up to date and has general coverage. Such books are normally available at your library, and the librarian will be glad to help you locate one. For entry-level positions, questions of appropriate difficulty are chosen -- neither highly advanced questions, nor those too simple. Such questions require careful thought but not advanced training.

If the position for which you are applying is technical or advanced, you will read more advanced, specialized material. If you are already familiar with the basic principles of your field, elementary textbooks would waste your time. Concentrate on advanced textbooks and technical periodicals. Think through the concepts and review difficult problems in your field.

These are all general sources. You can get more ideas on your own initiative, following these leads. For example, training manuals and publications of the government agency which employs workers in your field can be useful, particularly for technical and professional positions. A letter or visit to the government department involved may result in more specific study suggestions, and certainly will provide you with a more definite idea of the exact nature of the position you are seeking.

III. KINDS OF TESTS

Tests are used for purposes other than measuring knowledge and ability to perform specified duties. For some positions, it is equally important to test ability to make adjustments to new situations or to profit from training. In others, basic mental abilities not dependent on information are essential. Questions which test these things may not appear as pertinent to the duties of the position as those which test for knowledge and information. Yet they are often highly important parts of a fair examination. For very general questions, it is almost impossible to help you direct your study efforts. What we can do is to point out some of the more common of these general abilities needed in public service positions and describe some typical questions.

1) General information

Broad, general information has been found useful for predicting job success in some kinds of work. This is tested in a variety of ways, from vocabulary lists to questions about current events. Basic background in some field of work, such as sociology or economics, may be sampled in a group of questions. Often these are principles which have become familiar to most persons through exposure rather than through formal training. It is difficult to advise you how to study for these questions; being alert to the world around you is our best suggestion.

2) Verbal ability

An example of an ability needed in many positions is verbal or language ability. Verbal ability is, in brief, the ability to use and understand words. Vocabulary and grammar tests are typical measures of this ability. Reading comprehension or paragraph interpretation questions are common in many kinds of civil service tests. You are given a paragraph of written material and asked to find its central meaning.

3) Numerical ability

Number skills can be tested by the familiar arithmetic problem, by checking paired lists of numbers to see which are alike and which are different, or by interpreting charts and graphs. In the latter test, a graph may be printed in the test booklet which you are asked to use as the basis for answering questions.

4) Observation

A popular test for law-enforcement positions is the observation test. A picture is shown to you for several minutes, then taken away. Questions about the picture test your ability to observe both details and larger elements.

5) Following directions

In many positions in the public service, the employee must be able to carry out written instructions dependably and accurately. You may be given a chart with several columns, each column listing a variety of information. The questions require you to carry out directions involving the information given in the chart.

6) Skills and aptitudes

Performance tests effectively measure some manual skills and aptitudes. When the skill is one in which you are trained, such as typing or shorthand, you can practice. These tests are often very much like those given in business school or high school courses. For many of the other skills and aptitudes, however, no short-time preparation can be made. Skills and abilities natural to you or that you have developed throughout your lifetime are being tested.

Many of the general questions just described provide all the data needed to answer the questions and ask you to use your reasoning ability to find the answers. Your best preparation for these tests, as well as for tests of facts and ideas, is to be at your physical and mental best. You, no doubt, have your own methods of getting into an exam-taking mood and keeping "in shape." The next section lists some ideas on this subject.

IV. KINDS OF QUESTIONS

Only rarely is the "essay" question, which you answer in narrative form, used in civil service tests. Civil service tests are usually of the short-answer type. Full instructions for answering these questions will be given to you at the examination. But in case this is your first experience with short-answer questions and separate answer sheets, here is what you need to know:

1) Multiple-choice Questions

Most popular of the short-answer questions is the "multiple choice" or "best answer" question. It can be used, for example, to test for factual knowledge, ability to solve problems or judgment in meeting situations found at work.

A multiple-choice question is normally one of three types—
- It can begin with an incomplete statement followed by several possible endings. You are to find the one ending which *best* completes the statement, although some of the others may not be entirely wrong.
- It can also be a complete statement in the form of a question which is answered by choosing one of the statements listed.

- It can be in the form of a problem – again you select the best answer.

Here is an example of a multiple-choice question with a discussion which should give you some clues as to the method for choosing the right answer:

When an employee has a complaint about his assignment, the action which will *best* help him overcome his difficulty is to
- A. discuss his difficulty with his coworkers
- B. take the problem to the head of the organization
- C. take the problem to the person who gave him the assignment
- D. say nothing to anyone about his complaint

In answering this question, you should study each of the choices to find which is best. Consider choice "A" – Certainly an employee may discuss his complaint with fellow employees, but no change or improvement can result, and the complaint remains unresolved. Choice "B" is a poor choice since the head of the organization probably does not know what assignment you have been given, and taking your problem to him is known as "going over the head" of the supervisor. The supervisor, or person who made the assignment, is the person who can clarify it or correct any injustice. Choice "C" is, therefore, correct. To say nothing, as in choice "D," is unwise. Supervisors have and interest in knowing the problems employees are facing, and the employee is seeking a solution to his problem.

2) True/False Questions

The "true/false" or "right/wrong" form of question is sometimes used. Here a complete statement is given. Your job is to decide whether the statement is right or wrong.

SAMPLE: A roaming cell-phone call to a nearby city costs less than a non-roaming call to a distant city.

This statement is wrong, or false, since roaming calls are more expensive.

This is not a complete list of all possible question forms, although most of the others are variations of these common types. You will always get complete directions for answering questions. Be sure you understand *how* to mark your answers – ask questions until you do.

V. RECORDING YOUR ANSWERS

Computer terminals are used more and more today for many different kinds of exams.

For an examination with very few applicants, you may be told to record your answers in the test booklet itself. Separate answer sheets are much more common. If this separate answer sheet is to be scored by machine – and this is often the case – it is highly important that you mark your answers correctly in order to get credit.

An electronic scoring machine is often used in civil service offices because of the speed with which papers can be scored. Machine-scored answer sheets must be marked with a pencil, which will be given to you. This pencil has a high graphite content which responds to the electronic scoring machine. As a matter of fact, stray dots may register as answers, so do not let your pencil rest on the answer sheet while you are pondering the correct answer. Also, if your pencil lead breaks or is otherwise defective, ask for another.

Since the answer sheet will be dropped in a slot in the scoring machine, be careful not to bend the corners or get the paper crumpled.

The answer sheet normally has five vertical columns of numbers, with 30 numbers to a column. These numbers correspond to the question numbers in your test booklet. After each number, going across the page are four or five pairs of dotted lines. These short dotted lines have small letters or numbers above them. The first two pairs may also have a "T" or "F" above the letters. This indicates that the first two pairs only are to be used if the questions are of the true-false type. If the questions are multiple choice, disregard the "T" and "F" and pay attention only to the small letters or numbers.

Answer your questions in the manner of the sample that follows:

32. The largest city in the United States is
    A. Washington, D.C.
    B. New York City
    C. Chicago
    D. Detroit
    E. San Francisco

1) Choose the answer you think is best. (New York City is the largest, so "B" is correct.)
2) Find the row of dotted lines numbered the same as the question you are answering. (Find row number 32)
3) Find the pair of dotted lines corresponding to the answer. (Find the pair of lines under the mark "B.")
4) Make a solid black mark between the dotted lines.

VI. BEFORE THE TEST

Common sense will help you find procedures to follow to get ready for an examination. Too many of us, however, overlook these sensible measures. Indeed, nervousness and fatigue have been found to be the most serious reasons why applicants fail to do their best on civil service tests. Here is a list of reminders:

- Begin your preparation early – Don't wait until the last minute to go scurrying around for books and materials or to find out what the position is all about.
- Prepare continuously – An hour a night for a week is better than an all-night cram session. This has been definitely established. What is more, a night a week for a month will return better dividends than crowding your study into a shorter period of time.
- Locate the place of the exam – You have been sent a notice telling you when and where to report for the examination. If the location is in a different town or otherwise unfamiliar to you, it would be well to inquire the best route and learn something about the building.
- Relax the night before the test – Allow your mind to rest. Do not study at all that night. Plan some mild recreation or diversion; then go to bed early and get a good night's sleep.
- Get up early enough to make a leisurely trip to the place for the test – This way unforeseen events, traffic snarls, unfamiliar buildings, etc. will not upset you.
- Dress comfortably – A written test is not a fashion show. You will be known by number and not by name, so wear something comfortable.

- Leave excess paraphernalia at home – Shopping bags and odd bundles will get in your way. You need bring only the items mentioned in the official notice you received; usually everything you need is provided. Do not bring reference books to the exam. They will only confuse those last minutes and be taken away from you when in the test room.
- Arrive somewhat ahead of time – If because of transportation schedules you must get there very early, bring a newspaper or magazine to take your mind off yourself while waiting.
- Locate the examination room – When you have found the proper room, you will be directed to the seat or part of the room where you will sit. Sometimes you are given a sheet of instructions to read while you are waiting. Do not fill out any forms until you are told to do so; just read them and be prepared.
- Relax and prepare to listen to the instructions
- If you have any physical problem that may keep you from doing your best, be sure to tell the test administrator. If you are sick or in poor health, you really cannot do your best on the exam. You can come back and take the test some other time.

VII. AT THE TEST

The day of the test is here and you have the test booklet in your hand. The temptation to get going is very strong. Caution! There is more to success than knowing the right answers. You must know how to identify your papers and understand variations in the type of short-answer question used in this particular examination. Follow these suggestions for maximum results from your efforts:

1) Cooperate with the monitor

The test administrator has a duty to create a situation in which you can be as much at ease as possible. He will give instructions, tell you when to begin, check to see that you are marking your answer sheet correctly, and so on. He is not there to guard you, although he will see that your competitors do not take unfair advantage. He wants to help you do your best.

2) Listen to all instructions

Don't jump the gun! Wait until you understand all directions. In most civil service tests you get more time than you need to answer the questions. So don't be in a hurry. Read each word of instructions until you clearly understand the meaning. Study the examples, listen to all announcements and follow directions. Ask questions if you do not understand what to do.

3) Identify your papers

Civil service exams are usually identified by number only. You will be assigned a number; you must not put your name on your test papers. Be sure to copy your number correctly. Since more than one exam may be given, copy your exact examination title.

4) Plan your time

Unless you are told that a test is a "speed" or "rate of work" test, speed itself is usually not important. Time enough to answer all the questions will be provided, but this does not mean that you have all day. An overall time limit has been set. Divide the total time (in minutes) by the number of questions to determine the approximate time you have for each question.

5) Do not linger over difficult questions

If you come across a difficult question, mark it with a paper clip (useful to have along) and come back to it when you have been through the booklet. One caution if you do this – be sure to skip a number on your answer sheet as well. Check often to be sure that you have not lost your place and that you are marking in the row numbered the same as the question you are answering.

6) Read the questions

Be sure you know what the question asks! Many capable people are unsuccessful because they failed to *read* the questions correctly.

7) Answer all questions

Unless you have been instructed that a penalty will be deducted for incorrect answers, it is better to guess than to omit a question.

8) Speed tests

It is often better NOT to guess on speed tests. It has been found that on timed tests people are tempted to spend the last few seconds before time is called in marking answers at random – without even reading them – in the hope of picking up a few extra points. To discourage this practice, the instructions may warn you that your score will be "corrected" for guessing. That is, a penalty will be applied. The incorrect answers will be deducted from the correct ones, or some other penalty formula will be used.

9) Review your answers

If you finish before time is called, go back to the questions you guessed or omitted to give them further thought. Review other answers if you have time.

10) Return your test materials

If you are ready to leave before others have finished or time is called, take ALL your materials to the monitor and leave quietly. Never take any test material with you. The monitor can discover whose papers are not complete, and taking a test booklet may be grounds for disqualification.

VIII. EXAMINATION TECHNIQUES

1) Read the general instructions carefully. These are usually printed on the first page of the exam booklet. As a rule, these instructions refer to the timing of the examination; the fact that you should not start work until the signal and must stop work at a signal, etc. If there are any *special* instructions, such as a choice of questions to be answered, make sure that you note this instruction carefully.

2) When you are ready to start work on the examination, that is as soon as the signal has been given, read the instructions to each question booklet, underline any key words or phrases, such as *least, best, outline, describe* and the like. In this way you will tend to answer as requested rather than discover on reviewing your paper that you *listed without describing*, that you selected the *worst* choice rather than the *best* choice, etc.

3) If the examination is of the objective or multiple-choice type – that is, each question will also give a series of possible answers: A, B, C or D, and you are called upon to select the best answer and write the letter next to that answer on your answer paper – it is advisable to start answering each question in turn. There may be anywhere from 50 to 100 such questions in the three or four hours allotted and you can see how much time would be taken if you read through all the questions before beginning to answer any. Furthermore, if you come across a question or group of questions which you know would be difficult to answer, it would undoubtedly affect your handling of all the other questions.

4) If the examination is of the essay type and contains but a few questions, it is a moot point as to whether you should read all the questions before starting to answer any one. Of course, if you are given a choice – say five out of seven and the like – then it is essential to read all the questions so you can eliminate the two that are most difficult. If, however, you are asked to answer all the questions, there may be danger in trying to answer the easiest one first because you may find that you will spend too much time on it. The best technique is to answer the first question, then proceed to the second, etc.

5) Time your answers. Before the exam begins, write down the time it started, then add the time allowed for the examination and write down the time it must be completed, then divide the time available somewhat as follows:
    - If 3-1/2 hours are allowed, that would be 210 minutes. If you have 80 objective-type questions, that would be an average of 2-1/2 minutes per question. Allow yourself no more than 2 minutes per question, or a total of 160 minutes, which will permit about 50 minutes to review.
    - If for the time allotment of 210 minutes there are 7 essay questions to answer, that would average about 30 minutes a question. Give yourself only 25 minutes per question so that you have about 35 minutes to review.

6) The most important instruction is to *read each question* and make sure you know what is wanted. The second most important instruction is to *time yourself properly* so that you answer every question. The third most important instruction is to *answer every question*. Guess if you have to but include something for each question. Remember that you will receive no credit for a blank and will probably receive some credit if you write something in answer to an essay question. If you guess a letter – say "B" for a multiple-choice question – you may have guessed right. If you leave a blank as an answer to a multiple-choice question, the examiners may respect your feelings but it will not add a point to your score. Some exams may penalize you for wrong answers, so in such cases *only*, you may not want to guess unless you have some basis for your answer.

7) Suggestions
    a. Objective-type questions
        1. Examine the question booklet for proper sequence of pages and questions
        2. Read all instructions carefully
        3. Skip any question which seems too difficult; return to it after all other questions have been answered
        4. Apportion your time properly; do not spend too much time on any single question or group of questions

5. Note and underline key words – *all, most, fewest, least, best, worst, same, opposite*, etc.
6. Pay particular attention to negatives
7. Note unusual option, e.g., unduly long, short, complex, different or similar in content to the body of the question
8. Observe the use of "hedging" words – *probably, may, most likely*, etc.
9. Make sure that your answer is put next to the same number as the question
10. Do not second-guess unless you have good reason to believe the second answer is definitely more correct
11. Cross out original answer if you decide another answer is more accurate; do not erase until you are ready to hand your paper in
12. Answer all questions; guess unless instructed otherwise
13. Leave time for review

   b. Essay questions
   1. Read each question carefully
   2. Determine exactly what is wanted. Underline key words or phrases.
   3. Decide on outline or paragraph answer
   4. Include many different points and elements unless asked to develop any one or two points or elements
   5. Show impartiality by giving pros and cons unless directed to select one side only
   6. Make and write down any assumptions you find necessary to answer the questions
   7. Watch your English, grammar, punctuation and choice of words
   8. Time your answers; don't crowd material

8) Answering the essay question

Most essay questions can be answered by framing the specific response around several key words or ideas. Here are a few such key words or ideas:

M's: manpower, materials, methods, money, management
P's: purpose, program, policy, plan, procedure, practice, problems, pitfalls, personnel, public relations

   a. Six basic steps in handling problems:
   1. Preliminary plan and background development
   2. Collect information, data and facts
   3. Analyze and interpret information, data and facts
   4. Analyze and develop solutions as well as make recommendations
   5. Prepare report and sell recommendations
   6. Install recommendations and follow up effectiveness

   b. Pitfalls to avoid
   1. *Taking things for granted* – A statement of the situation does not necessarily imply that each of the elements is necessarily true; for example, a complaint may be invalid and biased so that all that can be taken for granted is that a complaint has been registered

2. *Considering only one side of a situation* – Wherever possible, indicate several alternatives and then point out the reasons you selected the best one
3. *Failing to indicate follow up* – Whenever your answer indicates action on your part, make certain that you will take proper follow-up action to see how successful your recommendations, procedures or actions turn out to be
4. *Taking too long in answering any single question* – Remember to time your answers properly

IX. AFTER THE TEST

Scoring procedures differ in detail among civil service jurisdictions although the general principles are the same. Whether the papers are hand-scored or graded by machine we have described, they are nearly always graded by number. That is, the person who marks the paper knows only the number – never the name – of the applicant. Not until all the papers have been graded will they be matched with names. If other tests, such as training and experience or oral interview ratings have been given, scores will be combined. Different parts of the examination usually have different weights. For example, the written test might count 60 percent of the final grade, and a rating of training and experience 40 percent. In many jurisdictions, veterans will have a certain number of points added to their grades.

After the final grade has been determined, the names are placed in grade order and an eligible list is established. There are various methods for resolving ties between those who get the same final grade – probably the most common is to place first the name of the person whose application was received first. Job offers are made from the eligible list in the order the names appear on it. You will be notified of your grade and your rank as soon as all these computations have been made. This will be done as rapidly as possible.

People who are found to meet the requirements in the announcement are called "eligibles." Their names are put on a list of eligible candidates. An eligible's chances of getting a job depend on how high he stands on this list and how fast agencies are filling jobs from the list.

When a job is to be filled from a list of eligibles, the agency asks for the names of people on the list of eligibles for that job. When the civil service commission receives this request, it sends to the agency the names of the three people highest on this list. Or, if the job to be filled has specialized requirements, the office sends the agency the names of the top three persons who meet these requirements from the general list.

The appointing officer makes a choice from among the three people whose names were sent to him. If the selected person accepts the appointment, the names of the others are put back on the list to be considered for future openings.

That is the rule in hiring from all kinds of eligible lists, whether they are for typist, carpenter, chemist, or something else. For every vacancy, the appointing officer has his choice of any one of the top three eligibles on the list. This explains why the person whose name is on top of the list sometimes does not get an appointment when some of the persons lower on the list do. If the appointing officer chooses the second or third eligible, the No. 1 eligible does not get a job at once, but stays on the list until he is appointed or the list is terminated.

X. HOW TO PASS THE INTERVIEW TEST

The examination for which you applied requires an oral interview test. You have already taken the written test and you are now being called for the interview test – the final part of the formal examination.

You may think that it is not possible to prepare for an interview test and that there are no procedures to follow during an interview. Our purpose is to point out some things you can do in advance that will help you and some good rules to follow and pitfalls to avoid while you are being interviewed.

What is an interview supposed to test?

The written examination is designed to test the technical knowledge and competence of the candidate; the oral is designed to evaluate intangible qualities, not readily measured otherwise, and to establish a list showing the relative fitness of each candidate – as measured against his competitors – for the position sought. Scoring is not on the basis of "right" and "wrong," but on a sliding scale of values ranging from "not passable" to "outstanding." As a matter of fact, it is possible to achieve a relatively low score without a single "incorrect" answer because of evident weakness in the qualities being measured.

Occasionally, an examination may consist entirely of an oral test – either an individual or a group oral. In such cases, information is sought concerning the technical knowledges and abilities of the candidate, since there has been no written examination for this purpose. More commonly, however, an oral test is used to supplement a written examination.

Who conducts interviews?

The composition of oral boards varies among different jurisdictions. In nearly all, a representative of the personnel department serves as chairman. One of the members of the board may be a representative of the department in which the candidate would work. In some cases, "outside experts" are used, and, frequently, a businessman or some other representative of the general public is asked to serve. Labor and management or other special groups may be represented. The aim is to secure the services of experts in the appropriate field.

However the board is composed, it is a good idea (and not at all improper or unethical) to ascertain in advance of the interview who the members are and what groups they represent. When you are introduced to them, you will have some idea of their backgrounds and interests, and at least you will not stutter and stammer over their names.

What should be done before the interview?

While knowledge about the board members is useful and takes some of the surprise element out of the interview, there is other preparation which is more substantive. It *is* possible to prepare for an oral interview – in several ways:

1) Keep a copy of your application and review it carefully before the interview

This may be the only document before the oral board, and the starting point of the interview. Know what education and experience you have listed there, and the sequence and dates of all of it. Sometimes the board will ask you to review the highlights of your experience for them; you should not have to hem and haw doing it.

2) Study the class specification and the examination announcement

Usually, the oral board has one or both of these to guide them. The qualities, characteristics or knowledges required by the position sought are stated in these documents. They offer valuable clues as to the nature of the oral interview. For example, if the job involves supervisory responsibilities, the announcement will usually indicate that knowledge of modern supervisory methods and the qualifications of the candidate as a supervisor will be tested. If so, you can expect such questions, frequently in the form of a hypothetical situation which you are expected to solve. NEVER go into an oral without knowledge of the duties and responsibilities of the job you seek.

3) Think through each qualification required

Try to visualize the kind of questions you would ask if you were a board member. How well could you answer them? Try especially to appraise your own knowledge and background in each area, *measured against the job sought*, and identify any areas in which you are weak. Be critical and realistic – do not flatter yourself.

4) Do some general reading in areas in which you feel you may be weak

For example, if the job involves supervision and your past experience has NOT, some general reading in supervisory methods and practices, particularly in the field of human relations, might be useful. Do NOT study agency procedures or detailed manuals. The oral board will be testing your understanding and capacity, not your memory.

5) Get a good night's sleep and watch your general health and mental attitude

You will want a clear head at the interview. Take care of a cold or any other minor ailment, and of course, no hangovers.

What should be done on the day of the interview?

Now comes the day of the interview itself. Give yourself plenty of time to get there. Plan to arrive somewhat ahead of the scheduled time, particularly if your appointment is in the fore part of the day. If a previous candidate fails to appear, the board might be ready for you a bit early. By early afternoon an oral board is almost invariably behind schedule if there are many candidates, and you may have to wait. Take along a book or magazine to read, or your application to review, but leave any extraneous material in the waiting room when you go in for your interview. In any event, relax and compose yourself.

The matter of dress is important. The board is forming impressions about you – from your experience, your manners, your attitude, and your appearance. Give your personal appearance careful attention. Dress your best, but not your flashiest. Choose conservative, appropriate clothing, and be sure it is immaculate. This is a business interview, and your appearance should indicate that you regard it as such. Besides, being well groomed and properly dressed will help boost your confidence.

Sooner or later, someone will call your name and escort you into the interview room. *This is it.* From here on you are on your own. It is too late for any more preparation. But remember, you asked for this opportunity to prove your fitness, and you are here because your request was granted.

What happens when you go in?

The usual sequence of events will be as follows: The clerk (who is often the board stenographer) will introduce you to the chairman of the oral board, who will introduce you to the other members of the board. Acknowledge the introductions before you sit down. Do not be surprised if you find a microphone facing you or a stenotypist sitting by. Oral interviews are usually recorded in the event of an appeal or other review.

Usually the chairman of the board will open the interview by reviewing the highlights of your education and work experience from your application – primarily for the benefit of the other members of the board, as well as to get the material into the record. Do not interrupt or comment unless there is an error or significant misinterpretation; if that is the case, do not hesitate. But do not quibble about insignificant matters. Also, he will usually ask you some question about your education, experience or your present job – partly to get you to start talking and to establish the interviewing "rapport." He may start the actual questioning, or turn it over to one of the other members. Frequently, each member undertakes the questioning on a particular area, one in which he is perhaps most competent, so you can expect each member to participate in the examination. Because time is limited, you may also expect some rather abrupt switches in the direction the questioning takes, so do not be upset by it. Normally, a board member will not pursue a single line of questioning unless he discovers a particular strength or weakness.

After each member has participated, the chairman will usually ask whether any member has any further questions, then will ask you if you have anything you wish to add. Unless you are expecting this question, it may floor you. Worse, it may start you off on an extended, extemporaneous speech. The board is not usually seeking more information. The question is principally to offer you a last opportunity to present further qualifications or to indicate that you have nothing to add. So, if you feel that a significant qualification or characteristic has been overlooked, it is proper to point it out in a sentence or so. Do not compliment the board on the thoroughness of their examination – they have been sketchy, and you know it. If you wish, merely say, "No thank you, I have nothing further to add." This is a point where you can "talk yourself out" of a good impression or fail to present an important bit of information. Remember, *you close the interview yourself.*

The chairman will then say, "That is all, Mr. _____, thank you." Do not be startled; the interview is over, and quicker than you think. Thank him, gather your belongings and take your leave. Save your sigh of relief for the other side of the door.

How to put your best foot forward

Throughout this entire process, you may feel that the board individually and collectively is trying to pierce your defenses, seek out your hidden weaknesses and embarrass and confuse you. Actually, this is not true. They are obliged to make an appraisal of your qualifications for the job you are seeking, and they want to see you in your best light. Remember, they must interview all candidates and a non-cooperative candidate may become a failure in spite of their best efforts to bring out his qualifications. Here are 15 suggestions that will help you:

1) Be natural – Keep your attitude confident, not cocky

If you are not confident that you can do the job, do not expect the board to be. Do not apologize for your weaknesses, try to bring out your strong points. The board is interested in a positive, not negative, presentation. Cockiness will antagonize any board member and make him wonder if you are covering up a weakness by a false show of strength.

2) Get comfortable, but don't lounge or sprawl

Sit erectly but not stiffly. A careless posture may lead the board to conclude that you are careless in other things, or at least that you are not impressed by the importance of the occasion. Either conclusion is natural, even if incorrect. Do not fuss with your clothing, a pencil or an ashtray. Your hands may occasionally be useful to emphasize a point; do not let them become a point of distraction.

3) Do not wisecrack or make small talk

This is a serious situation, and your attitude should show that you consider it as such. Further, the time of the board is limited – they do not want to waste it, and neither should you.

4) Do not exaggerate your experience or abilities

In the first place, from information in the application or other interviews and sources, the board may know more about you than you think. Secondly, you probably will not get away with it. An experienced board is rather adept at spotting such a situation, so do not take the chance.

5) If you know a board member, do not make a point of it, yet do not hide it

Certainly you are not fooling him, and probably not the other members of the board. Do not try to take advantage of your acquaintanceship – it will probably do you little good.

6) Do not dominate the interview

Let the board do that. They will give you the clues – do not assume that you have to do all the talking. Realize that the board has a number of questions to ask you, and do not try to take up all the interview time by showing off your extensive knowledge of the answer to the first one.

7) Be attentive

You only have 20 minutes or so, and you should keep your attention at its sharpest throughout. When a member is addressing a problem or question to you, give him your undivided attention. Address your reply principally to him, but do not exclude the other board members.

8) Do not interrupt

A board member may be stating a problem for you to analyze. He will ask you a question when the time comes. Let him state the problem, and wait for the question.

9) Make sure you understand the question

Do not try to answer until you are sure what the question is. If it is not clear, restate it in your own words or ask the board member to clarify it for you. However, do not haggle about minor elements.

10) Reply promptly but not hastily

A common entry on oral board rating sheets is "candidate responded readily," or "candidate hesitated in replies." Respond as promptly and quickly as you can, but do not jump to a hasty, ill-considered answer.

11) Do not be peremptory in your answers

A brief answer is proper – but do not fire your answer back. That is a losing game from your point of view. The board member can probably ask questions much faster than you can answer them.

12) Do not try to create the answer you think the board member wants

He is interested in what kind of mind you have and how it works – not in playing games. Furthermore, he can usually spot this practice and will actually grade you down on it.

13) Do not switch sides in your reply merely to agree with a board member

Frequently, a member will take a contrary position merely to draw you out and to see if you are willing and able to defend your point of view. Do not start a debate, yet do not surrender a good position. If a position is worth taking, it is worth defending.

14) Do not be afraid to admit an error in judgment if you are shown to be wrong

The board knows that you are forced to reply without any opportunity for careful consideration. Your answer may be demonstrably wrong. If so, admit it and get on with the interview.

15) Do not dwell at length on your present job

The opening question may relate to your present assignment. Answer the question but do not go into an extended discussion. You are being examined for a *new* job, not your present one. As a matter of fact, try to phrase ALL your answers in terms of the job for which you are being examined.

Basis of Rating

Probably you will forget most of these "do's" and "don'ts" when you walk into the oral interview room. Even remembering them all will not ensure you a passing grade. Perhaps you did not have the qualifications in the first place. But remembering them will help you to put your best foot forward, without treading on the toes of the board members.

Rumor and popular opinion to the contrary notwithstanding, an oral board wants you to make the best appearance possible. They know you are under pressure – but they also want to see how you respond to it as a guide to what your reaction would be under the pressures of the job you seek. They will be influenced by the degree of poise you display, the personal traits you show and the manner in which you respond.

ABOUT THIS BOOK

This book contains tests divided into Examination Sections. Go through each test, answering every question in the margin. We have also attached a sample answer sheet at the back of the book that can be removed and used. At the end of each test look at the answer key and check your answers. On the ones you got wrong, look at the right answer choice and learn. Do not fill in the answers first. Do not memorize the questions and answers, but understand the answer and principles involved. On your test, the questions will likely be different from the samples. Questions are changed and new ones added. If you understand these past questions you should have success with any changes that arise. Tests may consist of several types of questions. We have additional books on each subject should more study be advisable or necessary for you. Finally, the more you study, the better prepared you will be. This book is intended to be the last thing you study before you walk into the examination room. Prior study of relevant texts is also recommended. NLC publishes some of these in our Fundamental Series. Knowledge and good sense are important factors in passing your exam. Good luck also helps. So now study this Passbook, absorb the material contained within and take that knowledge into the examination. Then do your best to pass that exam.

EXAMINATION SECTION

THE "IN-BASKET" EXAMINATION

While the exact format of in-basket exercises will vary, they frequently involve each trainee in a group first individually assuming the role of a manager who is faced with a number of letters, memoirs, and notes to which he must respond in writing within a limited time period. For example, the trainee may be told that he has just returned from vacation and that he must leave on a trip in four hours, during which time he must respond in writing to all the items on his desk.

To further complicate the exercise, you, the trainee, may be told that you have just returned from vacation and must leave on a business trip in five hours. Also, it is a holiday and your secretary is home, and no one else is around the office to help you. There are more inquiries and problems to respond to than is possible in five hours and so you will have to determine the relative priority of the work to be done.

As you can see, the IN-BASKET EXERCISE demands good decision-making skills, rather than learning new facts or acquiring new skills. The time pressure factor may result in your finding out how well you perform under stress.

When these exercises are conducted in an oral format, and after each exercise is finished (time runs out), you may be asked to justify your decisions and actions to the examiner and the other participants when it is held as a group exercise, and then they in turn will evaluate your actions and critique it. The rating, of course, is done differently in competitive examinations.

The fact that this type of exercise can be given to groups of managerial trainees is considered an advantage to management, i.e., it is easier and cheaper to administer than other training methods. This training technique also tests managerial candidates for decision-making abilities, particularly due to the time constraints involved. This is considered a vital skill for most managerial candidates for decision-making abilities, particularly due to the time constraints involved. This is considered a vital skill for most managerial positions and, although other training techniques such as role playing can also provide stress, in-basket exercises do more so and are specifically designed for this purpose.

There are limitations, too. As with in-basket questions pertaining to case study examples, they are in large part hypothetical in nature, or static, in that the managerial candidate does not have to live or "die" with the consequences of a poor decision, except where he/she is rated poorly on an examination.

Some in-basket exercises provide guidelines or suggestions for solution. The candidate may be presented with a problem which requires a series of decisions and actions but is also presented with a number of alternate means of resolving the problem, from which he must choose the best option. Next, the problem may be further developed and you may be provided with a number of new choices to resolve this new, or expanded, problem. It may even be required a third time. Then comes the evaluation and critique.

So with this technique, the trainee receives information evaluating the consequences, good or bad, of his decisions at each decision point in the exercise.

In order to properly critique the trainee's decisions, the examiner must be highly skilled in conducting the exercise and in conducting the critique. At its extremes, the critique, as with performance evaluations, can be so general as to be meaningless or be so specific that the trainee becomes so overwhelmed as to render the whole training exercise pointless.

In-basket exercises are often used in on-the-job management group training programs, together with case studies.

IN-BASKET EXERCISE

SAMPLE TEST QUESTIONS

These questions consist of a scenario in which the test taker assumes the role of a supervisor returning from a vacation and reviewing memos and analyzing the situations, identifying relationships, and making connections among the pieces of information provided in the scenario and in-basket items. These questions relate to the test taker's solution, decision or action in response to a problem to achieve a specific objective.

You are to read the situation described below and the three numbered in-basket items that follow. Then respond to the three multiple-choice questions that follow the in-basket materials.

Scenario and Background

Assume that you are Casey Jones, a District Sales Supervisor in the Sales Division of a major pharmaceutical company.

You supervise a staff of three Sales Representatives, each of whom leads a professional team that includes two assistant representatives. Your immediate supervisor is the District Manager of the Sales Division, Terry Gibson. The Sales Division also includes two other Supervisors and their staffs.

Your Sales Representatives and their assignments are:

Scott Bailey, Sales Area One
Jesse Taylor, Sales Area Two
Shawn Richard, Sales Area Three

Scott is your most experienced and competent employee. Jesse was transferred to you from another Sales District about one year ago, and Shawn is your newest employee who is very competent, but still is working on being an effective team leader.

It is Monday morning, April 12, and you have just returned from a one-week vacation. The numbered items that follow represent the contents of your in-basket. These include memos, letters, and other information that came in while you were on vacation. Your plan for the morning is to review and take action on your in-basket items. In about an hour, you will go to the first of several meetings that will consume the remainder of the day.

Interoffice Memo #1

Date: Tuesday, April 6th

From: Scott Bailey
District Sales Representative, Area One

To: Casey Jones
District Sales Supervisor
Northeastern District

Subject: New Hires Training Program

Before you left, you approved the idea I had for the new training program and told me to proceed to order the new assimilation computers. However, the computer company, Technologies Expanding, assured me that they would arrive in time for our new hires to begin training. As you are aware, the training begins in one week, but I have not received the new computers yet. The customer service representative told me that the company has been having difficulties getting their orders out and could not guarantee that the computers would be in on time.

There is another company that can supply our computers, but the cost would be an additional $8,000. I recommend that we order from the other company and begin training on the old computers while we wait for the new computers. Although the new hires will not work on specific training for two weeks, we can at least start them on the product information part of the course.

Interoffice Memo #2

Date: Thursday, April 8th

From: Terry Gibson
          District Division Manager

To: Casey Jones
          District Sales Supervisor
          Northeastern District

Subject: New Company Policy

Beginning May 1st, there will be a new policy which requires all Sales Representative to have their clients fill out and sign the Form 2030. This form is for our inventory purposes. We had discussed using this form a couple of months ago and at the time found it to be quite tedious. But as our business is expanding and we are moving to other parts of the country, we need a more efficient way to keep track of what we are selling.

Our next inventory will be on May 30th. These forms must be filled out no later than May 15th so we can have the information to have a successful inventory. I know this is short notice, but it shouldn't long to go through your records of what your representatives have sold in the last six months. If you have any further questions or need any assistance you can contact my Administrative Assistant, Aaron Daigle, (x3632), who is collecting all the information.

Interoffice Memo #3

Date: Monday, April 5th

From: Jody Rogers
Assistant District Sales Representative, Area Four

To: Casey Jones
District Sales Supervisor
Northeastern District

Subject: Area Team Four

I am requesting an assignment to a different Area Team. I have been working on Shawn Richard's team for the past six months. I realize that Shawn is a new employee and has only been in this position for seven months, but he does not handle leadership in a professional manner.

He is not organized, and I feel that Dale Stevens and I are the ones who are compensating for him. He does not delegate responsibility and cannot manage the travel schedule, the appointments, or the distribution lists. I have tried to help him get organized while Dale helps with the arrangements, but our efforts have not helped. He cannot seem to manage his time effectively, which leaves his assistants, me and Dale, to keep our area serviced.

How am I ever going to move up professionally and to show my talents if my work is suffering due to Shawn's inability to manage his team?

In-Basket Questions

1. Which of the following is the most appropriate action to take in response to the issue of the training schedule in Item #1?

    A. Allow Scott to proceed with the training on the old computers and then interrupt training when the new computers arrive.
    B. Delay the training till the new computers arrive.
    C. Let the students finish the course with the old computers without the interruption of the new computers, and the next group of students will begin training with the new computers.
    D. Cancel the training altogether until the issue with the computers has been resolved.

2. Which of the following actions will have the best resolution to the problem with Technologies Expanding?

    A. Cancel the order with Technologies Expanding and proceed with the new order.
    B. Contact the president of Technologies Expanding and demand a discount because the company did not meet your expectations.
    C. Cancel the order and have the old computers updated.
    D. Call the customer service representative manager to verify the accuracy of the information Scott received and discuss your situation and the options that are available to you.

3. What would be the best action to take in response to Jody's compliant? (Item #3)

    A. No action is required because Jody tends to exaggerate.
    B. Tell Jody that it is important to be supportive of each other and you will enroll her in a teambuilding course.
    C. Move Jody to Scott's team so she can help with the training.
    D. Look into the matter and see if there is evidence of Shawn's behavior described by Jody, and also talk with Dale to gain further insight into the issue.

KEY (CORRECT ANSWERS)

1. C – The students will get the training they need to perform the duties of the job without the interruption of the installation of the new computers.
2. D – By calling the service manager you can get a better idea of exactly what the situation is and what options are available to you before you cancel the order.
3. D – You first need to determine if there is a valid complaint and if Shawn's behavior reflects Jody's complaint before you take any action.

Sample Test Material for:

THE IN-BASKET

Test material will be presented in a job simulation exercise format.

For more information about this format, please see the section titled *More Information on Job Simulation Exercises* that follows the Sample Job Simulation Exercise.

Test Task: You will be given **Background** information on a fictional agency and your role in the agency. You will then be presented with a series of situations. Each situation will be followed by a list of choices that represent possible responses one could make. You will need to read the information presented and select the best choice(s) to take to collect relevant information and/or resolve the problem(s) in the situation described.

SAMPLE JOB SIMULATION EXERCISE:

Background and Sections A and B:

BACKGROUND

A new bureau, the **Bureau of Communications,** has just been organized within the Department of Regulations. The Bureau Director is Rena Morgan. The Bureau's principal objective is the efficient and effective flow of communication and information within and among divisions in the Department and between the Department and its publics.

The **Bureau of Communications** is comprised of three groups:

- The **Public Relations Group** serves as the liaison between the Department's Commissioner and Executive Office, and the public -- primarily the media.
- The **Freedom of Information Group** maintains and processes requests from individuals and groups for information under the Freedom of Information Laws and Regulations.
- The **Central Communications Group** serves as an information and communication center for Department management and the general public.

You have recently been appointed as Head of the Central Communications Group within the Bureau of Communications. The principal functions and activities of your group are as follows:

- Make and coordinate presentations on Department issues to the public and other interest groups.
- Respond to letters and telephone inquiries on general issues pertinent to Department operations.
- Serve as liaison between the Department and Legislative staff.
- Produce Department publications.
- Design Department forms for public and internal use.
- Prepare Department annual report and other reports as assigned.
- Assist Public Relations Group staff with publicity issues.
- Review communication flow within the Department and recommend necessary improvements.
- Assist in drafting and disseminating Department policies and procedures.

Your supervisor is Rena Morgan, Director, Bureau of Communications.

As Head of the Central Communications Group, you supervise a secretary and three unit supervisors:

- Sandra Fineberg, Secretary 1
- Frank Williams, Supervisor, Agency Publication Unit
- Mary Walters, Supervisor, Agency Presentations Unit
- Bill Richards, Supervisor, Legislative Inquiries Unit

Frank Williams and Mary Walters are both experienced employees. Frank and Mary each supervise two professional staff. Bill Richards has recently been assigned to your group after spending the first 18 months of his agency employment in one of the Department's line divisions. Bill's unit has one professional staff position, which is currently vacant. In addition to working as your secretary, Sandra Fineberg also provides word processing support to Frank, Mary, and Bill and their unit staff.

You have been Head of the Central Communications Group for just under a month. After three days away from the office, you find the following items in your in-basket:

- a memo from Bill Richards to Rena Morgan, concerning a new training course
- a memo from Bill Richards to you, concerning his workload
- a memo from Sandra Fineberg to you, concerning Bill Richards

READ THE IN-BASKET MATERIALS WHICH FOLLOW.

IN-BASKET ITEM ONE
MEMORANDUM

TO: Rena Morgan, Director, Bureau of Communications
FROM: Bill Richards
SUBJECT: What this Department needs . . .

> **TO:** *You*
>
> *What is this about?*
> *Rena*

. . . is a new training course on "Ethical Decision Making."

From my experience in working with public inquiries and Department correspondence, it strikes me that our decisions are difficult, and the "best" solutions are seldom without costs. Yet we need to make these decisions without undue delay.

In one of my graduate courses, we studied F. Mosher, who emphasized the need for flexibility and value priorities in public decision-making. There is a high ethical content in governmental decisions - often they do not succumb neatly to factual analysis. Rarely are they totally right or totally wrong. And the public character of this Department's decisions adds complicating dimensions to ethical behavior.

Anyway, I have lots of ideas that would be useful for this course. I'd like to present it to interested Department employees in general and bureau staff in particular (they need it!).

I'm available to discuss this in further detail, at your convenience.

IN-BASKET ITEM TWO
MEMORANDUM

TO: You, Head, Central Communications Group
FROM: Bill Richards
SUBJECT: Workload

I am pleased to be assigned to this group, since the work involves critical activities occurring throughout the Department. I enjoy most of the work I have had to date, and am always eager for more.

However, I get the impression that you think some of my work is "incomplete" or has "erroneous" information. Let me point out that I probably produce more than Frank's and Mary's units combined. Maybe if they did more of their share of the work I would feel less rushed.

So far all of my assignments involve gathering information or preparing letters or reports under very tight deadlines. I would like to get some assignments that involve longer range planning or project development as well as get a chance to do some public speaking. Also, there are some divisions I am not familiar with. If I knew more about the work of these divisions, I'm sure my work would be even better.

I would appreciate the opportunity to discuss better ways of scheduling the workload with you as soon as possible. I had a course in workload scheduling if that will be of any help.

IN-BASKET ITEM THREE
MEMORANDUM

TO: You, Head, Central Communications Group
FROM: Sandra Fineberg, Secretary 1

Bill Richards has insulted me again, and I feel it is just not fair. I must do work for four people in this group, but Bill insists that his work is "top priority" and should be done first. He told me I am just too slow!

I don't need this. I am going to request a transfer if the situation continues.

Continue now with SECTION A

SECTION A

To address the most urgent of these three memos, you would first deal with: **(Choose ONLY ONE.)**

1. Bill's memo and Rena's note about Bill's proposed training course
2. Bill's memo about the group's workload
3. Sandra's memo about Bill

- Mark '**A**' on your answer sheet if you are **selecting** that choice or action.
- Mark '**B**' on your answer sheet if you are **not selecting** that choice or action.
- You **must** mark **A** <u>or</u> **B** for **each** choice presented.

Then, go to SECTION B on the next page.

SECTION B

Rena calls you and expresses her concern about Bill Richards' manner in working with others. Rena comments that Bill produces a substantial amount of work, but it is not always accurate. Rena also says that she considers Bill abrasive and argumentative. She asks you to talk with Bill further and then get back to her.

You would now: **(Choose UP TO TWO.)**

4. Review available records of Bill's work performance and relationships.
5. Ask Frank and Mary if they have had any personal problems working with Bill.
6. Check informally with others in the Department and see how they view Bill.
7. Briefly review Frank's, Mary's, and Bill's unit assignments and overall workload.
8. Ask Sandra for a written list of the problems she has had with Bill.
9. Contact the director of the line division where Bill was employed for the last 18 months.

- Mark '**A**' on your answer sheet if you are **selecting** that choice or action.
- Mark '**B**' on your answer sheet if you are **not selecting** that choice or action.
- You **must** mark **A** <u>or</u> **B** for **each** choice presented.

This is the end of the Sample Background and Sections A and B.

The Solutions to Sections A and B are found on the following page.

Solution to Sections A and B from the Sample Job Simulation Exercise:

In the preceding sample Section A, the *most important* memo to address first is choice 3, and this choice is valued at +1. The memos described in choices 1 and 2 will require attention, but are not as critical as the urgent concerns expressed in Sandra Fineberg's memo (choice 3). Therefore, choices 1 and 2 are valued at 0.

Listed below are all the choices presented in sample Section A and their assigned values:

1. Bill's memo and Rena's note about Bill's proposed training course **0**
2. Bill's memo about the group's workload **0**
3. Sandra's memo about Bill **+1**

In the preceding sample Section B, the most helpful steps to take in gathering information before talking with Bill are described in choices 4 and 7. Choice 4 offers more comprehensive information on the quality and quantity of Bill's work performance and relationships, and choice 7 provides objective information about the distribution of work, which Bill views as a problem (see preceding memo). Therefore, in this "Choose UP TO TWO" section, choices 4 and 7 are valued at +1. Choices 5, 6, 8, and 9 are either less effective or inappropriate; therefore, these choices are valued at 0.

Listed below are all the choices presented in sample Section B and their assigned values:

4. Review available records of Bill's work performance and relationships. **+1**
5. Ask Frank and Mary if they have had any personal problems working with Bill. **0**
6. Check informally with others in the Department and see how they view Bill. **0**
7. Briefly review Frank's, Mary's, and Bill's unit assignments and overall workload. **+1**
8. Ask Sandra for a written list of the problems she has had with Bill. **0**
9. Contact the director of the line division where Bill was employed for the last 18 months. **0**

Scoring Sections A and B from the Sample Job Simulation Exercise:

Section A is a **"Choose ONLY ONE"** section. There is only **one** positive choice in this section, choice 3, and that choice is valued at +1. There are two other choices in this section, choices 1 and 2, and they are valued at 0.

In a "Choose ONLY ONE" section, only one of the candidate's choices is scored. A choice with a value of 0 is scored before a choice with a value of +1.

- A candidate would receive the maximum credit for this section (+1) if the choice valued at +1 was selected and none of the choices valued at 0 were selected (i.e., if the candidate marked 'A' on the answer sheet for choice 3 and 'B' for choices 1 and 2).
- A candidate would receive a section score of 0 if either of the choices valued at 0 were selected.
- If a candidate selected **more than** one choice, only one choice would be scored. A choice valued at 0 would be scored and additional choices valued at 0 or +1 would **not** be scored.
- A candidate would receive a section score of 0 if **no** choices were selected.

Section B is a **"Choose UP TO TWO"** section. There are **two** positive choices in this section, choices 4 and 7, which are valued at +1. There are four other choices in this section, choices 5, 6, 8, and 9, and they are valued at 0.

In a "Choose UP TO TWO" section, only two of the candidate's choices are scored. Choices with a value of 0 are scored before choices with a value of +1.

Some of the possible scoring outcomes include the following:

- A candidate would receive the maximum credit for this section (+2) if the two choices valued at +1 were selected and none of the choices valued at 0 were selected (i.e., if the candidate marked 'A' on the answer sheet for choices 4 and 7, and 'B' for choices 5, 6, 8, and 9.)

- A candidate who selected two choices, one valued at +1 and one valued at 0, would receive a section score of +1, the sum of the two choices.

- A candidate who selected *only one choice* would receive the score associated with that choice (i.e., either +1 or 0).

- If a candidate selected **more than** two choices, only two choices would be scored. The choices valued at 0 would be scored first, then the +1 choice, up to a maximum of two choices total.

- A candidate would receive a section score of 0 if **no** choices were selected.

End of Sample Job Simulation Exercise

MORE INFORMATION ON JOB SIMULATION EXERCISES:

Job simulation exercises present candidates with situational judgment problems, similar to those encountered on the job, and many possible answer choices.

Each answer choice is numbered. Candidates must select the best answer choice(s) presented and, on the separate scannable answer sheet, mark 'A' for the choice(s) selected and 'B' for the choice(s) not selected. Candidates must mark each and every answer choice as either one they are selecting or one they are **not** selecting.

In the preceding Sample Job Simulation Exercise, each choice has a value of +1 or 0. In sections that specify the number of choices to select (e.g. Choose ONLY ONE or Choose UP TO THREE), only that number of choices are scored. In these sections, a candidate's choices with a value of 0 are scored before the candidate's choices with a value of +1. If a candidate has selected more than the specified number, only the number of choices specified are scored.

To compute subtest scores for a job simulation exercise, candidate section scores are totaled and scaled according to the range of possible points for the subtest (e.g., 0 to 15, 0 to 30, etc.)

Directions for Job Simulation Exercises:

The job simulation exercises will present you with situations that are similar to those you might encounter on the job. The job simulation exercise will start with **Background** information that will tell you about the job setting and your role in that setting. The Background may also include some job-related issues, situations, and/or resource materials for you to consider.

You will then be given a series of situations in simulation Sections. Each Section will present the situation and choices representing possible responses one could make in that situation. You are to read the information and select the best choice(s) to take to collect relevant information and/or resolve the problem(s) in the situation presented.

The job simulation exercise will start with **Section A**. The Sections will continue in alphabetical order (Section B, then Section C, etc.) to the end of the exercise. Each Section will present you with choices, and you are to select the most appropriate choice(s) from among those presented.

Instructions for Selecting Answer Choices:

Each section will include an instruction on **how many** choices to select in that section. The instructions may tell you to:

- choose a specific number of choices, e.g., **"Choose ONLY ONE."**
- choose **"up to"** a maximum number of choices, e.g., **"Choose UP TO THREE."** (Candidates may choose fewer than three, but should not choose more than three.)
- choose as many choices as are appropriate, e.g., **"Choose AS MANY as are appropriate."**

Follow the instructions to each section carefully. Failure to follow the instructions may result in a lower score.

Instructions for Marking Answer Choices:

In order to be scored, all your answers must be recorded on a separate, scannable answer sheet. Using a No. 2 pencil, you are to mark 'A' for the choices you select and 'B' for the choices you are not selecting. The following instructions will appear at the end of each Section:

- Mark '**A**' on your answer sheet if you are **selecting** that choice or action.
- Mark '**B**' on your answer sheet if you are **not selecting** that choice or action.
- You **must** mark **A** or **B** for **each** choice presented.

You must mark either **A** or **B** for each choice presented because your answer sheet will be optically scanned by a machine that reads the darkest filled-in circle next to a choice number as your selection for that choice number. Marking A for choices you select and B for choices you do not select will ensure that your choices are recorded accurately.

Complete instructions on how to mark your answer sheet will be provided with your test materials on the day of your test. Be sure to follow these instructions carefully to ensure that your answers are scored correctly.

JOB SIMULATION EXERCISE INSTRUCTIONS

This exercise is designed to measure the following:

- ability to detect errors or discrepancies in the entry of records, posting data, or other log entries;

- ability to transcribe numerical information from one document to another;

- ability to enter simple information on forms or to otherwise record data according to standardized instructions, such as dates, totals, and amounts;

- ability to read and follow instructions; and

- ability to read and comprehend simple instructions or information, such as work assignments or labels on containers.

During this exercise, you are to assume the role of an Administrative Support Assistant II in a fictitious department known as the Department of Business Licensing. Any similarities to any State agencies or any actual procedures used by you or others in actual jobs should be disregarded. Instead, you should concentrate only on the rules and procedures given to you in the instructions for this exercise. This agency was created solely for this exercise.

On the next few pages, you will find a brief outline of the function of the Department of Business Licensing. You will also find detailed instructions on how to process the various forms you will encounter during this exercise. To successfully complete your exercise, you must carefully follow the instructions you are given. To answer the questions in this work simulation exercise, you should mark your answer sheet according to the instructions given. The remainder of this booklet will contain instructions, forms, and procedures you must follow to complete this exercise.

THE DEPARTMENT OF BUSINESS LICENSING

This mission of the Department of Business Licensing (DBL) is to inspect the accounting records and physical locations of new businesses throughout the State. A primary function of this mission is the issuance of a business license so that the new business may legally operate. The cost of these licenses varies based on several factors.

You are to assume the role of an ASA II in an office of the DBL. In this position, you are to review the applications of new businesses for a business license. You must then calculate the cost of the license based on various guidelines, which will be provided to you. To perform your job, you must be familiar with the following forms:

- Business License Application Form
- Business License Summary Report Form
- Business Inspection Form
- Business Inspection Results Summary Form
- Business Licenses Cost Form Worksheet
- Business Licensing Cost Chart

This booklet contains detailed instructions on the procedures and rules you must follow in order to complete these forms and to correctly calculate the cost of the license.

I. Business License Application Form

Example A shows a copy of a completed Business License Application Form submitted by the ABC Pest Control Company. This form was completed by this business in order to obtain a business license.

Example A

Business License Application Form	
Application #: **99-1078**	
Name: **ABC Pest Control**	Annual Rent Expense: **25,000**
Number Employees: **16**	Business Zone: **A**
Estimated Annual Sales: **300,000**	Estimated Emp. Med. Insurance: **10,000**
Estimated Annual Payroll: **200,000**	Date: **10/29/09**

The following information must be contained on any Business License Application Form in order for the form to be processed by your office:

Application Number: This number is assigned to the application by your department.

Name: The name of the business should appear here.

Number of Employees: Here the business must indicate the number of employees who are drawing a salary from that business.

Estimated Annual Sales: This is the total sales the business believes it will achieve. This is an estimate. The business is new and is not yet fully operational so actual sales are not yet known.

Estimated Annual Payroll: This is the amount of money that the new business estimates it will pay to its employees over the next calendar year.

Annual Rent Expense: This is the amount of money a business is paying to rent, lease, or buy its present facilities. If the business currently owns the property and is not making any rent payments, the business should not write in the number "0" but instead should write the word "own" in this space.

Business Zone: In the State, each city with a population greater than 100,000 has been divided by the legislature into business zones. These zones represent an effort by the State Legislature to attract business into low-income, target zones. The letters A, B, and C designate the zones. Zone A is the highest priority for new business and, accordingly, is charged the least amount for a license. Zone B is the second priority level while Zone C, the third, pays the highest amount for a license.

Estimated Employee Medical Insurance: On this line, a business will enter the amount of money it estimates it will pay into its employees' medical insurance coverage fund. If the business does not offer medical insurance to its employees, the words "None Offered" should be written here; the number "0" should not be entered.

Date: This is the date on which the Business License Application Form was completed.

PROCESSING OF BUSINESS LICENSE APPLICATION FORM

A new business must complete a Business License Application Form and send it to your office. Once the form is received in your office, your job is to process the form and to notify the inspectors in your department of the request for a business license. The job of the inspector is to go to the business to inspect the facilities and to review the business operation's accounting records to ensure that the numbers provided on the Business License Application Form are accurate.

To process the Business License Application Form, you must follow these steps:

1. Review each entry on the form and ensure that all blanks are completed and that all information given is entered in the correct blank. Any unusual information should be circled on the application form for additional clarification.

2. Transfer the information shown on the Business License Application Form to the Business License Summary Report Form.

II. Business License Summary Report Form

The Business License Summary Report Form is an internal document created and used only in your office. The purpose of this report is to summarize the information from each Business License Application Form. Example B shows a completed Business License Summary Report Form.

Example B

Business License Summary Report Form						
Application Number	Employees	Sales	Payroll	Zone	Insurance	Approval
09-1078	16	300,000	200,000	A	10,000	A
09-1079	10	400,000	325,000	A	15,000	A
Totals	26	700,000	525,000		25,000	

You will note on this Business License Summary Report Form the following information: the Application Number, the Number of Employees, the Estimated Annual Sales, the Estimated Annual Payroll, the Business Zone, and the Estimated Medical Insurance Costs. Part of your job is to transfer the information from the Business License Application Form directly to the Business License Summary Report Form. At the end of the week, you must total all the information you have entered onto the summary report. Currently, your office is not highly automated. Therefore, you must manually calculate many things using an office calculator. One thing you will have to be able to do is manually calculate the information contained on the Business License Summary Report Form.

III. **Business Inspection Form**

A third form processed in your office is the Business Inspection Form. Example C shows a completed Business Inspection Form.

Example C

	Business Inspection Form		
	Name	Zone	Application Number
1)	ABC Pest Control	A	09-1078
2)	Perfect Pickles	A	09-1079
3)			

The inspectors in your office use this form as a source document to conduct inspections of new businesses. The purpose of these inspections is to review the information contained on the Business License Application Form and ensure this information is accurate. An inspector from your office visits each new business to review their accounting records, physical location, and number of employees. In order for the inspector to carry out these inspections, (s)he must first obtain the name of the business. You provide this information to the inspector on the Business Inspection Form that you complete. Information you provide on the Business Inspection Form must be accurate. Once the Business Inspection Form is completed, the inspector will take this form to the business and conduct the inspection. Businesses in Zone A are listed first on the Business Inspection Form. Businesses located in Zone A are inspected before those with B or C classifications. B-classified businesses are inspected before those classified in Zone C. If two businesses have the same business zone classification, they should be listed in alphabetical order on the Business Inspection Form. The inspector will follow the order of inspections on the Business Inspection Form, so you must make sure you list the correct order of inspections on the Business Inspection Form. Once the inspection is completed, the inspector will complete a Business Inspection Results Summary Form.

IV. **Business Inspection Results Summary Form**

A Business Inspection Results Summary Form is shown as Example D.

Example D

Business Inspection Results Summary Form	
Application #: **99-1078**	
Name: **ABC Pest Control**	Annual Rent Expense: **25,000**
Number Employees: **16**	Business Zone: **A**
Estimated Annual Sales: **300,000**	Estimated Emp. Med. Insurance: **10,000**
Estimated Annual Payroll: **200,000**	Date: **11/13**
Comments: **Approved for license**	

This form, completed by the inspector, shows the results of the inspection. This form is very similar to the Business License Application Form (with the exception of a comment line used by the inspector to make any notes about the inspections). As an ASA II, you must read over this form and determine if the inspector found the same information as the business originally submitted on its Business License Application Form. If there are any discrepancies between the information recorded by the inspector on the Business Inspection Results Summary Form and the information submitted by the business on the Business License Application Form, the information given by the inspector on the Business Inspection Results Summary Form must be used. You must carefully review the Business Inspection Results Summary Form information to make sure no discrepancies are found. The Business Inspection Results Summary Form also shows if the inspector feels that it is appropriate at this time to issue a license to the business. If the inspector does feel that it is appropriate to issue the license, your final role is to calculate the amount the business must pay for the license.

IV. **Business License Cost Form Worksheet**

To calculate the cost of the business license, a Business License Cost Form Worksheet must be completed. An example of this form is shown as Example E.

Example E

Business License Cost Form Worksheet	
Name: ABC Pest Control	Application #: 09-1078
Estimated Annual Sales:	300,000
Payroll Deduction:	-30,000
Rent & Medical Deduction:	-14,000
Net After Deductions:	256,000
Business Zone Adjustment A	-64,000
Net Total	192,000

This worksheet is designed to assist you in calculating the amount a business must pay to obtain its license. The information used to complete the Business License Cost Form Worksheet should always come from the Business Inspection Results Summary Form. Here is an explanation of how the cost of the license was calculated in Example E.

Name: The name of the company applying for the license goes here.

Application Number: This is the application number from the Business Inspection Results Summary Form.

Estimated Annual Sales: This figure comes directly from the Business Inspection Results Summary Form.

Payroll Deduction: The payroll deduction is calculated in the following way: Multiply the Estimated Annual Payroll from the Business Inspection Results Summary Form by 15% (.15). Example: 200,000 × .15 = 30,000. Then, transfer the answer to the payroll deduction line on the worksheet.

Rent and Medical Deduction: The rent and medical deduction is calculated in a similar way to the payroll deduction. Begin by (1) multiplying the Annual Rent Expense shown on the Business Inspection Results Summary Form by 12% (.12). Then, (2) multiply the Estimated Medical Insurance Cost by 10% (.10). Finally, (3) add this answer to the original Estimated Medical Insurance Cost and to the number calculated for the rent deduction.

Example: (1)   25,000 × .12 = 3,000
           (2)   10,000 × .10 = 1,000
           (3)   1,000 + 10,000 + 3,000 = 14,000

This sum becomes the rent and medical deduction.

Net After Deductions: The net after deductions is calculated by subtracting the payroll deduction and the rent and medical deduction from the estimated annual sales. In Example E, the net after deductions is $256,000.

BUSINESS ZONE ADJUSTMENT

As mentioned earlier, cities are divided into three business zones: A, B, and C.

Business Zone A: Zone A is an area in the city in which businesses are encouraged to open. Accordingly, businesses in Zone A pay less for their business license. To calculate the business zone adjustment for a business in Zone A, multiply the net after deductions (in Example E, 256,000) by 25% or .25.

Example: $256,000 × .25 = 64,000

This number should then be subtracted from the net after deductions to obtain the net total.

Business Zone B: Businesses in the city designated as Zone B are not especially encouraged to open. Accordingly, there is no deduction for a business opening in Zone B. Therefore, no calculation is necessary. The number placed onto the form should be "0" for Zone B businesses.

Business Zone C: The opening of a business in Zone C is highly discouraged. Accordingly, businesses opening in Zone C must pay a higher price for their business license. To calculate a business zone adjustment for a business opening in Zone C, (1) multiply the estimated annual sales by 25% or .25. Then, (2) add this number to the net after deductions to determine the net total.

> Example: (1) 300,000 × .25 = 75,000
> (2) 75,000 + 256,000 = 331,000

IV. **Business Licensing Cost Chart**

To arrive at a final license cost, refer to the Business Licensing Cost Chart shown as Example F.

Example F

	Business Licensing Cost Chart	
	Net Total	Cost of License
1)	0 – 24,000	100
2)	25,000 – 75,000	500
3)	76,000 – 125,000	1000
4)	126,000 – 135,000	1300
5)	136,000 – 150,000	1650
6)	151,000 – 200,000	1900
7)	201,000 – 250,000	2250
8)	251,000 – 300,000	2500
9)	301,000 – Above	1% of Sales

For ABC Pest Control, the net total was $192,000. Looking to the table shown as Example F, you see a range of numbers in line 6 between $151,000 and $200,000. Our example's total of $192,000 falls within this range of numbers. Therefore, the amount the business must pay for the business license is $1,900.

COMPLETING THE BUSINESS LICENSE SUMMARY REPORT FORM

Once a cost is calculated, you should put the letter "A" in the approval column on the Business License Summary Report Form. This final approval will ensure the business will receive its license. If, at this time, the business does not meet the requirements for the license, you should put the letter "D" on the Business License Summary Report Form.

EXAMINATION SECTION
Inbox Examination #1: TEST 1

Senior Technical Writer/Content Director, Interaxion

You are T. SMITH, the senior technical writer/content director for an eight-year-old business service provider, Interaxion. The primary services provided to its clients are Web hosting, security services, high-capacity Internet access, and information system audits. You and your staff of 4 writers and 2 assistants have recently completed a draft of customer use manuals for a new addition to the service line: a dedicated storage network for clients with large amounts of data. Within the next several months, Interaxion also intends to launch a new download hosting service that will help clients place large files and applications on their own dedicated servers for access.

Interaxion is a medium-sized company that aggressively competes with larger business-to-business service organizations, much of them sprung from existing computer or telecommunications companies. To hold its market share, Interaxion offers a level of service and individual client attention that goes beyond the norm.

The president and CEO of your company, Marlane Liddell, is the engine behind Interaxion's aggressive approach. She is anxious to make Interaxion into a one-stop destination for any and all business-to-business networking services, which explains the rapid schedule of new product/service rollouts—now occurring at a pace of nearly two per year. Many employees privately complain that the grueling pace of development and launch makes work more stressful and error-prone, but the business is growing steadily. While some errors do occur in implementing and documenting services, the departments are managed well enough to correct these mistakes before they cause a significant loss of up-time for clients—if they weren't managed this well, Interaxion would have real problems in customer relations.

As the head of the technical writing department, you are accountable to the Vice President of Customer Relations, Branch Stuckey. He's known as a calm, reasonable man who nevertheless keeps the pressure steady—if his memos or phone calls are not answered within a reasonable amount of time, he is sure to pay a personal visit to ask why. Both he and you share the vision of the technical writing department as the most important medium through which customers receive information about Interaxion's products and services.

You and your staff are responsible for writing the promotional materials and specifications that anchor every service's marketing campaign, and for writing easy-to-follow manuals for their use. You're also accountable for maintaining and updating the Interaxion Web site.

You and Stuckey have jointly decided that the clientele would be well-served by two additional projects. The first, a general technical glossary, is to be available both in print and from Interaxion's Web site, and will help customers to understand the increasingly complex jargon involved in implementing the company's services. You and Stuckey have set a deadline of six months for the launch of this glossary.

Another document you've decided will be helpful is a Frequently Asked Questions (FAQ)/Troubleshooting guide for each of the company's line of services. This will require close collaboration with both the Technical Support and Communications departments. This a project that is of particular interest to the president, who wants a progress report submitted at the end of each month.

As a matter of principle, you try to work no more than a standard 8-to-5 workday. The three-day focus for this exercise is the Monday-Wednesday span of the 23rd through the 25th. The items you find in your in-box are items 1 through 10 and a general information folder compiled by your trusted assistant, Fred. On Tuesday afternoon, a meeting is scheduled from 2 p.m. to 4. p.m. that will include the marketing staff and your department, to discuss reasons why the marketing campaign for Interaxion's security services is not doing well. Tina Niu, Vice President of Marketing, seems to believe it's because the promotional material is too technical and jargony. You met briefly with your staff on Friday to prepare a response to this, but were unsatisfied with the results. You'd like at least another two hours with your writers before meeting with the marketing department.

On the following pages are a list of important departments and personnel at Interaxion, a to-do list, messages, memos, and a planner covering the three-day period. Read the instructions below, then assume you have just arrived Monday morning to find these items in your in-basket.

1. *Look over the list of officers, the planner, the to-do list, and in-basket items quickly, to get an idea of the tasks to be done.*

2. *In the spaces provided in the left margin of the to-do list, indicate the priority of each item, and note how you would dispose of each. Priorities should be labeled in the following manner:*

    AB priorities = those that are both important and urgent
    A priorities = those that are important, but not particularly urgent (can be deferred)
    B priorities = those that are urgent, but not so important
    X priorities = neither urgent nor important

3. *After reading the in-basket items, do the following:*

    a. *First, decide which items can be delegated, and to whom. Use Form B, Delegated Calls and Correspondence, to list and prioritize these items.*
    b. *Next, prioritize the items to which you must respond personally on Form C, Personal Calls and Correspondence.*

4. *Take the planning guide and schedule the tasks you have in front of you. Be sure to allow some "flexible time" to handle any interruptions or crises.*

Interaxion

Important Departments/Personnel:

President/CEO: Marlane Liddell
VP Marketing: Tina Niu
- Marketing Director: Brian Paulsen
- General Sales Manager: Maxine Patton

VP Service Delivery: Owen Stark
- Director of Engineering: Anna Karpov
- Chief Information Architect: Juan Machuca
  - (Various Project Managers)

VP Finance: Tom Wilson
- Treasurer: Mary Stravinsky
- Comptroller: Barbara Bernstein
  - John Slingsby, Director of Cost Analysis
  - Ruth Nielsen, Director of Budgeting and Accounting

VP Administration and Human Resources: Tariq Nayim
- Director of Human Resources: Amos Otis
- Director of Administration: Nancy Frank

VP Customer Relations: Branch Stuckey
- Director of Communications: Alvin Gehring
- Director of Technical Support: Hollis Holt
- **Chief Technical Writer: T. SMITH**
  - Terry Appleton, Technical Writer
  - Samir Naramayan, Technical Writer/Web Designer
  - Jim Mason, Technical Writer
  - Tracy Livingston, Associate Writer
    - Fred Cummings, Assistant to **T. SMITH**
    - Stacia Cocker, Office Assistant

Things to Do:

Priority   *Item*

_____   •attend meeting on downtime of hosting service. Some clients have fallen below the promised 99.999% uptime, and the company needs to devise ways to improve performance.

   Disposition: _____

   _____

   _____

_____   •meet with technical writing staff for input on the promotion of security services.

   Disposition: _____

   _____

   _____

_____   •meet with staff to outline promotional copy for download hosting service —now looks as if it will be rolled out in about 8 months.

   Disposition: _____

   _____

   _____

_____   •see what's up with Mason's overtime.

   Disposition: _____

   _____

   _____

Things to Do (cont'd):

_____ •contact people who sent in resumes for associate writing job--Sanchez looked best of all, but I'll interview Larkin, too. Reject Yancey and Crespin.

Disposition: _____

_____

_____

_____ •meet with writers to assign updates to manuals for each of the security services. Should take about an hour.

Disposition: _____

_____

_____

_____ •check on the progress of the technical glossary--Mason is falling way, way behind.

Disposition: _____

_____

_____

_____ •check with human resources and budgeting to ask about availability for part-time position, to compile the FAQ/Troubleshooting guide—even with new associate, not enough staff time to devote to this.

Disposition: _____

_____

_____

_____ •proofread/line-edit customer manual (8 hours work at least) for storage network operation, and send it to the printer. Must be done by you personally, and by Thursday morning! Several customers have already purchased network and are waiting.

Disposition: _____

_____

Item 1

NOTE TO: T. SMITH
DATE: 20th   TIME: 4:50 p.m.

WHILE YOU WERE OUT

M: Janet Yancey

OF: _____

PHONE (____) _____ _____
      AREA CODE   NUMBER   EXTENSION

	Telephoned	✓	Please Call
	Called to See You		Will Call Again
	Wants to See You		Returned Your Call

Message: Anxious to speak w/ you about associate writer position.

Item 2

Memorandum

To: T. SMITH
CC: Hollis Holt, Director of Technical Support
From: Alvin Gehring, Director of Communications
Date: 20th
Re: Web site e-mail service

I've been contacted a few times in the past couple of weeks by customers who have visited our Web site and wanted to e-mail us a question. Apparently some of them have clicked on the "e-mail us" hypertext button from a product description page, and nothing has happened.

I know that this is probably a very small-scale problem, and that the more persistent customers will know to simply e-mail us using their own mail programs. But I can't help thinking we might be losing some potential customers without this direct link.

Can you look into this and see what the problem is? I'd like to find out as soon as possible.

Item 3

Memorandum

To: T. SMITH
CC:
From: Marlane Liddell, CEO and President
Date: 23rd
Re: Updates on troubleshooting guide and arrangement with Sturdevant

---

Just a note to remind you that I'll want to meet with you soon to talk about progress on the FAQ/Troubleshooting Guide.

I've also recently received a letter from Sturdevant Publishing about our arrangement with them. Their $6500 payment is figured into our revenues for the quarter, so we'll need to meet that contract deadline.

Let me know when you're available to meet—and when we do meet, make sure you're ready with the good news.

Item 4

NOTE TO: T. SMITH
DATE: 23rd
TIME: 9:00 am

WHILE YOU WERE OUT

M: Philip Larkin

OF:

PHONE: ( ) — AREA CODE — NUMBER — EXTENSION

✓	Telephoned		Please Call
	Called to See You		Will Call Again
	Wants to See You		Returned Your Call

Message: Wants to know your decision about associate writer position.

Memorandum

To: T. SMITH
CC: Terry Appleton, Samir Naramayan, Jim Mason, Technical Writers
From: Tracy Livingston, Associate Writer
Date: 23rd
Re: Security services/marketing

I hope this doesn't sound too compulsive, but I know we all worked very hard on the specs and promotional materials for security services, and I can't accept the idea that people aren't buying in because they don't understand our copy.

I conducted a little of my own market research over the weekend — interviewing purchasers from about a dozen clients who've bought other services from us, but went with another company for security. There were a few different reasons, but many clients seem to have placed the blame on some questionable architecture.

When pressed, a few said that they did find some parts of the promotional copy a little hard to follow — but added that it wasn't the factor that affected our buying decision.

We'll need to be careful about how we present this, so it doesn't appear we're shifting blame to Service Delivery. This can be one of the things we decide together when we meet (when are we meeting again? Isn't the meeting with Marketing tomorrow afternoon?).

Before we do meet, I hope you'll all take a look at some of the results of the interviews, enclosed here. It should take about a half-hour to get through them.

Item 6

NOTE TO: T. SMITH
DATE: 23rd   TIME: 8:24 a.m.

WHILE YOU WERE OUT

M Jim Mason

OF

PHONE ( ) AREA CODE   NUMBER   EXTENSION

✓	Telephoned		Please Call
	Called to See You		Will Call Again
	Wants to See You		Returned Your Call

Message: Will come in at 10:30 a.m. today — had to take his wife to a rescheduled hospital appointment. Says he's sorry — the only time he could do it.

Item 7

Memorandum

To: All Department Heads
CC:
From: Marlane Liddell, President and CEO
Date: 23rd
Re: Meeting on hosting service downtime

A reminder: our meeting on resolving the hosting service downtime problem will be this Wednesday, the 25th, from 1 p.m. to 4 p.m.

Enclosed is a short examination of issues, compiled by Alvin Gehring Hollis Holt, and Owen Stark, that will need to be addressed if we are to improve the uptime of our Web hosting service. This is probably the most important problem facing our company today, and we'll all need to work together to resolve it as soon as possible.

Please take a look through the enclosed 30 pages to get an idea of what's holding us back, and try to have some ideas for resolution ready by the time we meet Wednesday.

Item 8

2642 Avenue of the Americas

New York, NY 00000

Sturdevant Publishing

November 10

T. SMITH
Chief Technical Writer
Interaxion
3445 Newton Ave.
Cambridge, MA 00000

Dear T. SMITH:

We at Sturdevant are pleased you've decided to contribute to our forthcoming publication, *The Encyclopedia of Technical Publishing*, to be compiled over the next 9 months and released early next year.

Last month, you agreed to send us a general profile of your company and a specific description of the different forms of writing (manuals, proposals, letters, specifications, etc.) performed by your department, along with a few recent samples of your work.

As you know, payment of $6500 to Interaxion was contingent on the delivery of this information by the end of the current month. We expect that you have every intention of honoring this contract, but we haven't heard from you recently and wanted to extend a reminder to you in any case.

Sincerely,

Bob Francis

Editorial Director

Item 9

Memorandum

To: T. SMITH
CC: Jim Mason, Technical Writer; Barbara Bernstein, Comptroller
From: Ruth Nielsen, Director of Budgeting and Accounting
Date: 23rd
Re: Overtime

Our records show an unusual amount of overtime charged to the company by your department over the last month. In order to meet our budget targets for the quarter, you'll need to work with your employees to reduce the number of hours they work each week.

If you're unable to reduce these hours, it may be necessary to conduct an internal audit in order to verify their necessity. Of course this is simply adding time and expenditure to the situation, and we'd like to avoid it entirely.

Please let us know how this situation is resolved.

Item 10

NOTE TO: T. SMITH
DATE: 23rd   TIME: 7:50 a.m.

WHILE YOU WERE OUT

M: Janet Yancey
OF:
PHONE: ( )

	Telephoned	✓	Please Call
	Called to See You	✓	Will Call Again
	Wants to See You		Returned Your Call

Message: Wants to speak w/ you ASAP about associate writer position — will keep calling.

General Information Folder:

1. Additional interdepartmental memos—about a dozen of them. Don't need a response but should be read for information. Should take about a half hour.

2. Eight news and trade newspapers and magazines—about two hours' worth of reading.

3. About 20 items of junk mail—should be reviewed. Will take about 30 minutes.

4. A detailed report—in addition to Liddell's 30-page report and Livingston's interviews—that need to be studied for possible action. It's a compilation of customer-satisfaction ratings for the company's other services, including their ratings of the documentation for each on a broad range of criteria, including readability, ease of understanding, and thoroughness. This should require about an hour.

DELEGATED CALLS AND CORRESPONDENCE

Priority   *Item*   *Delegated to:*

_____

_____

_____

_____

_____

_____

_____

_____

PERSONAL CALLS AND CORRESPONDENCE

Priority *Item* *Response:*

_____

_____

_____

_____

_____

_____

_____

_____

19

	23 Monday	24 Tuesday	25 Wednesday
7 AM			
8			
9			
10			
11			
12 PM			
1			
2			
3			
4			
5			
6 PM			
7			

KEY (CORRECT ANSWERS)

Discussion of Inbox Examination #1:

Senior Technical Writer/Content Director, Interaxion

One of the first things you should realize, when looking over all the information in front of you, is that there won't be enough time within the next three days for you to do the things on your list, as well as the tasks required by your in-box items. This is hardly surprising for a senior worker at a mid-sized company, but you'll have to decide quickly what can be either eliminated from your schedule, or postponed.

To-Do List:

In this case, the prime candidate for elimination is the three-hour meeting on the downtime of the company's hosting service. While the president is anxious about it, and wants input from people from all departments, there's really not much a technical writing staff can do about the problem. You should try to free up these three hours—speaking with the president personally and explaining what needs to be done by you and your staff in the next three days, and offering to send a representative to the meeting who will report back to you.

As chief technical writer, there are two situations that are both important and urgent: your meeting with marketing department to discuss the quality of your staff's promotional materials, and the huge task of editing the manual for Interaxion's storage network users. Since some customers have already purchased the network, they'll need the manual as soon as possible. The meeting with Marketing is on Tuesday, and you have two tasks to complete before then: read through the information supplied by Tracy Livingston, and call the afternoon meeting with the writers on Monday—they'll need to drop everything in the afternoon for this.

Once the most important and urgent items are taken care of, you should turn your attention to tasks that are important, but not as pressing. You'll need to meet with the staff for two further purposes: outlining promotional copy for the company's downloading hosting service (not that urgent, since the rollout isn't for another 8 months), and assigning updates for the manuals for security service users. Since your copy on the promotional materials for these services is being questioned by the marketing department, it's probably best to schedule this meeting after you've met with Marketing and these questions have been resolved. You'll also need to see if you can find a way to hire part-time help for compiling the FAQ/Troubleshooting guide, since this is of extreme importance to the president.

Urgent matters that aren't quite as significant as the others facing you right now are the progress of the technical glossary—not due out for another six months—and the related problem of Jim Mason's excessive overtime. His memo about taking his wife to the hospital hints that he might be going through some personal problems, and if they're affecting his work, this situation needs to be resolved soon.

Discussion (cont'd)

Delegated Calls and Correspondence:

Janet Yancey may insist on speaking with you personally, but it may simply be that she wants a yes or no answer regarding her hiring. For now, it should be enough to have your assistant send her a letter. Assuming Fred is informed about the progress of your arrangements with Sturdevant—and assuming the contract is being honored—he can also send a reply to them. The e-mail problem, presented in the memo from Hollis Holt, is best left to the expertise of your Web designer, Samir Naramayan.

Personal Calls and Correspondence:

It appears that the news on the progress of the FAQ/Troubleshooting guide is not that good, but you'll need to set up a meeting with the president anyway to tell her so. It might be a good time to state your case about needing more help. You should send a memo to set a meeting time, and to reassure her about the arrangement with Sturdevant.

Since you do intend to interview Philip Larkin about the associate writer position, you should probably call him personally to set this up—though some managers might leave this to an assistant. It's acceptable to include this in the "delegated" column as well.

The memo from the president is simply a re-statement of your obligation to attend the hosting service downtime meeting—and you've determined you can't do this. You should make every attempt to speak with the president personally, to explain why, and to see if sending your assistant is acceptable. You should also give the 30-page report to your assistant, Fred, to have him either outline it for you or see if any of it is relevant to the technical writing staff at all.

Jim Mason appears to be in some trouble, and he may need your help to resolve it—especially since his problems are being noticed by the budgeting department. Since it would be best to discuss it privately, out of the office, you might meet him somewhere for lunch and try to work things out. He'll have to find a way to get things done within a regular 40-hour week.

Planner:

Filling in the planner can be done in a number of ways—as long as everything on your to-do list and in your inbox gets taken care of, and in an appropriate sequence. The most difficult thing to schedule will probably be the meeting with the writers about promotional copy for the security services. It's a short-notice meeting, for one thing, and you'll need to look over Livingston's interviews first. The meeting must happen before the Tuesday meeting with marketing—and Since Jim Mason won't be in until 10:30 on Monday, it will have to take place after that. The tight window requires that the meeting happen Monday afternoon or Tuesday morning. Items such as progress on other projects can be discussed briefly, toward the end of scheduled meetings.

In addition, it wouldn't make sense to schedule the other meeting—regarding the updates to existing security service manuals—until after some of the questions raised by both the marketing department and Livingston's interviews have been resolved. This will have to take place some time on Wednesday.

Things to Do: 22

Priority	Item

___X___ • attend meeting on downtime of hosting service. Some clients have fallen below the promised 99.999% uptime, and the company needs to devise ways to improve performance.

Disposition: _Contact Marlane Liddell personally to explain why you can't make the meeting. Ask if you can send an assistant to take notes, promise to review them later and get back to her with ideas._

___AB___ • meet with technical writing staff for input on the promotion of security services.

Disposition: _Schedule meeting for Monday, the 23rd, after Mason gets in._

___A___ • meet with staff to outline promotional copy for download hosting service — now looks as if it will be rolled out in about 8 months.

Disposition: _Schedule after more urgent meetings — maybe combine with manual update meeting._

___B___ • see what's up with Mason's overtime.

Disposition: _Meet with him soon and privately, away from other writers._

___A___ • contact people who sent in resumes for associate writing job--Sanchez looked best of all, but I'll interview Larkin, too. Reject Yancey and Crespin.

Disposition: _Have Fred send letter to Yancey and Crespin; call Larkin and Sanchez personally to set up interviews_

Things to Do (cont'd):

A • meet with writers to assign updates to manuals for each of the security services. Should take about an hour.

Disposition: _Schedule meeting after all other concerns regarding security services documentation have been cleared up—no sooner than Wednesday._

B • check on the progress of the technical glossary--Mason is falling way, way behind.

Disposition: _A quick check that can be slipped in at the end of another meeting—try for Monday or Wednesday._

A • check with human resources and budgeting to ask about availability for part-time position, to compile the FAQ/Troubleshooting guide—even with new associate, not enough staff time to devote to this.

Disposition: _Contact them personally, during flex time, before scheduling meeting with Marlane Liddell._

AB • proofread/line-edit customer manual (8 hours work at least) for storage network operation, and send it to the printer. Must be done by you personally, and by Thursday morning! Several customers have already purchased network and are waiting.

Disposition: _Try to fit in big time blocks to devote to this—give it your full attention._

DELEGATED CALLS AND CORRESPONDENCE

Priority	Item	Delegated to:
X	#1 — Yancey call	Fred
A	#2 — Holt memo	Samir
X	#8 — Sturdevant letter	Fred will write response
X	#10 — Yancey call	Fred

25

PERSONAL CALLS AND CORRESPONDENCE

Priority	Item	Response:
A	#3—Liddell memo	Brief memo
A	#4—Larkin call	Phone call for interview
AB	#7—Liddell memo	Personal visit
A	#9—Nielsen memo	Meet w/ Mason and write memo

	23 Monday	24 Tuesday	25 Wednesday
7 AM			
8	flex-time: delegate, make calls, set up meeting	flex-time: reading, sorting work on storage network manual	read customer sat. report
9	reading: interdept. memos, trade publications		flex-time: schedule interviews
10			work on storage network manual
11			
12 PM		lunch, meeting w/ Mason	
1	flex-time: examine Livingston interviews	flex-time: sort through junk mail	meeting w. writers: •assign updates to manuals,
2	meeting w. writers:	meeting w/ Marketing	•outline download promo copy
3	•ideas for response to marketing,		work on storage network manual
4	•progress of tech. glossary,	work on storage network manual	
5	•FAQ/Troubleshooting guide		
6 PM			
7			

EXAMINATION SECTION
IN-BASKET

Senior Graphic Designer, Callens New Media

You are B. GARCIA, the senior graphic designer of Callens New Media, a small publisher of materials (newsletters, meeting planners, city guides, and more) for those who organize and attend trade conventions. You have a background both in art and in computer technology, and because the company is small, you play a dual role as both a project manager for the publications and a troubleshooter/technical support resource when there are problems with the publishing software or the company Web site, which you designed and now maintain.

Because of your company's size, its success has relied primarily on occupying this smaller niche in the business publishing market. Your boss, Reynold Callens, would like to draw upon your technological knowledge and expand services to include Web design and servicing, and eventually to include such things as hosting and downloading services for professional associations who conduct merchandising operations from their Web sites. In your last evaluation, you and your boss set an objective to produce a Web-based demonstration of the services that will be available to anyone who visits the company Web site. The deadline for completion of this project has been left open, but your boss is pressing you to show him results soon.

The organizational structure of the company is somewhat loose, due to its size, and could use some readjustment. There are no vice presidents; simply a few team leaders, each overseeing a few workers. Though each team leader reports directly to Reynold Callens, you are often approached by people from other departments for input on solutions, because you were one of the company's first employees and have more knowledge about clients and products, as well as some working knowledge of the earlier and simpler versions of the company's computer networks. Though you don't resent being thought of as a "catch-all" for projects or problems that don't fit neatly into the company's departmental structure, you believe your own responsibilities are keeping you busy enough. The added pressures from other departments is getting stressful for both you and your staff, whom you sense are becoming slightly indignant at the repeated encroachments on their time.

You and your staff bear much responsibility for the timeliness and completeness of the company's current operations. Your responsibilities include making sure the publications are proofread and camera-ready, making arrangements with the printers, arranging for distribution of your company's products to individual conferees, and offering the final say for photos, illustrations, or maps in every publication. Traditionally, you have been the one who communicates with customers directly about certain projects, answering questions or addressing concerns—though these are tasks which should logically fall to your production assistant, Craig Long.

The company's size also means that you have no office assistant. Any calls that come in are handled either by you or your staff of three—your associate graphic artist, Sally

Montrose, your technical writer/content provider, Stan Lee, or your production assistant, Craig Long. You hired all three of them, and you're generally pleased with their work so far—though you admit to having a hard time delegating tasks that can be handled by one or more of them. This is due, you admit, to your own reluctance to surrender control of details, and not with any problem you have with their work thus far.

The three-day focus is the Monday-Wednesday span of the 16th through the 18th—a period that coincides with the beginning of a convention in Cincinnati, to which Craig Long has been dispatched to oversee the distribution of materials to individual participants on Monday and early Tuesday. The items you find in your in-box are items 1 through 10 and a general information folder that you have compiled yourself, which contains items that you believe will need your attention, sooner or later.

On Tuesday afternoon from 1 p.m. to 3 p.m., you are meeting with your boss and an outside consultant, both to check on the progress of the demonstration and to discuss the resources that will be needed to make the proposed Web services available to clients. You'll need to supply an idea of manpower and work-hour needs for different types of sites—and you'll need to get input from your staff to do this, which you estimate will take an hour. Since Craig Long is in Cincinnati, the meeting will have to be a conference call.

On Wednesday morning from 9 a.m. to 11 a.m. you are meeting one-one-one with Callens to more clearly define two things: First, what your own personal responsibilities are, now that the company is growing and your title of "graphic designer" doesn't seem to quite encompass all the managerial tasks you've been taking on. Second, the extent and limit of what your team members are expected to do. You will need to go to this meeting armed with four proposed job descriptions: for yourself, which you will need to write before the meeting (anticipated time: 2 hours), and for Montrose, Lee, and Long, who have already been assigned to write their own. You'll need to meet together with them for an hour, to go over their written descriptions, before you present them to the boss.

You and your staff like to work a normal eight-hour day whenever possible. The day begins at 8 and ends at 5, so an hour-long lunch is the custom, though because of the recent pressures at the workplace it's often much shorter than that.

On the following pages are a list of important departments and personnel at Callens New Media, a to-do list, messages, memos, and a planner covering the three-day period. Read the instructions below, then assume you have just arrived Monday morning to find these items in your in-basket.

1. *Look over the list of officers, the planner, the to-do list, and in-basket items quickly, to get an idea of the tasks to be done.*

2. *In the spaces provided in the left margin of the to-do list, indicate the priority of each item, and note how you would dispose of each. Priorities should be labeled in the following manner:*

   AB priorities = those that are both important and urgent
   A priorities = those that are important, but not particularly urgent (can be deferred)
   B priorities = those that are urgent, but not so important
   X priorities = neither urgent nor important

3. *After reading the in-basket items, do the following:*

   a. *First, decide which items can be delegated, and to whom. Use Form B, Delegated Calls and Correspondence, to list and prioritize these items.*
   b. *Next, prioritize the items to which you must respond personally on Form C, Personal Calls and Correspondence.*

4. *Take the planning guide and schedule the tasks you have in front of you. Be sure to allow some "flexible time" to handle any interruptions, crises, or new issues or correspondence.*

Callens New Media

Important Departments/Personnel:

Owner/CEO: Reynold Callens

Marketing and Sales Team:
Marketing and Sales Director: Roland Brooks (team leader)
Sales Region 1: Tom Spencer
Sales Region 2: Lorna Stans

Administrative Team:
Accounting Officer: Terry Spath (team leader)
Budget and Accounting Assistant: Ed Stein
Information Architect: Gordon Wayne
Manager, Enterprise Systems: Frank Luntz
Director of Human Resources: Monica Torres

Production/Customer Relations Team:
Senior Graphic Designer: B. Garcia (team leader)
Associate Graphic Artist: Sally Montrose
Technical Writer/Content Provider: Stan Lee
Production Assistant: Craig Long

Things to Do:

Priority   *Item*

_____   • check and respond to e-mails, especially any from clients, hotels, or Craig Long in Cincinnati. Time required: half an hour

Disposition: _____

_____

_____

_____   •write job description for Wednesday meeting. Would like to have this done before meeting with Callens on Tuesday, in order to be ready if there is time. Two hours.

Disposition: _____

_____

_____

_____   •update the company Web site to add newly hired personnel, and to more accurately reflect the company's products and services. Estimated time: 3 hours—one hour design and layout, one hour writing content, one hour formatting/coding.

Disposition: _____

_____

_____

_____   •deliver proofs for newsletter to local printer, for next month's radiologists' convention in Cleveland. Should take about a half hour.

Disposition: _____

_____

_____

Things to Do (cont'd):

_____   •respond to customer requests for information about upcoming projects and publications (requests for proofs, information about content, requests for edits, etc.). Should take about an hour and a half.

Disposition: _____

_____

_____

_____   •find illustrations, maps and photos for meeting planner, for next month's convention in Denver. Already been designed. Needs to be ready for printer within two weeks. Should take about two hours.

Disposition: _____

_____

_____

_____   • call temp agency, hotels to arrange for drops (hotel charges for doorman to make drops) for Philadelphia convention that begins this Thursday and runs through Sunday. Should take about an hour.

Disposition: _____

_____

_____

_____   •perform design and layout for a meeting planner and city guide for an upcoming convention in Nashville. Initial design must be done by you and should take about 8 hours total; you need to spend at least 3 hours on it before Thursday to stay on schedule.

Disposition: _____

_____

_____

General Information Folder:

1. Several articles in trade journals, flagged by Reynold Callens to be read by you and discussed with him at a later, unspecified date. Should take about an hour

2. About 30 items of junk mail—should be scanned. About an hour's worth of reading.

3. Additional interdepartmental memos—ten or so. Don't require a response but should be read for information. Should take about a half hour.

4. A written proposal from a software vendor detailing the newest features of the latest version of their desktop publishing suite. They are not your vendor but want you to switch to their line. You want to consider it. It's about an hour and a half of reading.

FORM B: DELEGATED CALLS AND CORRESPONDENCE

Priority　　　　　　　　*Item*　　　　　　　　　　　*Delegated to:*

_____

_____

_____

_____

_____

_____

_____

_____

_____

FORM C: PERSONAL CALLS AND CORRESPONDENCE

Priority   *Item*   *Response:*

_____

_____

_____

_____

_____

_____

_____

_____

Item 1

From: smontrose@cnm.com
Date: June 15, 7:22:39 PM EST
Subject: Monday
To: clong@cnm.com, bgarcia@cnm.com

Wanted to let you both know in advance that I'll be leaving the office tomorrow (Monday), after lunch. My son is sick and has an appointment with the doctor in the afternoon. I haven't forgotten our meeting—I'll be back first thing Tuesday morning.

Item 2

Memorandum

To: All Team Leaders
CC:
From: Reynold
Date: June 14
Re: The Future

I've been thinking a lot over the past month about the direction this company is taking, and I think you're all right, to a degree: We've outgrown the informal structure that was in place when we first started. Roles aren't as clearly defined as they need to be, and there is some overlap in responsibilities. I realize the potential for conflict here, and I'm grateful that you've all been able to bear these growing pains so graciously. You'd tell me if you were having any problems with each other, right?

Anyway, I think it's time we sat down together and had a serious talk about the future of this company—how it is structured, what each of our roles is going to be, an d where we out to be investing our resources in the coming years. It's a serious subject that deserves your serious consideration. I'm tentatively scheduling a leadership meeting for 1-4 on Wednesday. If there's some reason why that won't work—I know the Philadelphia convention begins the next day, but I'm assuming we're on top of that—then let me know. Otherwise, bring your best ideas.

--Reynold

Item 3

NOTE TO: B. Garcia
DATE: Friday, June 13th   TIME: 7:00 pm

WHILE YOU WERE OUT

M: Horst, concierge
OF: Cincinnati Hampden Court Hotel
PHONE: (513) 888-7777 EXTENSION: 55

[X] Telephoned
[ ] Called to See You
[ ] Wants to See You
[ ] Please Call
[ ] Will Call Again
[ ] Returned Your Call

Message: Materials haven't arrived yet for next week's convention — can't get hold of printer. Call back ASAP!
— Sally

Item 4

From: glesst@ana.org
Date: June 16, 8:07:12 AM EST
Subject: meeting
To: bgarcia@cnm.com

I have the advance proofs of the newsletter for our convention next month in Denver—thanks for sending them along so promptly. I have some questions. First, a general question about the style guide your staff uses (I'm curious about some of the choices you've made in indentation and layout—I think I might like a few changes to be made here). I also have a few corrections to make about the details of the convention and some of the bios that appear on the last page.

Thanks again—I hope I'll hear from you soon.

--Teresa Gless

Item 5

From: clong@cnm.com
Date: June 16, 8:07:12 AM EST
Subject: meeting
To: smontrose@cnm.com, bgarcia@cnm.com

I know we have to have a conference call today or tomorrow, but things are getting hairy here in Cincinnati and I'm going to need to stay on top of things nearly around the clock. I can be available today from 3-5 pm or tomorrow from 8-9 in the morning. Give me a call on the cell at either of those two times.

I'll be back in the office no later than 3 p.m. on Tuesday. See you both then.

Item 6

                                                 1947 Nautilus Ct.
                                                 Mystic, CT 00000

June 8

Production Department
Callens New Media
7875 Shore Drive
Tampa, FL 00000

To Whom it May Concern:

I'm a Printing Technology Professional with many years of experience in the printing trade. As you will see from my attached resume, I have a plethora of skills which are directly related to the mission of a printing or marketing firm.

My skills in printing, graphic arts, web site design and customer service would be an excellent fit with any company utilizing the printing arts.

With over 12 years in commercial printing and 20 years of involvement with computers, it is my hope that your company could use a person with my expertise.

I am a very positive individual with excellent people skills and have previously been an inspiring force in team situations.

I'd like a chance to convince you that my skills and energy would be an asset to your firm. If needed, I can also provide a comprehensive portfolio that exhibits my greatest accomplishments in the last 10 years of my career, as well as letters of recommendation from previous employers.

                                                      Sincerely,

                                                    Fred G. Moose

Item 7

NOTE TO: B. Garcia
DATE: Friday, June 13th
TIME: 9:00 a.m.

WHILE YOU WERE OUT

MS. Vivian Wu
OF Hood Printing, Oregon
PHONE (503) 555-2424

✓	Telephoned		Please Call
	Called to See You		Will Call Again
	Wants to See You		Returned Your Call

Message: Questions about sizing, res of photos for DHA convention in Portland next week, (25th?)

— Lorna

Item 8

NOTE TO: B. Garcia
DATE: Monday, June 16th   TIME: 8:11 am

WHILE YOU WERE OUT

MS: Merman
OF: National League of Dental Hygienists
PHONE: (212) 777-1234 EXT: 203

X	Telephoned		Please Call
	Called to See You		Will Call Again
	Wants to See You		Returned Your Call

Message: Doesn't have confirmation that materials have arrived at hotel and are ready for distribution at Philadelphia Convention. Begins on Thurs., 19th.

—Sally

Item 9

Memorandum

To: B. GARCIA
CC: Reynold Callens, President
From: Roland Brooks, Director of Marketing and Sales
Date: June 13
Re: Marketing our new services

B.:

I'm going to be meeting with our sales staff next week about how to begin planting the seeds of interest in our new Web services to our clients—especially the national medical groups. The problem is, I'm not yet very knowledgeable about what these services are going to be and how, exactly, they are going to serve our clients. I'll be grateful if I could be brought up to speed on the technical details, but most especially I'll be interested in being able to explain, in layman's terms, what each of these proposed services is going to enable our clients to do.

Would it be possible to meet for an hour or so this week to talk about this? Thanks in advance.

Item 10

NOTE TO: B. Garcia
DATE: Monday, June 16th   TIME: 7:45 am

WHILE YOU WERE OUT

M: Horst, concierge
OF: Cincinnati Hampden Court Hotel
PHONE: (513) 888-7777 EXTENSION: 55

X	Telephoned		Please Call
	Called to See You		Will Call Again
	Wants to See You		Returned Your Call

Message: materials are there at front desk, but hasn't heard from anyone at CNM about distribution. Conferees calling to ask about it. Not his job! Call back ASAP!

— Sally

	20	
16 Monday	**17 Tuesday**	**18 Wednesday**

7
8
9
10
11
12
1
2
3
4
5
6
7

KEY (CORRECT ANSWERS)

Discussion of Inbox Examination

Senior Graphic Designer, Callens New Media

There are 24 total work hours in these three days, and the four meetings listed in the introduction—with your staff, to discuss the requirements of the Web services demonstration; with Reynold Callens and the consultant; with the staff to go over job descriptions; and with Callens again—consume six of these hours, leaving you with 18 hours in which to handle everything else. It's not enough time—and so it's time for you to do what you've been reluctant to do so far: delegate.

To-Do List:

Since the convention in Cincinnati begins on the 16th, you should check your e-mails to see if any are concerned with it—and it turns out a couple of them are. This task should be done before any others, so that you can perform the necessary follow-up.

There are two other tasks on the To-Do List that are both important and urgent: the second (writing your job description, which you'd like to have ready in case Callens is ready to discuss it at Tuesday's meeting) and the seventh (arranging the details for the Philadelphia convention). The job description should be done as soon as possible on Monday. Ordinarily, the details of the Philadelphia convention should be delegated to Craig Long, your production assistant, but since the convention begins Thursday, and he won't return until Tuesday afternoon, you'd be better off taking care of it yourself, and soon.

There are several possibilities for delegation on the list. The third item—updating the company Web site—is a team effort that should involve all members. Design and layout should be Montrose's input, and it's Lee's job to write the content. Long can help them when he returns. Since you are the most technically proficient, you can handle the formatting and coding. You don't have three hours to spend on this—your commitment should not exceed one hour.

The fifth task—responding to customer requests—is specifically mentioned in the introduction as the kind of job you should be turning over to your production assistant, Craig Long. This isn't urgent and can be done by him when he returns from Cincinnati.

Another task that should be delegated to Lee or Montrose, or both, is the sixth item: finding graphic content for the Denver planner. It is a job well within their responsibilities.

The fourth task, delivering the Cleveland proofs, could be delegated to Long when he returns, but it's not a time-consuming job—it could probably be done on the way home from work, if you leave a little early.

The last task—three hours of design and layout for Nashville—is all yours. You will need to fit in your three hours somewhere during these three days.

Discussion (cont'd)

Delegated Calls and Correspondence:

Item 4, Teresa Gless's inquiry about the Denver materials' content, is best left to the person who wrote it. We can assume that was Stan Lee. Similarly, item 7 is a question about illustrations, and so should go to Sally Montrose.

It shouldn't be your job at all to answer an unsolicited letter of application to employment in your department. You should send item 6 straight to Monica Torres, human resources director.

You can admire Roland Brooks' enthusiasm for promoting the new Web services, but it should be obvious to anyone that the company hasn't even made the final decision about what these services will be. Instead of a one-on-one meeting with him, you should invite him to Tuesday's discussion with the consultant, or talk about it over lunch.

Personal Calls and Correspondence:

Nearly all of the in-box items that should be handled personally are both important and urgent. Items 1 and 5—emails from Long and Montrose about their availability for the conference call—simply require the quick response that the only possible time for the conference call about the work requirements for the demonstration is 8-9 Tuesday morning. You should remember this when filling out your planner.

Items 3 and 10 are your most urgent—the convention in Cincinnati is under way and the conferees don't have their newsletters or meeting planners yet. You need to get in touch with Long or the printer in Cincinnati to work this out immediately.

Item 8 presents a similar situation. Ordinarily, you should consider having Craig Long look into this, but since the convention begins Thursday, you probably ought to just take care of it.

The trickiest item, 2, takes a huge and unexpected chunk of important time away from your work this week. It's tricky because it's a memo from your boss, who should understand the irony of calling a meeting to eliminate role conflict and redundancies in the company—three hours after he has scheduled a one-on-one meeting with you to do basically the same thing.

You don't really have three hours to give for this meeting. You should suggest that most of your input on this issue will be presented during Wednesday's morning meeting, and that you'll still attend in the afternoon if he requires it—but you have a lot of work to do to keep things running smoothly. When filling out your planner, tentatively schedule things for 1-4 Wednesday that can, if needed, be put off.

Discussion (cont'd)

Planner:

There are many ways to fill out the planner, as long as the items on the to-do list and in your in-box are taken care of, and in a sequence that works. Fill in your four required meetings first. Here are some points to consider:

Montrose is out for Monday afternoon, which leaves only 8-9 Tuesday morning (the only other time Craig Long is available) for the staff conference call on the work requirements for the Web services demonstration.

You want your job description ready before Tuesday's meeting with Callens, in case he asks about it. Because you only have two hours total left to you on Tuesday morning, you should probably schedule this task for some time Monday.

Montrose is out Monday afternoon, and there are no meetings scheduled. This is a good time to work on the design and layout for the Nashville materials.

Flex-time is best scheduled at the margins of meetings, in case they begin early or run long.

As mentioned previously, you should try to convince Callens that your attendance at both Wednesday meetings is superfluous. Assume that he'll agree with you, but schedule tasks that can be postponed in case he insists.

Your input on the Web site updates—formatting and coding the changes made by your staff—should be done after you've given them a chance to provide the design and content. Try to schedule your work as late as possible during this time frame.

Things to Do:

Priority   *Item*

___A___   • check and respond to e-mails, especially any from clients, hotels, or Craig Long in Cincinnati. Time required: half an hour

Disposition: <u>Do this first, to head off any potential troubles in Cincinnati</u>

___AB___   •write job description for Wednesday meeting. Would like to have this done before meeting with Callens on Tuesday, in order to be ready if there is time. Two hours.

Disposition: <u>Given the way time is shaping up, this should be done some time Monday.</u>

___A___   •update the company Web site to add newly hired personnel, and to more accurately reflect the company's products and services. Estimated time: 3 hours — one hour design and layout, one hour writing content, one hour formatting/coding.

Disposition: <u>Take responsibility for formatting and coding, and delegate the rest to those who can do the work. Plan to spend an hour on it.</u>

___A___   •deliver proofs for newsletter to local printer, for next month's radiologists' convention in Cleveland. Should take about a half hour.

Disposition: <u>If you can make time, do this toward the end of one of your work days. If not, have Long do it.</u>

Things to Do (cont'd):

__B__ •respond to customer requests for information about upcoming projects and publications (requests for proofs, information about content, requests for edits, etc.). Should take about an hour and a half.

Disposition: <u>Delegate this to Craig Long—it's why you hired him.</u>

__A__ •Find illustrations, maps and photos for meeting planner, for next month's convention in Denver. Already been designed. Needs to be ready for printer within two weeks. Should take about two hours.

Disposition: <u>Have your staff handle this—Lee and Montrose, or both.</u>

__AB__ • call temp agency, hotels to arrange for drops (hotel charges for doorman to make drops) for Philadelphia convention that begins this Thursday and runs through Sunday. Should take about an hour.

Disposition: <u>Since the convention is Thursday, and this has been your job in the past, you should simply handle this as soon as you can.</u>

__B__ •perform design and layout for a meeting planner and city guide for an upcoming convention in Nashville. Initial design must be done by you and should take about 8 hours total; you need to spend at least 3 hours on it before Thursday to stay on schedule.

Disposition: <u>Try to find a long interrupted period of time to do this work.</u>

DELEGATED CALLS AND CORRESPONDENCE

Priority	Item	Delegated to:
A	4—Gless e-mail	Lee
X	6—Applicant cover letter	Torres
A	7—Hood Printing call	Montrose
X	9—Brooks memo	Callens, or lunch meeting

PERSONAL CALLS AND CORRESPONDENCE

Priority	Item	Response:
AB	1—Montrose e-mail	Brief reply: schedule conference call for 8-9 Tues. morning
A	2—Callens memo	Discuss w/him—try to cover this in Wed. morning meeting
AB	3—Cincinnati hotel call	Try to reach Long or the printer immediately
AB	5—Long e-mail	Brief reply: schedule conference call for 8-9 Tues. morning
AB	8—NLDH call	Check with the hotel and/or printer, then reply
AB	10—Cincinnati hotel call	Call Long or the printer immediately

	16 Monday	17 Tuesday	18 Wednesday
7			
8	flex-time: Cincinnati mess	demo meeting with staff	flex-time
	check additional e-mails		"
9	write job description for	flex-time	Callens meeting about job
	Tues. meeting	"	definitions
10	"	call temp. agencies, hotels,	"
	"	etc. for Philadelphia	"
11	read trade journal articles	scan junk mail	flex-time
	for Callens	"	"
12	lunch	lunch w/Brooks	lunch
	"		
1	design and layout, Nash-	demo meeting w/Callens,	respond to customer inqui-
	ville	consultant	ries (or delegate to Long)
2	"	"	"
	"	"	read software proposal
3	"	flex-time	"
	"	"	"
4	read dept. memos	job descriptions meeting	format and code Web site
	deliver Cleveland proofs	w/staff	updates
5			
6			
7			

EXAMINATION SECTION
TEST 1

DIRECTIONS: Each question or incomplete statement is followed by several suggested answers or completions. Select the one that BEST answers the question or completes the statement. PRINT THE LETTER OF THE CORRECT ANSWER IN THE SPACE AT THE RIGHT.

Use the following management description as well as the accompanying documents and correspondence to answer the questions in this exam section.

Deputy Director of Human Services, Orange County

You are Jackson White, the Deputy Director of Human Services for Orange County, California. Having served this role for four years, you are responsible for the financial planning of the County Human Services Division, overseeing and monitoring the fiscal reporting of grants given to the Human Services Division and evaluating all programs run through the HSD. You report to John Williams, the Director of Human Services and your superior, as well as Marlene Troubleau, the County Director of Finance, for fiscal implications of services related to policy decisions and contracts.

As you know, Orange County is the third largest county in California, and one of the largest in the United States, with a population of over 2.5 million. One of your many challenges is balancing the amount of people living in the county with the numerous attractions and popular cities within its borders. From Anaheim and Huntington Beach to Disneyland and Fashion Island, there are a lot of tourists and local residents that require your attention as well as the many Orange County employees that you oversee on a daily basis.

Your boss, John Williams, is the inspiration behind why the "OC" has been so successful in its programs and endeavors, due to his aggressive approach to marketing and promoting the county and its many attractions. He is especially anxious to make Orange County even more of a destination for people from all walks of life, which explains the amount of opportunities and money spent on getting residents and tourists alike involved in the County's programs.

Due to the programs allowed and the times employees are asked to work, some employees complain of being underpaid for the work expected of them and also complain that they are understaffed. As a result of these concerns, you have been talking with Ms. Troubleau to see what kind of money is available to bring in more help and/or possibly allocate raises to current employees. Currently, no raises have been given and there is still a hiring freeze in place.

In addition to the above-mentioned roles, you are tasked with finding a way to include more residents with new programs or advertising that attracts them to current ones. So you have begun to work on a committee with Mr. Williams, and Mariela Suarez, who is the Director of Program Activities.

2 (#1)

You have three important meetings this week in which vital decisions will be made that will affect the organizational focus and direction for the foreseeable future. Your first meeting, on Monday at 11 a.m., will be with Ms. Troubleau to discuss the budget, specifically focusing on financial availability for programs, pay raises and ending the hiring freeze. On Tuesday, at 2:30 p.m., you will be with chosen representatives of the employee union to discuss pay raises as well as ending the current hiring freeze. Lastly, you have a committee meeting on Thursday at 9 a.m., with Ms. Suarez, Mr. Williams and others to determine what new programs can be added, which ones are no longer feasible and how to promote current and new programs.

Attn: All Staff

From: Jackson White

Date: October 12th

Subject: Julie Rodriguez

I wanted to take a moment to recognize Ms. Rodriguez's efforts over the past few months in our Parks and Rec department. She has had to oversee a number of programs often short staffed and in a county as large as ours, that is not an easy thing to accomplish. If you see Ms. Rodriguez please let her know how much you appreciate her work ethic and upbeat, positive attitude. I know I have!

From: jacksonwhite@orangecounty.gov

To: julierodriguez@orangecounty.gov

Subject: Your efforts and pay raise

Date: 10/16

Ms. Rodriguez,

First let me say the all staff memo was not an attempt to cover up the issues we face as a staff. I understand all of your concerns about pay and hiring freezes, and to show you it was an authentic gesture of recognition, I have been authorized by Ms. Troubleau to grant you a $2,000 pay raise to your annual salary. Before you can argue, this pay raise will not come at the cost of hiring any new employees.

Respectfully,

Jackson White

1. According to equity theory, after you gave Ms. Rodriguez her raise and public recognition of her work ethic, what is the next step she will hopefully take in the motivation process?   1._____
    A. She will renegotiate new valued rewards for her next performance period
    B. She will compare her reward with a self-selected comparison group or person
    C. She will reduce her productivity briefly while enjoying the earned reward
    D. She will expect an increase in future rewards

3 (#1)

2. Based on the memo and e-mail, which of the following BEST characterizes Ms. Rodriguez's relationship with you and the rest of her superiors?   2._____
    A. She trusts that you will give her the resources she needs
    B. Ms. Rodriguez dislikes you and her superiors so much that she could get fired
    C. Based on recent history, she has trouble trusting that you and your superiors will give her the things she needs to be successful
    D. Ms. Rodriguez doesn't trust management, but then again she doesn't trust anyone so it's not that much of a problem

---

To: jacksonwhite@orangecounty.org

From: tina@leadershipmanagement.com

Subject: Confirmation #1233224

Date: November 22

Hello, this is an e-mail to confirm your December 1st workshop titled "Theories in Management and Leadership". We know our workshops are successful and guarantee that you will be a better leader and manager in the future because of your dedication to your craft. Here are some of the details for you to be aware of on the day of your workshop:

1. Be on time. Many of our consultants have other workshops and seminars to attend so we start right at 7:45. Donuts and coffee will be provided.

2. Bring your own lunch. Lunch is not provided for you so please bring your own lunch or plan on picking up food from local restaurants. A full list of places to eat is attached to this e-mail.

3. Come prepared! We like it when you ask questions and even challenge our speakers. Please come having read the materials provided to you so that you can ask whatever questions you need to in order to become a better leader!

We look forward to seeing you at the workshop.

Sincerely,

Tina Balachowski

To: Jackson White
Date: December 1   Time: 9:34am
While you were out…

M: Ms. Susan Flanagan
Of: Your office secretary
Phone: N/A

Telephoned		Please Call	X
Called to See You		Will Call Again	
Wants to See You		Urgent	X
Returned Your Call			

Message: Jackson – there was an incident with Ms. Suarez and Ms. Rodriguez this morning. Ms. Suarez wants Ms. Rodriguez fired and Ms. Rodriguez is threatening harassment against Ms. Suarez. Mr. Williams has indicated that you should adjudicate this issue as soon as you can.

3. You show a willingness to update your knowledge on current theories in management and leadership in order to become more effective in your managerial role. At your workshop, you come to realize that some managers have low concern for services and high concern for staff. Which style of management have you learned from the workshop?
    A. Organization Man
    B. Impoverished Management
    C. Team Management
    D. Country Club Management

4. After you leave your workshop, you receive the message up above (While You Were Out…). If you adhere to many conflict resolution specialists, including experts like Louis Pondy, how should you feel about the conflict between Ms. Suarez and Ms. Rodriguez?
    A. If there is no conflict in your organization, then the organization has no reason for being
    B. Your organization is in deep trouble if you have conflict
    C. Conflict always drains the creative energy from any organization
    D. None of the above

5. After meeting with Ms. Rodriguez and Ms. Suarez, you are having difficulty deciding what to do. Which of the following interventions would be BEST for your organization moving forward?
    A. Have the dispute settled with litigators and let the legal process play out
    B. Assign an in-house mediator to resolve the dispute quietly
    C. Mandate both parties attend interpersonal conflict management workshops and see if they can work out their differences afterwards
    D. Hire an arbitrator who will assist the involved parties in reaching their own decision

To: jacksonwhite@orangecounty.org

From: gerrycarlson@orangecounty.org

Subject: What do I do?

Date: January 23rd

Hi Mr. Jackson, first let me say thank you for hiring me as an Assistant Program Director. I know there were more experienced candidates, so it was really wonderful to get an opportunity to manage right out of college. With that said, I was hoping you could help me resolve a few issues. Many of the employees that work directly under me seem to resent the fact that they are more seasoned and experienced in this field than I am. They question and sometimes outright challenge leadership to the point of insubordination. I cannot help but feel that some of this is because they do not think I have "earned my stripes" as the saying goes. Anyway, I was hoping you could give me some ideas of how to change the morale around or in the event that certain employees become belligerent, do I have the authority to terminate their contracts? Please let me know what the appropriate approach is for this situation.

Thanks,

Gerry Carlson

6. Gerry is your youngest program director and many of the employees under her, as noted in the e-mail, or senior to her, have been very hostile. Gerry feels challenged and is the scapegoat for everything that doesn't go well. Which of the following actions would be BEST for her to take?

    A. Continue to seek help from you and your boss, Mr. Williams
    B. Disregard what she feels and continue to work through the conflict
    C. Quit her job and find work in another field
    D. Identify the source of the conflict and understand the points of friction

6._____

The following dialogue took place between you and your boss earlier today:

Mr. Williams: "Jackson, we need to talk about a few employees in our advertising department."

You: "Okay, which employees, and what is the issue?"

Williams: "Well, some of our highest performing teams of employees have been underperforming in minor ways the last few weeks."

You: "Hmm, do we know why? Has anyone asked what the issue is?"

Williams: "No, not yet. That's partially why I wanted to talk to you. No one has made mention of anything but Jasmine Kelly and Michael Huffington are two of our best ad sales people and they have not met their goals three out of the last four weeks. I'd like you to figure out the best way to reach them and get the two back on track to meet their goals from here to the rest of the quarter."

You: "Okay, I'll take care of it by the end of the day."

To: jasminekelly@orangecounty.org, michaelhuffington@orangecounty.org

From: jacksonwhite@orangecounty.org

Subject: Recent performance

Date: January 30

Hey guys, I noticed that the last few weeks have been kind of rough in terms of ad sales. Your manager tells me you've missed sales goals in four out of five weeks. Before you get worried, no your job is not on the line. Rather, I want to take time now, before it is really an issue, to figure out what is going on. Normally, you two are top of the list in terms of sales, so if there is an issue or conflict that we are unaware of please let me know.

Like I said, you two are my all-stars, so please tell me how I can help get you back on track.

Respectfully,

Jackson White

7. In the above scenario, you chose to send an e-mail to the two individuals whose sales had been down recently. What would be the BEST way to handle a situation like this in the future?
    A. You handled the situation the way it should have been handled. Not all individuals are performing badly.
    B. Call the whole ad sales department together to discuss the need for better performance
    C. Ask one of your more experienced and trusted employees in ad sales to talk to the underperformers
    D. Do nothing at this stage because performance has not suffered that badly

7.____

8. Two days after the e-mail was sent to Ms. Kelly and Mr. Huffington, Ms. Kelly requests a private meeting. During the meeting she confides that Mr. Huffington has become hostile toward her, which makes working as a tandem difficult. Which of the following pieces of information, if true, would explain the sudden aggression and possibly lead to a resolution of conflict if explained to both parties?
    A. Ms. Kelly accidently embarrassed Mr. Huffington in a sales department meeting
    B. Mr. Huffington recently broke up with his girlfriend of four years and did not tell anyone about it
    C. Ms. Kelly threw Mr. Huffington a surprise party when he celebrated his third year in the department
    D. Mr. Huffington felt like Ms. Kelly really understood him when he told her about his financial problems

8.____

You arrive to work one morning, check your voicemail, and hear the following message:

> "Hello Mr. Jackson, my name is John Jefferson with the Department of Consumer Information and Insurance Oversight, and I am calling about one of your employees who claims she is not receiving Workers Compensation as a result of an incident on October 22nd of last year. Can you please call me back at your earliest convenience to ensure that the employee is in fact entitled to her Workers Compensation? Thanks, and have a good day."

Upon looking into the issue, you realize that employees in your Human Resources department have been negligent and did not process the injured employee's claim like they should have.

You send out the following memo to everyone in the HR department:

> Attn: HR Department
>
> From: Jackson White
>
> Date: February 22nd
>
> Subject: Workers Compensation
>
> If someone is injured at work, you do not have a choice in whether you process their workers compensation or not. Please make sure we file all claims as soon as possible to avoid compliance problems with the federal government. We could get in trouble, with sanctions and possible terminations, if we do not adhere to federally regulated insurance benefits. If you have any questions please let me know immediately.

9. Benefits like Workers' Compensation that are required by law to be provided to all employees are referred to as
    A. medical
    B. direct
    C. involuntary
    D. statutory

9._____

10. Which of the following could happen if you continued to neglect the employee's claim of Workers' Compensation?
    A. You could have to pay the expenses out of pocket
    B. The state may levy taxes against you
    C. You could be sent to jail for up to 6 months
    D. Nothing. The Consumer Information and Insurance Oversight Department can only issue warnings not actual fines.

10._____

> To: jacksonwhite@orangecounty.org
>
> From: hilaryegan@orangecounty.org
>
> Subject: Program Analysis
>
> Date: February 23rd
>
> Hi Mr. White, I am trying to remember what processes you want us to take with the new program project. There were a lot of ideas thrown out at the meeting and now that I am back with my team I find it is hard to remember exactly what was said. Would you mind meeting with me sometime this week so I can be sure my project and team are on the same page?
>
> Thanks, Hilary
>
> To: hilaryegan@orangecounty.org
>
> From: jacksonwhite@orangecounty.org
>
> Subject: Re: Program Analysis
>
> Date: February 23rd
>
> Hi Ms. Egan, thank you for letting me know of your team's confusion as quickly as you did. I am available tomorrow at 9:30 am to meet with you about the project. Please let me know if this works for you.

Two days after you meet with Hilary and go over the project's timeline and processes, you get this e-mail.

To: jacksonwhite@orangecounty.org

From: hilaryegan@orangecounty.org

Subject: Program Analysis (Again)

Hi Mr. White, sorry for being such a pain, but some of the points of emphasis from this project are still not clear. My team is struggling to figure out how exactly to best accomplish this project in the timeline you set out in our meeting. I feel like the information I bring to them is not quite what you told me verbally, but I am not sure if it is just me or if something is getting lost in translation. Anyway, could we please schedule another meeting to make sure we get on track once and for all?

Thanks, Hilary

---

11. At this point, extensive use of which type of communication would most likely aid in solving the complex issue raised by Ms. Egan and her team?   11._____
    A. Verbal
    B. Written
    C. Formal
    D. Nonverbal

12. If there continues to be communication blockers and miscommunication as this project moves along, which of the following would most likely be the result?   12._____
    A. The project is delayed
    B. Trust level is increased
    C. Conflict occurs
    D. Senior management is displeased

March 3, 2016

Mr. Jackson White
Human Services Department, Orange County
13042 Old Myford Rd
Irvine, CA 92692

Dear Mr. White,

On February 15th, I signed up my child to be a part of the youth basketball program run by your department and as of yesterday, I have received no contact from a coach or program sponsor as to where and when my child will be involved with the activity. We have always been a part of the community sports programs without issue so it is surprising that now there is a problem.

To resolve this problem, I would appreciate an explanation as to why I have not been contacted, and I would like to see my child take part in the program. Enclosed are copies of my payment for the activity and the initial confirmation e-mail stating that I had signed up successfully.

Again, this is the first time this has happened, but I have not gotten anywhere with e-mails to your subordinates, which is why I have lodged this formal complaint. I anticipate and appreciate your timely response to this issue.

Sincerely,
Dana Wilkerson

To: jacksonwhite@orangecounty.org

From: williamcollete@orangecounty.org

Subject: Parent sign-up issue

Date: March 5, 2016

Hello Mr. White, thank you for letting me know about the issue with Ms. Wilkerson. I had not realized she was having trouble with contacting us regarding signing her child up for the basketball program. I can assure you that it was an oversight and will not happen again. Unfortunately, all of the spots for the program are now filled, so I am unsure of what we should do to correct this issue. According to her confirmation letter, and receipts, it would appear she signed up before many of the residents whose children are currently a part of the program. Please let me know how I should respond to Ms. Wilkerson or if you wish to handle this case personally, please let me know what the outcome of that interaction is. Again, on behalf of my program I apologize for the mistake.

Respectfully,

William Collete

13. Based on the information and type of correspondence from Dana Wilkerson, what kind of tone can you safely assume she has adopted and how should you respond?

13._____

   A. She is concerned, but not angry. As she has been a loyal participant, you should make sure her concerns are taken care of as soon as possible.
   B. She is overreacting and aggressive. You should wait a week or two for her to calm down then address her concerns.
   C. She is being a little dramatic but not too aggressive. You can take care of her concerns right away, but if you have more urgent issues, take care of them first.
   D. It doesn't matter what her tone is. She is not someone who should be contacting you about an issue like this.

14. As the manager, you have final say in how this matter is resolved. Which of the following is the BEST way to resolve the issue?

14._____

   A. Have Mr. Collete inform Ms. Wilkerson that we are sorry for the inconvenience and will refund her the money, but her son will not be able to participate in the activity this time.
   B. Inform Ms. Wilkerson yourself that you will refund her money, and her son will not be able to participate in the activity.
   C. Have Mr. Collete make space for Ms. Wilkerson's son, and have him call the parents of the child who will lose his or her spot in the activity. You will call Ms. Wilkerson yourself to tell her you've corrected the mistake.
   D. Call Ms. Wilkerson yourself to inform her that her son will be involved in the activity; tell Mr. Collete to e-mail you the name of the child who has lost his or her spot so you can inform the parents of that child yourself.

To: jacksonwhite@orangecounty.org

From: ahmedjohnson@orangecounty.org

Subject: SS

Date: March 22nd

Hello, Mr. White, I would like to request a private meeting with you concerning some of the work habits of my team. As you know, our project has been delayed somewhat due to some rising contentions. I would love your feedback and approach to this matter, so could you please let me know when you are available to have a conversation?

Thanks,

Ahmed Johnson

11 (#1)

Three days later, your scheduled meeting with Ahmed takes place:

Ahmed: "I am not getting along with the new person to our project, Sharon. I am doing my best to work with her, but every exchange and interaction is awkward and tense. I know you hired her and put her on my team, so I would love to know how to handle this situation."

You: "It's great that you recognize that it's a difficult working relationship, and I appreciate that you've brought the situation to my attention. My recommendation is to approach the situation differently. Try not to go into conversations with Sharon expecting awkward exchanges and tense interactions. Put yourself in a neutral place before you approach her or when she approaches you. If that doesn't work, consider having a direct conversation with Sharon about the situation. If you feel uncomfortable doing so, I'd be happy to facilitate a conversation to make the working relationship more at ease."

15. Which active listening skill is demonstrated in this conversation? 15._____
    A. Be in the moment and engrossed
    B. Let the employee speak
    C. Provide feedback
    D. Recognize feelings behind the words

Use the following scenario to answer questions 16-17:

Steven created a project schedule based on input from Mo and Anya on the team. Donna and Sarah feel like their input was ignored. Due to being younger and newer to the team, they believe Steven has marginalized their concerns about the timeline for the project. They challenged the schedule, stating that it was impossible to achieve and was setting up the team for failure. Meanwhile, Sarah was arguing with Anya over who should lead the database design and development effort for the project. While Sarah admits Anya has more experience than she does in database development, she only agreed to be on this project in order to take a lead role and develop her skills further so she could apply for managerial roles later on in the year. If she knew Anya was going to be the lead she wouldn't have bothered joining this project team. Additionally, Mo appears to be operating on his own, not letting the others know of his progress nor keeping his information up to date on the site. No one really knows what he has been working on or how much progress is being made.

You had initially taken a side role during these exchanges, hoping that the team would work it out for themselves. However, you know from past experience managing many project teams that it is important to take control and guide the team through this difficult time. You decide to convene all of the team members for a virtual meeting to go over their roles and responsibilities (which were agreed to in the kick-off meeting) and to ensure that they understand the goals and objectives of the project. You made some decisions since the team couldn't come to agreement. You determined that Anya would lead the database development design component of the project, working closely with Sarah so she can develop further experience in this area. You reviewed the schedule that Steven created with the team, making adjustments where necessary to address the concerns of Donna and Sarah. You reminded Mo that this is a team effort and he needs to work closely with the others on the team.

Over the next few weeks, you notice that arguments/disagreements are few to none and when they did occur, they were worked out quickly by the team, without your involvement being necessary. Still, you monitored how things were going and held regular virtual meetings to ensure the team was moving in the right direction. On a monthly basis, you bring the team together for a face-to-face meeting. As the working relationships of the team members started improving, you start seeing significant progress on the project.

16. According to most accepted team-building experts, there are five stages of team building. Based on the above scenario, in which stage does the team seem to be?
    A. Forming
    B. Storming
    C. Performing
    D. Adjourning

16._____

17. Which of the following key ingredients for accountability and engagement in a team are indicated in the scenario?
    A. Energy of team members and their attitude
    B. Team members' emotional intelligence
    C. Clarity of individual goals
    D. The social networks in the team

17._____

To: Jackson White
Date: April 2nd Time: 8:40 am

While you were out...

M:
Of:
Phone: N/A

Telephoned	X	Please Call	X
Called to See You		Will Call Again	
Wants to See You	X	Urgent	
Returned Your Call			

Message: Mike McCoy called and I have copied down his message into writing for your convenience.

John and I work in the same department. As you know I am a new employee, while John has worked here for a long time. Due to the fact that we have very similar roles, we work together quite often. John has had a routine here for a while and he is not afraid to share those routines with me.

Because he's been here so long, he thinks he knows how to do things and he tells others about it, whether or not they ask. I try hard to follow company rules. I am quiet, and follow the rules always clocking in within five minutes of my shift start. Even though there is no way to track clocking in at our own buildings, I think John always clocks in at another building so he won't be marked tardy, usually coming at least 10 minutes late. People continually ask me where John is and frankly, sir, I am tired of covering for John as I have for a while.

This all came to a head yesterday as John showed up 20 minutes late. I had to cover for him twice yesterday, and when he finally showed up I confronted him about it. His response was as follows: "Hey, I clocked in. I've been doing this for years. As long as you do not say anything to anyone, nobody will ever know. Just shut up and do your job." We started yelling at one another and I'm afraid John would've hit me had I not walked away. Please do something about this volatile situation.

13 (#1)

The following day, you receive a message from John Hopkins, the man Mike McCoy mentioned in his voicemail message:

To: jacksonwhite@orangecounty.org

From: johnhopkins@orangecounty.org

Subject: Disputation

Date: 3/31

Hey White, listen, I overheard that McCoy sent you a message yesterday and I wanted to make sure you got my side of the story. Listen, he is flat out lying to you!!! Every day I strive to get better at the job and you know you've never had any complaints about me. I know that sniveling snake is trying to take my job which is why he made up a story about me threatening him. We did argue, it's true, but trust me it was a mutual disagreement, not me bullying him. What are we in high school? Is he tattling on me to the principal now? I trust you are smart enough to see through this lie you've been told.

Thanks,

Hopkins

---

18. Based on the above information from each side, what should you do to remedy the situation?
    A. Nothing; this is an issue that the two men need to work out on their own
    B. Side with John; he has been here longer and requires less training for his job and thus costs less money. You know his work history and he has never had a complaint before this.
    C. Side with Mike; it is clear John has been abusing the system for a while and Mike seems like a more diligent worker. While training him will cost money up front, it will be better in the long run because he will work harder thus increasing production.
    D. Warn them that further issues involving verbal threats or abuse will lead to possible termination. Though it will cost money to hire and train new employees, it is better than fights breaking out and the cost of potential litigation.

18._____

19. If you decide to avoid the situation above and stall Mike and John, which of the following is likely to happen?
    A. Both parties win and go back to working normally
    B. Resentment will build
    C. The issue will go away permanently
    D. The issue will come up under another guise

19._____

> April 24, 2016
>
> TO: HR Department
>
> FROM: Jackson White
>
> RE: Conflict Resolution Training Session
>
> Please read the mandatory annual 'Conflict Resolution' seminar pamphlet. Fill out the Pre-training Survey as well.
>
> *Have you ever found yourself hoping that conflicts with your coworkers or team members will just work themselves out? Unfortunately, conflicts are rarely self-healing conditions. This course will show you how to deal with conflicts and give you specific steps for turning conflict into a challenge to grow. Please plan to attend our training session on conflict resolution skills. The session will be held May 2nd at 9:00am. During the session, we'll cover how to:*
>
> - *Ask questions to draw out the other side of the conflict.*
> - *Listen without judging.*
> - *Avoid interrupting, blaming, and arguing.*
> - *Give periodic feedback to check understanding.*
> - *Ask for feedback to check understanding of your viewpoint.*
> - *Set goals, create an action plan, and follow up on your solution.*
>
> The training will be tailored to your specific needs, so please take a few minutes to complete the enclosed Pre-training Survey and return it to me by (Insert Date). Be candid! I'll use the responses to develop a program that addresses critical areas participants have identified.
>
> Please mark your calendar so that you may attend this very important training session.

Two weeks after your HR team attends the conference, you receive the following note from Eric, who relays an incident that happened earlier this week in one of the meeting rooms:

> Jill, Sue, Ray, and I were sitting around a table with Jill and Ray on one side and Sue and me on the other. Jill was talking forcefully, while Ray was looking down and it was pretty obvious he was upset about something. Ray tells me privately that he and Jill were fine with one another until they were on the same team. In the meeting, Jill forcefully recommended that we take the survey ahead of making the recommendation. Ray stated that he felt like they asked for our opinion and not a full-*blown proposal. Jill didn't like that because she thought that* was the equivalent of throwing something together off the tops of our heads and she was clearly not going along with that.
>
> At this point, Ray seemed to resign himself to the fate of listening to whatever Jill decided, but then Sue spoke up saying that she agreed with Ray that we should give our opinion without making a big deal out of it. Not wanting a situation, I hastily agreed with Jill so that it would seem like she was not being ganged up

on. At that point Ray sighed and got up to leave, clearly disagreeing, but unwilling to fight it. *Jill, unwilling to let it go, jumped up and told Ray that it wasn't about her survey, it was about doing something the right way.*

Ray waved off her comment, turned to leave, in an attempt to avoid confrontation, but Jill was obviously still upset. Sue and I exchanged frustrated glances and commented that this team was not working well together. At that point, I decided to come to you privately to seek your advice. Please let me know *what we should do...*

20. What is the result of Eric's attempt to avoid open disagreement with Jill? 20.____
    A. The team was able to stick together and avoid an HR nightmare
    B. Formation of team factions and lowered morale
    C. Loss of respect for and confidence in each other, and a breakdown of working relationships
    D. Both B and C

21. If you forced Jill to patch things up with Ray, what should she avoid doing when trying to make things more cohesive? 21.____
    A. Become defensive when Ray tells her what bothered him about her
    B. Actively listen to what Ray is saying and rephrase each of his points to make sure she clearly understands him
    C. Tell Ray he has faults of his own to account for and shouldn't only shoulder all of the blame on her
    D. Ask Ray questions about specific things that he wants her to avoid doing in the future

Jamie Wilkes works as a Parks and Recreation Manager with a team that consists of two assistant managers, four camp counselors, a bookkeeper and a part-time volunteer. You assigned them the task of creating a new program for Orange County. Jamie has sent out the following memorandum to her team explaining their objectives:

Memo

From: Jamie Wilkes

To: Parks and Recreation New Horizons Team

Date: May 12, 2016

Re: New Horizons Directives

As an extension of the unprecedented guidelines in place for our New Horizons project, we are taking another important step towards transparency with our efforts for the Orange County community and our bosses. Each day we meet with our bosses, community and each other to figure out the best transition for this project both orally and in writing. We need to make sure we give the people of Orange County a "seat at the table" and that we receive the benefit of their feedback.

Accordingly, any documents we create will be posted on our website for people to review and comment on. Everyone deserves a "seat at the table" and in addition to that we will record all meetings and make those times available to the public.

Please let me know if you have any questions about the direction of our new project.

Glad to have you all on board.

After the previous memo was sent out, some of Jamie's staff came to see her and ask for clarification about the memorandum.

22. Jamie held a meeting with the work team to determine what had gone wrong. It was determined that members of the work team had many varied experiences working for Orange County, different backgrounds, and varying emotions about working on the assignment. These differences among the work team members created _____ for Jamie's communication.
    A. encoded messages
    B. noise
    C. decoding
    D. feedback

23. Jamie's ability to actively listen and communicate effectively with regards to her team goes a long way toward
    A. determining whether or not the situation is resolved to the team's satisfaction
    B. making sure the problem doesn't surface again
    C. making sure no team members have any hard feelings towards Jamie or other teammates
    D. whether or not the team works together again

17 (#1)

Johnny, a recent graduate from Stanford University, has recently been hired as your information systems manager. As you know, Orange County programs have been running for a long time and you've hired Johnny to inform you and your team of how to better incorporate technology in an effort to make county programs more efficient. Johnny has recently called a meeting with senior management to address a few of the issues he has seen. The following is an amended transcript of that meeting:

```
Johnny: Okay, so I know all of you are busy so I will get right to the point.
We need to upgrade our technology in a bad way.

You: Alright, Johnny one step at a time. Tell me what you mean by this.

Johnny: Well, boss, the websites are clunky and confusing, and it is pretty
difficult to message program directors about inquiries that community members
may have. And that's the tip of the old iceberg.

Mariela Suarez: Johnny, thank you for bringing this up, but I do not want my
program directors being assaulted with communications from overbearing
parents. They have more important work to do.

Johnny: Listen Ms. Suarez, I am not saying we actively encourage parents to
seek out counselors and whatnot, but just that if there is a conflict or a
question about program policies, it is virtually impossible to figure out how
to contact someone and actually receiving a response.

You: Alright, so how do we fix this issue then, Johnny?

Johnny: You'll need to spend beaucoup bucks to overhaul the systems you guys
are using. You'll also need a crack IT staff to update the websites and get
all employees trained on using electronic communication. You do realize how
much money we're losing by all these paper memos constantly being sent out.
But I digress…
```

24. James, a camp program director, wants to know about electronic communication tools for directors, like himself, that find e-mail slow and cumbersome. Johnny tells James that _____ messaging is a communication tool that is defined as an interactive real-time communication that takes place among computer users who are logged onto the computer at the same time.

    24._____

    A. extended
    B. data code
    C. instant
    D. passive

25. After this meeting concludes, you realize you need to discipline certain members of the team. Upon reflection, who should you talk to and what admonishment should you give them?
    A. You should talk to Mariela and tell her not to be so hard on the IT guy, especially because she was only complaining due to the cost and access to her employees
    B. You should talk to Johnny and tell him he needs to be more formal in meetings, using less slang and nicknames for people, including you
    C. You should talk to both Johnny and Mariela and tell them they need to work out whatever problem they have between them privately or it could cost them their jobs
    D. You should not talk to anyone; the mistakes made were not egregious enough to warrant a formal complaint

25.____

———

KEY (CORRECT ANSWERS)

1. B
2. C
3. C
4. A
5. D

6. D
7. A
8. A
9. D
10. A

11. B
12. C
13. A
14. D
15. C

16. B
17. A
18. D
19. D
20. D

21. A
22. B
23. A
24. C
25. B

———

INTRODUCTION TO THE WRITTEN SIMULATION TEST

This booklet will discuss the Written Simulation Test you will be taking. Since it is unlike the multiple-choice tests you may have taken in the past, this booklet will explain the way it works.

WHAT IS THE WRITTEN SIMULATION TEST?

The Written Simulation Test you will be taking consists of two problems which involve you in situations like those you would encounter on the job for which you are being tested. Each problem is interactive and unfolds as a result of decisions you make about how to handle the situations. The situations may not change in the same way for everyone who takes the test. Different people will have different ways of solving problems and managing situations. The differences may cause the problem to unfold in different ways. The Written Simulation Test is written so that actions you choose usually produce outcomes, eventually leading to a conclusion.

HOW DOES THE WRITTEN SIMULATION TEST WORK?

The Written Simulation Test consists of a **Written Simulation Test Booklet**, a Response Booklet, an **Answer Sheet packe**t, and a **developer pen**:

Written Simulation Test Booklet (Blue Cover)

The Written Simulation Test Booklet introduces you to the setting of each problem. Every candidate sees the same Opening Scene. This scene tells you what is happening, and what your role is. Usually, it also presents you with the first situation that requires you to do or find out something.

After the Opening Scene there are numerous sections, identified by letters of the alphabet. The Opening Scene will send you to a section, which is often (though not always) Section A. In the section you will often see additional information about the situation; you will always see instructions on what to do in the section (e.g., choose only one, choose as many as you consider appropriate). It is CRUCIAL that you follow these instructions. In the section you will also find a list of different things you could do or information you might want to know in responding to the situation presented in the Opening Scene. Some of the things in the list are good responses to the situation, while others may be neutral or even bad. You must select the choice (or choices, if you are permitted to choose more than one) which you judge to be the best.

Written Simulation Answer Sheet Packet

Once you have selected a choice (either the one you think is best in a "choose only one" section or any of your choices in a "choose as many" section) you must then go to the Answer Sheet Packet.

1A		11D	
2A		12D	
3A		13D	
4A		14D	
5B		15D	

FIGURE 1

This packet contains answer sheets which have numbers and letters with blank boxes to the right of them (see Figure 1 above). The visible number/letter combinations correspond to the choices in the Written Simulation Test Booklet; the number is that of the choice, and the letter corresponds to the section of the problem in which that choice is found. The blank boxes also contain numbers, but they cannot be seen until they are exposed with the special developer pen. These numbers do not have letters attached to them.

1A		11D	
2A		12D	
3A		13D	
4A	#15	14D	
5B		15D	

FIGURE 2

When the developer pen is lightly rubbed across the space next to the choice you have selected, the latent response number becomes visible (see Figure 2 above). Be very sure that you have accurately identified the box corresponding to your choice and be sure you apply the developer pen **only** to the space next to your choice. Use a gentle, steady stroke from left to right. Do NOT rub the pen back and forth, as you might rub off the latent response number. You should also make sure you have exposed the <u>entire</u> number in the box.

Once you have exposed the response number, you are ready to learn the outcome of your choice.

(You should be aware that the latent response number may be the same for more than one choice. For example, there could be several choices which show "#1" in the box you expose next to the choice number. This is not a typographical error. When you look up #1 in the Response Booklet, it may be "yes" or "no" or some other response appropriate to a number of choices.)

Response Booklet (Yellow Cover)

The next step in the process is to find in the Response Booklet the response which has the same number as the latent number you have exposed. The Response Booklet contains statements and/or directions which help lead you through the Written Simulation problem. Its pages look like this:

#13. END OF PROBLEM. MAKE NO MORE CHOICES IN THIS PROBLEM.

#14. This is likely to cause a fire rather than prevent one.

#15. No one answers.

FIGURE 3

DO NOT CONFUSE THE NUMBER OF THE RESPONSE WITH THE NUMBER OF THE CHOICE IN THE TEST BOOKLET. In Figure 2, we selected choice 4A and exposed #15. It is important to find response #15 in the Response Booklet, NOT response #4.

As you can see from these examples, responses provide information and/or directions for working through the problem. Unless you are told otherwise, you should always return to the section in the Test Booklet in which you made your choice for instructions on how to proceed in the problem. You should not go to a new section until you are specifically instructed to do so by directions in the Response Booklet or the Test Booklet.

In the example that has been presented here, we began by selecting choice 4A. By uncovering the box to the right of this choice in the Answer Sheet Packet, you were directed to response #15 in the Response Booklet. Response #15 provides some information: "No one answers." Since the choice (4A) was in Section A, you would return to Section A for instructions on how to proceed. The example above also shows other types of responses you can expect to see as you work through the problem, including an END OF PROBLEM statement. Note that until you see this statement you have not finished the problem.

In most simulation problems you will see that the sections appear in alphabetical order in the Test Booklet, but there is no section "I" or "O". These are oat missing sections. They have been purposely omitted so they will not be mistaken for the numbers "1" and "0".

You will not be directed to sections in the order in which they occur in the Written Simulation Test Booklet, and not everyone will necessarily go through every section. Consequently, care must be taken to GO ONLY TO THOSE SECTIONS TO WHICH YOU HAVE BEEN DIRECTED.

HOW IS THE WRITTEN SIMULATION TEST SCORED?

Now that you know how a Written Simulation Test works, it is important to understand something about how it is scored and how to make sure you obtain the best score you can.

ONLY THE EXPOSED RESPONSE NUMBERS WILL BE SCORED. Only the response numbers marked on the Answer Sheets will be used to determine your test score. Nothing you may write in the Written Simulation Test Booklet or the Response Booklet will be counted toward your final score.

Similarly, EVERYTHING YOU EXPOSE WILL BE TAKEN INTO ACCOUNT IN SCORING. Be very careful in using the developer pen on the Answer Sheets. Avoid making stray marks or smudges with the developer pen. Whatever is exposed on these pages -- EVEN CHOICES EXPOSED ACCIDENTALLY -- will be scored, except in cases where exposing additional response numbers contrary to instructions would advantage a candidate.

All the choices in the Written Simulation Test are valued positively, negatively or neutrally. You record the choices which you select on the Answer Sheet(s) when you use the developer pen. In order to achieve the best score you can, you should choose only the choices which you consider positive. In those sections which allow you to make more than one choice, you should choose all the choices which you consider positive, while taking care not to choose poor choices. Selection of neutral choices in a "choose as many" section will neither help nor hurt your score.

EXAMPLE: PORTIONS OF A WRITTEN SIMULATION PROBLEM
(Discussion/instructions interspersed in the example will be printed in italics.)

The opening scene and the Sections would be located in the Written Simulation Test Booklet. The opening scene is important. Read it carefully, as it gives you the setting within which you will be operating in the problem.

OPENING SCENE

You run a unit which has a variety of work (including public contact and paperwork-oriented tasks) that can be assigned fairly flexibly among staff members. Your boss interviewed and hired a new person to work in the unit. You were not at the interview, nor could you talk with your boss about it before she went on vacation. Your new employee has just arrived from the Personnel Office.

CONTINUE NOW WITH SECTION A

The opening scene will end with a direction to go to a Section in the problem — in this case, SECTION A, which is reproduced below. Relevant parts of an answer sheet and a response booklet appear on the next page, to allow you to carry through on responding to Section A. (In the actual test material, the numbers in the boxes to the right of the choices would be blank until developed. Here they are all visible so that you can follow the logic of the problem. Just ignore those response numbers that you would not expose in a real testing situation.) Try working through this portion of the problem, bearing in mind the instructions on the preceding pages.

SECTION A

You have oriented the new employee to the office and have chatted a few minutes to set him at ease. In order for you to prepare to assign him work, it is time for you both to share some information. You would now: (Choose **AS MANY AS** you consider appropriate.)

1 A. Ask him what he and your boss discussed in the interview

2 A. Tell him about the personalities of the other workers in the office.

3 A. Describe the various assignments in the unit to him.

4 A. Ask him what kinds of assignments interest him.

AFTER YOU HAVE CHOSEN AS MANY AS YOU CONSIDER APPROPRIATE, HAVE EXPOSED (ON THE ANSWER SHEET) THE RESPONSE NUMBER FOR EACH CHOICE YOU SELECTED, AND HAVE READ THE RESPONSES, EXPOSE 5A ON THE ANSWER SHEET

ANSWER SHEET

The Answer Sheet would be part of the Answer Sheet Packet.

1A	#7
2A	#1
3A	#5
4A	#8
5A	#2
6B	#12

RESPONSES

Responses would be found in the Response Booklet.

1. Your choice has been recorded; it may have a positive, negative or neutral value in the problem. No new information is presented as a result of making this choice. **Return to the section you were just In and follow the directions given there.**

2. GO TO SECTION D IN THE TEST BOOKLET.

3. He says he likes "people" work.

4. No.

5. He listens intently and asks good questions.

6. GO TO SECTION F IN THE TEST BOOKLET.

7. He says he and your boss discussed available work assignments and his preferences.

8. He mentions enjoying record keeping and writing reports, and adds that he hates public contact work.

    Did you follow instructions and choose as many as you thought were appropriate? Did you follow through on your choices? For example, if you selected 3A and 4A, did you look to the right of 3A on the Answer Sheet (in the test material you would expose the number at the right), see #5, and go to #5 in the Responses to read the response "He listens intently and asks good questions"? Did you then repeat the process for 4A, i.e., look to the right of 4A, see #8, and go to #8 in the Responses to read the response "He mentions enjoying record keeping and writing reports, and adds that he hates public contact work"? Did you "expose" (read) 5A after you selected all the choices you wanted to, go to #2 in the Responses, and read that you should go to Section D in the test booklet? If not, go back and work with this material again. Then (as you are directed) go to Section D, which is reproduced on the next page along with the relevant portions of the Answer Sheet and Response Booklet. (In the actual Test Booklet. to get to Section D you will have to turn past Sections B and C.)

SECTION D

It is time to assign some work to your new subordinate. You would now: (Choose ONLY ONE unless otherwise directed.)

    11D.   Have him work with another staff member on some overdue reports.

    12D.   Have him work with another staff member doing routine follow-up telephone calls.

ANSWER SHEET

11D	#17
12D	#20

RESPONSES

    # 17.   GO TO SECTION C IN THE TEST BOOKLET.

    # 18.   He says he doesn't know how.

    # 19.   He doesn't come back after lunch.

    # 20.   After half a day, he appears at your desk, visibly upset, and asks for a reassignment.

    GO TO SECTION M IN THE TEST BOOKLET.

Did you pick only one response? (In the test, you could lose points if you choose more than one when not so directed.) Did you end up being directed to either Section C (if you chose 11D) or Section M (if you chose 12D)? If not, it might be wise to reread the general portion of the information booklet and then work through the problem again.

DISCUSSION OF THE EXAMPLE

There are a few important points that the portions of a problem you just went through illustrate:

- *It is critical that you develop the response number next to your choice number on the Answer Sheet and then read the appropriate response in the Response Booklet. Not only is the Answer Sheet the only record of your answers, but the Response Booklet often gives you information upon which to base your later actions. In Section A, for example, 4A is a good action to take. If you exposed the box next to it on your Answer Sheet, you would receive positive points. However, if you don't follow through on that choice by reading response #8, you don't find out the information that your new employee likes record keeping and writing reports, but hates public contact work. Without that information, you are not in a good position to make an assignment in Section D.*

- *It is critical to be accurate in going from the Answer Sheet to the Response Booklet. In Section A, choice 3A is a good choice. However, if you make the mistake of going directly to #3 in the Responses instead of to #5 (the response number "developed" on the Answer Sheet), you get information that could lead you astray in making your decision in Section D. (NOTE: Response #3 may attach to a choice from an entirely different Section dealing with an entirely different employee.)*

- *During the course of a problem there will be choices (like 2A in the example) which yield no new information or directions in the Response Booklet. Your choice has, however, been recorded on the Answer Sheet. If the choice was a good one, you would receive points for having selected it. If the choice was poor (as 2A is) it would be scored negatively. What you should understand, both about these "neutral" responses and other responses, is this:* **the responses you read aren't scored; <u>choices</u> you record on the Answer Sheet are scored.**

HELPFUL HINTS

When you take the test you must manage two test booklets and the Answer Sheet Packet. If you have adequate space, you may want to spread the test material in front of you. If you find this awkward. you might wish to try holding the Response Booklet on your lap while keeping only the Written Simulation Test Booklet and the Answer Sheet Packet on the desk top.

Another thing you may wish to do is keep track of your progress through the problem so that you can go back to review the events of the problem in the order they occurred. The Answer Sheet will help you in this process. Remember, the choices have been given letters as well as numbers. These letters tell you the section in the Test Booklet in which the choice is found. The Answer Sheet itself allows you to check quickly on the sections of the problem through which you have gone simply by looking at the letters to the left of the latent responses you have exposed. For example, by looking at the Answer Sheet on the next page you could tell that you had been through Sections A and D However, it does not tell you the order in which you went through them; you might want to track your path on a piece of scrap Paper

FIGURE 4

1A		11D	
2A		12D	#7
3A	#4	13D	
4A	#15	14D	#1
5A		15D	#1

FIGURE 4

Your test score will only be calculated from the responses exposed in the Answer Sheet Packet. You can feel free to make any notations you wish in both the Written Simulation Test Booklet (Blue Cover) and the Response Booklet (Yellow Cover); such notations may be useful in helping you review more easily what you've done.

If you follow the instructions given here, you should have no difficulty in working through the test problems.

Remember:

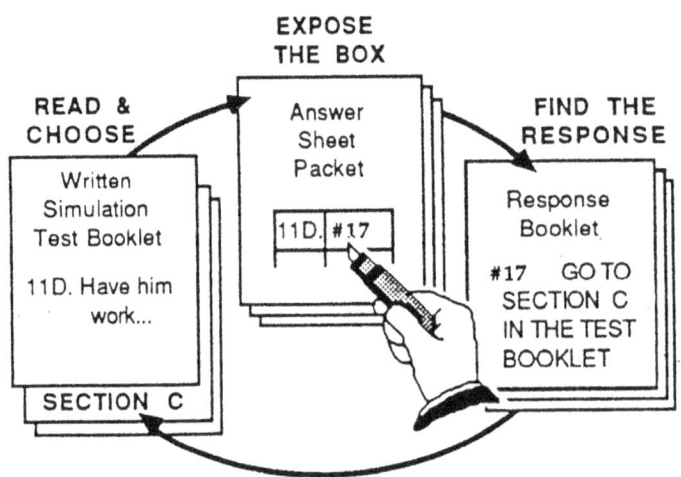

WRITTEN SIMULATION EXERCISES

As the name implies, written simulations reflect reality, but in a controlled manner. These written simulation tests consist of problems which involve you in realistic situations like those you would encounter as a first-line supervisor, manager or administrator. You will be required to work your way through each situation, making decisions about the best course of action to solve the problem that is presented. A problem unfolds as a result of decisions you make about how to handle the situations. Different people will have different ways of solving problems and managing situations. These differences may cause the problem to unfold in different ways. The written simulation test is designed so that actions you choose give you information or produce outcomes, eventually leading to a conclusion.

OPENING SCENE

When you open the Test Booklet, the problem will begin with an opening scene.

The opening scene introduces you to the problem. It tells you what your role is and what is happening. At the end of the opening scene, you will usually find the direction **Continue now with Section A**. Section A follows the opening scene.

> **Sample Problem**
>
> Assume you are a new supervisor in a unit that has an assignment to provide seminars to the public about your agency's programs. Joan, who reports to you, held the first session last Friday. On Monday, you receive an e-mail from your supervisor who indicates that the Commissioner has received complaints from participants at the seminar who indicated that there were not sufficient seats and handouts for the participants at the Friday session. Joan is currently holding the second session with a different group at the seminar site, which is located outside the office.
>
> **Continue now with Section A.**

PROBLEM SECTIONS

All sections of the written simulation problem contain choices. Each section is identified by a letter of the alphabet. Section A is the first section presented in the problem. You will generally not be directed to other sections in alphabetical order. (For example, you may be directed from A to Q to H to C, etc.). Also, you may not be directed to every section in the problem. GO ONLY TO THOSE SECTIONS TO WHICH YOU ARE DIRECTED. Some sections may have more than one page. Be sure that you start with the first page of the section. Also, make sure that you look at every page in a multi-page section.

In each section, you will find a list of things you could do or information you might want to know to respond to the situation. Some of the things are good choices, while others are neutral or even poor. In some of the sections, you will see additional information about the situation. In every section, you will see instructions for selecting choices. Some sections require you to **Choose ONLY ONE** of the choices; others permit you to **Choose AS MANY** as are appropriate, to **Choose UP TO** a specified number or to **Choose A SPECIFIC NUMBER**. Failure to follow these instructions could negatively affect your score on the test.

Section A

You would now: **(Choose ONLY ONE, unless otherwise directed.)**

1. Leave a message on Joan's desk for her to see you tomorrow.

2. Call your supervisor to find out more about the incident.

3. Talk to the Commissioner's staff about the complaints.

4. Go to the seminar and talk to Joan immediately.

5. Contact someone else from your unit who attended the session on Friday.

6. Contact the seminar site and leave a message for Joan to call you.

In answering a **Choose ONLY ONE** section you should assume that you will be allowed to make only one choice. You should evaluate all the choices and choose the one you believe is better than all the others. Occasionally, the response to that choice may direct you to make another choice in the same section. This does not necessarily mean that you have made a poor choice. It may be the preferred choice. However, you should **never assume** that you will have the opportunity to make a second choice.

In answering a **Choose AS MANY** section you will have the opportunity to make several choices. Not all the choices represent proper actions to take. You should evaluate all the choices and choose all those that you believe represent proper actions while not choosing any of those that you believe represent inappropriate actions.

In answering a **Choose UP TO** section you will be told the maximum number of choices you can make (e.g., **Choose UP TO FOUR**). You do not have to choose four but you cannot choose any more than four. If you do choose more than four, you will receive credit for the four lowest valued choices and may receive a lower score.

In answering a **Choose A SPECIFIC NUMBER** section you will be told the exact number of choices you must make (e.g., **Choose THREE**). You should not leave this section without making three choices. If you make more or fewer choices (four choices or two choices), you may receive a lower score. If you cannot find three choices that you believe are positive steps, you should look for choices that you believe will not be negative steps so that you can make the required three choices.

A **Choose AS MANY**, a **Choose UP TO** or a **Choose A SPECIFIC NUMBER** section will generally end with a numbered direction that begins: "**After you have chosen....**" This numbered direction does NOT count as one of the number of choices you may make in the section. You should make the appropriate number of choices in the section before following the instructions in the final numbered direction.

ANSWER SHEETS

Once you have made a selection, you must find the response for that choice. The answer sheet serves as the place for you to record your choices. It also tells you which response number to look up to find the outcome of a particular choice.

A	1		11		21		31		41
	2		12		22	F	32	H	42
	3		13		23		33		43
	4	C	14		24		34		44
	5		15	E	25		35		45
	6		16		26		36		46
B	7		17		27	G	37		47
	8	D	18		28		38		48
	9		19		29		39		49
	10		20		30		40		50

The answer sheets contain numbers with blank boxes to the right of them. Letters that identify each of the sections are positioned to the left of the first choice in that section. The visible numbers correspond to the choices in the Test Booklet. The boxes to their right contain "latent information": numbers, words, or checkmarks that cannot be seen until they are exposed with the special developer pen. Because each answer sheet is designed for a specific problem, it is essential that you use the answer sheet that corresponds to the problem you are working on.

When you lightly rub the developer pen across the box next to your choice number, you will expose the latent information. TAKE CARE TO EXPOSE ONLY THE BOX WHICH CORRESPONDS TO YOUR CHOICE. When exposing material on the answer sheet, rub the developer pen once over the area you wish to develop. The image will appear in one to two seconds. **DO NOT** repeatedly rub an area. Repeated rubbing may cause the image to be scrubbed off the paper and become unreadable. This will make it difficult for you to continue with the test and may result in your getting a lower score than you would have gotten otherwise.

Using the developer pen on a choice box creates a record of your choice. Unlike a multiple-choice test, there is no way you can erase a choice once you make it. As in real life, once an action is taken, it is not possible for it to be rescinded. Subsequent steps can be taken to counteract the action, but the original action remains.

When you expose the box on the answer sheet that corresponds to the number of the choice you selected in the Test Booklet, you will see one of three things: a **checkmark**, a **GO TO** statement or a three-digit **number**, as indicated in the following example.

A 1		11		21	183	31		41	
2		12		22	180	F 32		H 42	
3		13		23		33	178	43	✔
4		C 14	161	24	GO TO F	34		44	
5	156	15		E 25		35		45	
6	GO TO G	16		26		36		46	✔
B 7		17		27		G 37		47	
8		D 18	173	28		38		48	
9		19	153	29		39		49	
10		20		30		40	164	50	152

If a **checkmark** appears, continue to follow directions in the SAME section in which you are working in the Test Booklet. The checkmark merely means that your answer has been recorded, but no new information is presented to you as a result.

If a **GO TO** statement appears, go to the indicated lettered section in the Test Booklet. Be sure to develop the ENTIRE box, because some sections may be labeled with double letters (AA, BB, etc.).

If a three-digit **number** appears, look up that numbered response in the Response Booklet, read the response, and follow the directions at the end of the response.

In sections that allow more than one choice, make your choices one at a time. READ THE RESPONSE (IF ANY) TO EACH CHOICE BEFORE MAKING YOUR NEXT CHOICE.

RESPONSE BOOKLET

The Response Booklet contains the responses, which provide both feedback on your choices and directions for proceeding through the written simulation problem.

The following illustration shows the kinds of responses and directions you can expect to see.

If the directions send you to another section **(GO TO SECTION D)**, go immediately to that section and make no more choices in the section in which you were working. If the directions tell you to **Make another choice in the same section**, you must return to the section in which you were working and make another choice. If the directions tell you to **Return to the section you are working in and continue,** return to that section, make any additional choices that are appropriate and follow any further directions you are given.

> 181. He says he hopes so.
>   **GO TO SECTION D**.
>
> 182. There have been none. **Make another choice in the same section**.
>
> 183. She says she was prepared to make her presentation.
>   **Return to the section you are working in and continue.**

Responses provide information and/or directions for working through the problem. HOWEVER, not all the responses in the booklet are actual parts of the problem you are working on. Some responses present information which may be false or misleading. These have been included to prevent candidates from trying to piece the problem together by reading only the responses. The best course of action for you to take is to pay close attention ONLY to the responses to which you have been directed.

SCORING

CHOICES, NOT RESPONSES, ARE SCORED. Every time you use the developer pen on a box, you are recording a <u>choice</u>. Only the boxes exposed on the answer sheets will count toward your test score. Nothing you write in the Test Booklet or in the Response Booklet will be counted toward your final score.

EVERYTHING YOU EXPOSE ON THE ANSWER SHEET(S) WILL BE TAKEN INTO ACCOUNT IN SCORING. Be very careful using the developer pen on the answer sheet. Avoid making stray marks or smudges with the developer pen. When you expose a box, make sure it is the one that corresponds to your choice. Whatever you expose on an answer sheet - EVEN BOXES THAT YOU EXPOSED ACCIDENTALLY - will be scored, except in those cases where exposing additional response numbers contrary to instructions would advantage you. You will NOT be allowed to change or cross out exposed boxes. If you cross them out, they will be scored anyway. You will NOT be allowed to obtain a fresh answer sheet to make different selections.

Each choice in the written simulation test is valued positively, negatively or neutrally. In order to achieve the best score you can, you should select only the choices that you consider to be positive. In those sections that allow you to make more than one choice, you should select all the choices that you consider to be positive, while taking care not to select poor choices.

You may not be able to tell from the response to a choice whether that choice has a positive, negative or neutral value. As in real life, you may make the right decision but not immediately get good results. It is also possible to make a poor decision but have things appear to turn out all right in the short run. Do not become discouraged if a response to one of your choices suggests that the situation is not improving.

HINTS

Because you will be working the problem by going back and forth between the Test Booklet, the Answer Sheet Packet, and the Response Booklet, you could lose your place in the problem. You may find it helpful to leave your Test Booklet open to the section you are working in while you mark the answer sheet or look up responses so that you can return to the correct Test Booklet section quickly and easily. This is especially true of **Choose AS MANY** and **Choose UP TO** sections where you may go back and forth several times before being directed to another section.

You may find it helpful to track your path on a separate piece of paper by listing, in order, the sections to which you have been directed. This will enable you to review the events of the problem in the order they occurred and to keep track of your progress. You can also make any notations you wish in the rest of the Test Booklet. Although the answer sheets will show the sections in which you have exposed choices, they will not give you information on the order in which you have gone through the sections.

You should NOT make notations or stray marks on the answer sheets.

You should keep working on a problem until you are directed to a response that tells you it is the **END OF PROBLEM**.

IF YOU DON'T KNOW WHERE TO GO NEXT IN THE PROBLEM...

. . . follow the steps below. You are responsible for keeping track of where you are in the problem. The monitor is not permitted to assist you in finding your place.

If you find that you have answered only a few sections of the problem, and don't know where to go next, you've almost certainly missed a direction. If you become lost, LOOK FIRST in that section of the Test Booklet in which you're working:

- If the section directs you to **Choose AS MANY, Choose UP TO**, or **Choose A SPECIFIC NUMBER**, you may have missed the very last choice in the section that will usually tell you what box to expose next on the answer sheet in order to find the response that tells you where to go next.

- If the section directs you to **Choose ONLY ONE**, the box you exposed on the answer sheet either will have a GO TO statement, or will direct you to a response number. That numbered response either will have a GO TO statement at the end or will direct you to make another choice in the same section. If the response does neither, MAKE SURE you have exposed the correct numbered box on the answer sheet. If you have, then MAKE SURE you have read the correct numbered response in the Response Booklet.

If you still find yourself not knowing where to go next in the problem, the SECOND thing to do is retrace your path through the problem to make sure you haven't gone to a wrong section by mistake.

The last thing to remember, should you become lost, is not to give up. Entering a wrong section is not fatal. Back yourself up and pick up again where you went off the track.

A SAMPLE PROBLEM

We will now present a complete sample simulation problem. We will show all of the choices in the problem, the full answer sheet for the problem and all of the responses for the problem. We will discuss how to select choices in a section, and how to use the answer sheet to go to the responses that relate to the choices that are selected. We will show how to proceed through a section and how a problem progresses from section to section. Finally, we will show a fully exposed answer sheet so that you can see the responses associated with each of the choices and how making different choices could affect how a problem develops.

TAKING THE TEST

During an actual test, the simulation problem typically requires you to use three separate booklets:

Test Booklet - This booklet presents the problem situations and the possible choices that you can select. Pages 22 through 26 of this Promotion Test Battery Guide show the type of material that you will find in the Test Booklet.

Answer Sheet Packet - This small booklet contains the answer sheets for the different problems. Page 27 of this Promotion Test Battery Guide shows a sample answer sheet before any of the choices have been exposed. During the actual test you will need to use the special developer pen in order to mark a choice on the answer sheet, which may reveal other directions or information.

Response Booklet - Pages 28 through 30 of this Promotion Test Battery Guide show the type of material that you will find in the Response Booklet. When you select a choice, the answer sheet may indicate a numbered selection for you to read in the Response Booklet. The numbered selection in the Response Booklet will often provide additional information about the problem, and will give you directions to either continue in the section you are working in, or go to a different section of the Test Booklet.

Look over the sample Test Booklet, Answer Sheet and Response Booklet in this Promotion Test Battery Guide, and then go to page 31 of this Guide for a "walk-through" of the sample problem.

SAMPLE PROBLEM TEST BOOKLET

On the following pages are the opening scene and all the sections (A through H) of a sample problem.

SAMPLE PROBLEM

Assume you are a new supervisor in a unit that has an assignment to provide seminars to the public about your agency's programs. Joan, who reports to you, held the first session last Friday. On Monday, you receive an e-mail from your supervisor who indicates that the Commissioner has received complaints from participants at the seminar who indicated that there were not sufficient seats and handouts for the participants at the Friday session. Joan is currently holding the second session with a different group at the seminar site, which is located outside the office.

Continue now with Section A.

Section A

You would now: **(Choose ONLY ONE, unless otherwise directed.)**

1. Leave a message on Joan's desk for her to see you tomorrow.

2. Call your supervisor to find out more about the incident.

3. Talk to the Commissioner's staff about the complaints.

4. Go to the seminar and talk to Joan immediately.

5. Contact someone else from your unit who attended the session on Friday.

6. Contact the seminar site and leave a message for Joan to call you.

Section B

You would now: **(Choose ONLY ONE, unless otherwise directed.)**

7. Explain to your supervisor why the information that the Commissioner received was incorrect.

8. Draft a letter to the participants explaining the situation.

9. Direct Joan to make the changes she suggested.

10. Reassign Joan from the project.

11. Meet with your staff to resolve the dispute.

12. Tell Mike he must do what Joan has asked.

13. Tell your supervisor that you are unable to resolve the situation.

Section C

You would now say to Mike: **(Choose ONLY ONE, unless otherwise directed.)**

14. You appreciate him thinking about the problem and you want to hear what he has to say.

15. In light of Friday's problems, he is no longer going to be working on arrangements for seminars.

16. He should have done that in time to keep the problem from happening.

17. He will get a chance to explain it directly to the Commissioner.

Section D

When you speak with Joan, you would: **(Choose UP TO FOUR)**

18. Tell her about the complaint.

19. Ask her how the sessions are going today.

20. Tell her you are upset with her over the way she handled the situation.

21. Ask her if she was prepared on Friday.

22. Ask her what happened on Friday.

23. Ask her if she has any thoughts on how to avoid problems like those on Friday.

24. **After you have chosen UP TO FOUR, have marked your choices on the answer sheet, and have read the responses, EXPOSE 24 ON THE ANSWER SHEET.**

Section E

Your supervisor says he received a couple of calls complaining about the lack of seats and handouts. You would also want to ask him: **(Choose AS MANY as are appropriate.)**

25. whether he is aware of any other complaints

26. whether Joan has held seminars like this before

27. how Joan's work performance is in general

28. whether he wants you to discipline Joan

29. if the Commissioner wants to talk to Joan

30. if you should conduct the remaining seminars yourself

31. **After you have chosen as many as are appropriate, have marked your choices on the answer sheet, and have read the responses, EXPOSE 31 ON THE ANSWER SHEET.**

Section F

You would now: **(Choose ONLY ONE, unless otherwise directed.)**

32. Inform your supervisor that Mike caused the problem.

33. Discuss the situation with Mike.

34. Tell your supervisor that you have learned some things about Friday's seminar.

35. Ask Mike if he has any ideas about why there was a problem with Friday's seminar.

36. Schedule a meeting with your supervisor to discuss Mike and Joan's behavior.

Section G

Before speaking with Joan you would: **(Choose ONLY ONE, unless otherwise directed.)**

37. Ask for the evaluation sheets from Friday's seminar.

38. Tell your supervisor that you are going to straighten out the mess Joan has made.

39. Make a list of all the things Joan appears to have done wrong.

40. Make a list of the various questions you plan to ask Joan.

41. Ask if any complaints about Friday's seminar have come directly to your office.

Section H

You would plan to discuss the following with Mike: **(Choose AS MANY as are appropriate.)**

42. whether he was deliberately trying to embarrass Joan

43. whether he realized they were short seats and handouts Friday

44. whether he knows why more people appeared Friday than he had prepared for

45. whether he has any ideas on how to prevent a recurrence of Friday's problems

46. whether he has talked to Joan about what happened Friday

47. that you think your supervisor is overreacting

48. whether setting up the proper number of places was too much effort

49. that you are upset over the way he mishandled the situation

50. **After you have chosen as many as are appropriate and have marked your choices on the answer sheet, EXPOSE 50 ON THE ANSWER SHEET.**

SAMPLE PROBLEM ANSWER SHEET

Below is the answer sheet for the sample problem with no responses exposed.

Sample Problem
Answer Sheet

A	1		11		21		31		41
	2		12		22	F	32	H	42
	3		13		23		33		43
	4	C	14		24		34		44
	5		15	E	25		35		45
	6		16		26		36		46
B	7		17		27	G	37		47
	8	D	18		28		38		48
	9		19		29		39		49
	10		20		30		40		50

SAMPLE PROBLEM RESPONSE BOOKLET

On the following pages are the responses, numbered 151 through 183, for the sample problem. Pay special attention to the note at the beginning of the responses. It says that not all of the responses listed are actually part of the problem. Be sure that you read only the responses to which you have been directed.

RESPONSES

PLEASE BE AWARE: Not all of the responses below are actually a part of the problem you are working on. They may state accurate names and plausible events, but the information they present is misleading. These responses have been included to keep you from being able to piece the problem together by reading only the responses. The best course of action for you to take is to pay close attention ONLY to the responses to which you have been directed.

151. **There are no instructions in this problem that direct you to this section. You may have made an error in following the directions from the box on the answer sheet or from the response; or you may not have completely exposed a direction in the choice box. Go back over your choices, the directions in the responses, and any notes you have made to determine where you should be in the problem. You will not be penalized for exposing this box on your answer sheet.**

152. Mike tells you he thinks he knows what went wrong Friday and how to keep it from happening again. **GO TO SECTION C.**

153. She says they seem to be going well. **Return to the section you are working in and continue.**

154. Joan says she has a number of personal issues which may be affecting her performance. **Return to the section you are working in and continue.**

155. They have no additional information about the complaints. **Make another choice in the same section.**

156. No one is available. **Make another choice in the same section.**

157. Joan says she will not tolerate Mike treating her like this. **Return to the section you are working in and continue.**

158. She says she did the best she could under the circumstances. **Return to the section you are working in and continue.**

159. He says she has. **Return to the section you are working in and continue.**

160. He suggests that Mike does not usually cause problems. **Make another choice in the same section.**

161. He explains how the problem occurred and offers a good solution to keep it from happening again. **This is the end of the sample problem. Make no more choices in this problem.**

162. Mike says he made that suggestion to Joan several times but she ignored him. **Return to the section you are working in and continue.**

163. He says that doesn't seem necessary. **Return to the section you are working in and continue.**

164. You compile a short list of questions. **GO TO SECTION D.**

165. He asks to meet with you. **GO TO SECTION H.**

166. He suggests you meet with Mike to better find out what happened. **GO TO SECTION H.**

167. He says she is a good employee. **Return to the section you are working in and continue.**

168. She says she has been thinking about it. **Return to the section you are working in and continue.**

169. He says he is not. **Return to the section you are working in and continue.**

170. He looks very dejected and walks away. **This is the end of the sample problem. Make no more choices in this problem.**

171. He says that's good and you should continue your investigation. **Make another choice in the same section.**

172. Joan and Mike say they cannot reconcile their differences. **Return to the section you are working in and continue.**

173. She says she is not surprised that there was a complaint. **Return to the section you are working in and continue.**

174. He says he does not. **Return to the section you are working in and continue.**

175. Mike says he would rather transfer to another unit. **Return to the section you are working in and continue.**

176. They are not available. **GO TO SECTION D.**

177. He says that seems premature. **Return to the section you are working in and continue.**

178. Mike says that he would like to meet with you. **GO TO SECTION H.**

179. You decide you do not have enough information to do this. **GO TO SECTION D.**

180. She says that Mike, who works for you, was responsible for setting up the room the previous day and for having the handouts ready. When she arrived on Friday there were chairs and handouts for 30 people, but 45 people actually showed up. She got a few extra chairs from another room, and asked people to share the handouts. **Return to the section you are working in and continue.**

181. He says he hopes so. **GO TO SECTION D.**

182. There have been none. **Make another choice in the same section.**

183. She says she was prepared to make her presentation. **Return to the section you are working in and continue.**

WORKING THROUGH THE SAMPLE PROBLEM

TAKING THE SAMPLE PROBLEM

Working with these three parts of the problem - the test sections, the answer sheet and the list of responses - we will now proceed through the sample simulation test as we might in a real test situation. Always begin by reading the introductory material. For a real simulation problem it may be several pages long. For the sample problem, it is the paragraphs below.

SAMPLE PROBLEM

Assume you are a new supervisor in a unit that has an assignment to provide seminars to the public about your agency's programs. Joan, who reports to you, held the first session last Friday. On Monday, you receive an e-mail from your supervisor who indicates that the Commissioner has received complaints from participants at the seminar who indicated that there were not sufficient seats and handouts for the participants at the Friday session. Joan is currently holding the second session with a different group at the seminar site, which is located outside the office.
Continue now with Section A.

The introduction concludes by directing us to Section A. Introductory material in a real simulation problem will also direct you to Section A. Section A of the sample problem is shown next.

Section A

You would now: **(Choose ONLY ONE, unless otherwise directed.)**

1. Leave a message on Joan's desk for her to see you tomorrow.

2. Call your supervisor to find out more about the incident.

3. Talk to the Commissioner's staff about the complaints.

4. Go to the seminar and talk to Joan immediately.

5. Contact someone else from your unit who attended the session on Friday.

6. Contact the seminar site and leave a message for Joan to call you.

Candidates are directed to choose only one of the choices presented. The choices in Section A tend to fall into two categories - - those that propose an action to contact Joan and those that attempt to get additional information. We'll decide to get additional information before doing anything directly with Joan. We'll select choice 5. We then go to the answer sheet and, using the developer pen, expose the box immediately to the right of the number 5. Information will appear as shown next.

A	1			11			21			31			41	
	2			12			22		F	32		H	42	
	3			13			23			33			43	
	4		C	14			24			34			44	
	5	156		15		E	25			35			45	
	6			16			26			36			46	
B	7			17			27		G	37			47	
	8		D	18			28			38			48	
	9			19			29			39			49	
	10			20			30			40			50	

The number 156 has appeared in the box. We now go to the list of responses and read response number 156. It reads as follows:

156.   No one is available. **Make another choice in the same section.**

Note that in addition to the information given, the response also directs candidates to make another choice in the same section. Even though the initial directions in the section said choose only one, we have now been directed to return to section A and make another choice. This time, we'll select choice 6 and expose the box to the right of number 6 on the answer sheet. The answer sheet now looks like the following:

A	1			11			21			31			41	
	2			12			22		F	32		H	42	
	3			13			23			33			43	
	4		C	14			24			34			44	
	5	156		15		E	25			35			45	
	6	GO TO G		16			26			36			46	
B	7			17			27		G	37			47	
	8		D	18			28			38			48	
	9			19			29			39			49	
	10			20			30			40			50	

The exposed box contains the words GO TO G. These are directions to go to Section G in the test. We should stop working in Section A and go directly to Section G. Section G is shown next.

Section G

Before speaking with Joan you would: **(Choose ONLY ONE, unless otherwise directed.)**

37. Ask for the evaluation sheets from Friday's seminar.

38. Tell your supervisor that you are going to straighten out the mess Joan has made.

39. Make a list of all the things Joan appears to have done wrong.

40. Make a list of the various questions you plan to ask Joan.

41. Ask if any complaints about Friday's seminar have come directly to your office.

Section G begins by asking what you would want to do before speaking to Joan. Candidates must now choose one of the options presented. We'll choose choice 40 and expose the box to the right of 40 on the answer sheet. The answer sheet now looks like the following:

A	1	
	2	
	3	
	4	
	5	156
	6	GO TO G
B	7	
	8	
	9	
	10	

	11	
	12	
	13	
C	14	
	15	
	16	
	17	
D	18	
	19	
	20	

	21	
	22	
	23	
	24	
E	25	
	26	
	27	
	28	
	29	
	30	

	31	
F	32	
	33	
	34	
	35	
	36	
G	37	
	38	
	39	
	40	164

	41	
H	42	
	43	
	44	
	45	
	46	
	47	
	48	
	49	
	50	

The number 164 has appeared in the box. We go to the list of responses and read response 164 which reads as follows:

164. You compile a short list of questions. **GO TO SECTION D.**

This response directs the candidates to go to Section D. It may be tempting to go back into Section G and select choice 37. However, this is not a good thing to do. In exposing the box to the right of number 37 on the answer sheet, we may receive a lower score or directions that take us to a different section of the problem and leave us faced with conflicting directions on how to proceed. This could result in our having difficulty completing the problem or in receiving a lower score than we would otherwise receive. Once we have made a choice, exposed the answer sheet and come to a response that directs us to another section, we go immediately to that section without making any additional choices in the section in which we are currently working.

We are now in Section D, which is shown next.

Section D

When you speak with Joan, you would: **(Choose UP TO FOUR)**

18. Tell her about the complaint.

19. Ask her how the sessions are going today.

20. Tell her you are upset with her over the way she handled the situation.

21. Ask her if she was prepared on Friday.

22. Ask her what happened on Friday.

23. Ask her if she has any thoughts on how to avoid problems like those on Friday.

24. **After you have chosen UP TO FOUR, have marked your choices on the answer sheet, and have read the responses, EXPOSE 24 ON THE ANSWER SHEET.**

Section D is different from the first two sections we have worked in because it now directs us to choose up to four of the choices offered. Even though we can choose up to four choices, we will choose one choice at a time, expose the answer sheet and read the corresponding response before going on to making any additional choices. We will begin by choosing number 18, and exposing the answer sheet. The answer sheet now looks like the following:

A	1			11			21			31			41	
	2			12			22		F	32		H	42	
	3			13			23			33			43	
	4		C	14			24			34			44	
	5	156		15		E	25			35			45	
	6	GO TO G		16			26			36			46	
B	7			17			27		G	37			47	
	8		D	18	173		28			38			48	
	9			19			29			39			49	
	10			20			30			40	164		50	

We are directed to response number 173 which reads:

> 173. She says she is not surprised that there was a complaint. **Return to the section you are working in and continue.**

We then decide to choose response 19. After exposing the box on the answer sheet, the answer sheet now looks like the following:

	#			#			#			#			#	
A	1			11			21			31			41	
	2			12			22		F	32		H	42	
	3			13			23			33			43	
	4		C	14			24			34			44	
	5	156		15		E	25			35			45	
	6	GO TO G		16			26			36			46	
B	7			17			27		G	37			47	
	8		D	18	173		28			38			48	
	9			19	153		29			39			49	
	10			20			30			40	164		50	

We are directed to response 153 which reads as follows:

> 153. She says they seem to be going well. **Return to the section you are working in and continue.**

We then decide to choose response 22. After exposing the box on the answer sheet, the answer sheet now looks like the following:

A	1			11			21			31			41	
	2			12			22	180	F	32		H	42	
	3			13			23			33			43	
	4		C	14			24			34			44	
	5	156		15		E	25			35			45	
	6	GO TO G		16			26			36			46	
B	7			17			27		G	37			47	
	8		D	18	173		28			38			48	
	9			19	153		29			39			49	
	10			20			30			40	164		50	

We are directed to response 180 which reads as follows:

> 180. She says that Mike, who works for you, was responsible for setting up the room the previous day and for having the handouts ready. When she arrived on Friday there were chairs and handouts for 30 people, but 45 people actually showed up. She got a few extra chairs from another room, and asked people to share the handouts. **Return to the section you are working in and continue.**

At this point we have selected three responses from Section D. We are allowed four, so we will select one more choice. We decide to take response 21. After exposing the box on the answer sheet, the answer sheet now looks like the following:

A	1			11			21	183		31			41	
	2			12			22	180	F	32		H	42	
	3			13			23			33			43	
	4		C	14			24			34			44	
	5	156		15		E	25			35			45	
	6	GO TO G		16			26			36			46	
B	7			17			27		G	37			47	
	8		D	18	173		28			38			48	
	9			19	153		29			39			49	
	10			20			30			40	164		50	

We are directed to response 183 which reads as follows:

> 183. She says she was prepared to make her presentation. **Return to the section you are working in and continue.**

At this point we have made four choices and four is the maximum number of choices allowed in this section.

Choice 24 tells us that after we have chosen up to four, and have marked the choices on the answer sheet and read the responses, to expose the box to the right of number 24 on the answer sheet. We do this and the answer sheet now looks like the following:

A	1			11			21	183		31			41	
	2			12			22	180	F	32		H	42	
	3			13			23			33			43	
	4		C	14			24	GO TO F		34			44	
	5	156		15		E	25			35			45	
	6	GO TO G		16			26			36			46	
B	7			17			27		G	37			47	
	8		D	18	173		28			38			48	
	9			19	153		29			39			49	
	10			20			30			40	164		50	

The box to the right of number 24 contains the directions to GO TO F. At this point we will make no more choices in Section D and will go immediately to Section F which is shown next.

> **Section F**
>
> You would now: **(Choose ONLY ONE, unless otherwise directed.)**
>
> 32. Inform your supervisor that Mike caused the problem.
>
> 33. Discuss the situation with Mike.
>
> 34. Tell your supervisor that you have learned some things about Friday's seminar.
>
> 35. Ask Mike if he has any ideas about why there was a problem with Friday's seminar.
>
> 36. Schedule a meeting with your supervisor to discuss Mike and Joan's behavior.

Section F asks us to choose only one of the choices offered. We will choose number 33. After exposing the answer sheet, the answer sheet now looks like the following:

	#			#			#			#			#	
A	1			11			21	183		31			41	
	2			12			22	180	F	32		H	42	
	3			13			23			33	178		43	
	4		C	14			24	GO TO F		34			44	
	5	156		15		E	25			35			45	
	6	GO TO G		16			26			36			46	
B	7			17			27		G	37			47	
	8		D	18	173		28			38			48	
	9			19	153		29			39			49	
	10			20			30			40	164		50	

The number 178 has appeared on the answer sheet. We go to the list of responses and read response number 178 which reads as follows:

> 178. Mike says that he would like to meet with you. **GO TO SECTION H.**

The response provides us with some information. It also directs us to go immediately to Section H which is shown next.

27

> **Section H**
>
> You would plan to discuss the following with Mike: **(Choose AS MANY as are appropriate.)**
>
> 42. whether he was deliberately trying to embarrass Joan
>
> 43. whether he realized they were short seats and handouts Friday
>
> 44. whether he knows why more people appeared Friday than he had prepared for
>
> 45. whether he has any ideas on how to prevent a recurrence of Friday's problems
>
> 46. whether he has talked to Joan about what happened Friday
>
> 47. that you think your supervisor is overreacting
>
> 48. whether setting up the proper number of places was too much effort
>
> 49. that you are upset over the way he mishandled the situation
>
> 50. **After you have chosen as many as are appropriate and have marked your choices on the answer sheet, EXPOSE 50 ON THE ANSWER SHEET.**

Section H is different from the first four sections we have worked in because it now directs us to choose AS MANY of the choices offered as you consider appropriate. We will make each choice separately and expose the answer sheet before moving on to any additional choices. We will start by choosing number 43. The exposed answer sheet now looks like the following:

A	1			11			21	183		31			41
	2			12			22	180	F	32		H	42
	3			13			23			33	178		43 ✓
	4		C	14			24	GO TO F		34			44
	5	156		15		E	25			35			45
	6	GO TO G		16			26			36			46
B	7			17			27		G	37			47
	8		D	18	173		28			38			48
	9			19	153		29			39			49
	10			20			30			40	164		50

All that has appeared is a checkmark. As stated earlier, a checkmark tells us that our answer has been recorded but no new information is presented. We continue to work in the same section. Our second choice is number 46. The exposed answer sheet now looks like the following:

A	1			11			21	183		31			41	
	2			12			22	180	F	32		H	42	
	3			13			23			33	178		43	✓
	4		C	14			24	GO TO F		34			44	
	5	156		15		E	25			35			45	
	6	GO TO G		16			26			36			46	✓
B	7			17			27		G	37			47	
	8		D	18	173		28			38			48	
	9			19	153		29			39			49	
	10			20			30			40	164		50	

Again, a checkmark has appeared showing that our answer has been recorded. We decide that these two things are all we need to discuss with Mike and we move to choice 50 which tells us that after we have made as many choices as are appropriate and have marked the answer sheet, to expose box 50 on the answer sheet. The exposed answer sheet now looks like the following:

A	1			11			21	183		31			41	
	2			12			22	180	F	32		H	42	
	3			13			23			33	178		43	✓
	4		C	14			24	GO TO F		34			44	
	5	156		15		E	25			35			45	
	6	GO TO G		16			26			36			46	✓
B	7			17			27		G	37			47	
	8		D	18	173		28			38			48	
	9			19	153		29			39			49	
	10			20			30			40	164		50	152

The number 152 has appeared in the answer sheet. Response 152 reads as follows:

| 152. | Mike tells you he thinks he knows what went wrong Friday and how to keep it from happening again. **GO TO SECTION C.** |

The information and response in 152 tells us that Mike believes he knows what the problem was on Friday. We are then directed to go immediately to Section C. Again, if we had arrived at response 152 without choosing choices 43 and 46, we should not go back into Section H and choose them later. Without knowing what information will be exposed when we go to the answer sheet, we cannot be sure that it will not create serious problems for us continuing with the problem. We are now in Section C, which is shown next.

Section C

You would now say to Mike: **(Choose ONLY ONE, unless otherwise directed.)**

14. You appreciate him thinking about the problem and you want to hear what he has to say.

15. In light of Friday's problems, he is no longer going to be working on arrangements for seminars.

16. He should have done that in time to keep the problem from happening.

17. He will get a chance to explain it directly to the Commissioner.

We are again directed to make only one choice. We will choose number 14. After exposing the box on the answer sheet, the answer sheet now looks like the following:

A	1			11			21	183		31			41	
	2			12			22	180	F	32		H	42	
	3			13			23			33	178		43	✓
	4		C	14	161		24	GO TO F		34			44	
	5	156		15		E	25			35			45	
	6	GO TO G		16			26			36			46	✓
B	7			17			27		G	37			47	
	8		D	18	173		28			38			48	
	9			19	153		29			39			49	
	10			20			30			40	164		50	152

The number 161 has appeared in the answer sheet. When we read response number 161, it reads as follows:

> 161. He explains how the problem occurred and offers a good solution to keep it from happening again. **This is the end of the sample problem. Make no more choices in this problem.**

This response tells us that the problem has been concluded. At this point, we should make no more choices in the problem. A similar statement will appear when you have concluded a real simulation problem. Once you read that statement, make no more choices in the problem and be sure to follow any other directions that appear in the response.

SCORING THE SAMPLE PROBLEM

All choices in a simulation problem have a value of plus (+), minus (-) or zero (0). Below is a list of all the choices in this test along with their respective values.

SCORING TABLE

	Choice	Value		Choice	Value		Choice	Value		Choice	Value		Choice	Value
A	1	-1		11	0		21	0		31	0		41	+1
	2	+1		12	0		22	+1	F	32	-2	H	42	-1
	3	0		13	0		23	+1		33	+2		43	+1
	4	-2	C	14	+2		24	0		34	0		44	+1
	5	+1		15	-2	E	25	+1		35	+2		45	+1
	6	+2		16	-1		26	+1		36	-2		46	+1
B	7	0		17	-2		27	+1	G	37	+1		47	-1
	8	0	D	18	+1		28	-1		38	-2		48	-1
	9	0		19	+1		29	-1		39	-1		49	-1
	10	0		20	-1		30	-1		40	+2		50	0

Let's score ourselves on the test we just took. We chose choices 5, 6, 14, 18, 19, 21, 22, 24, 33, 40, 43, 46, and 50. Those choices are listed below along with their corresponding values from the table above.

Choice	Value	Choice	Value
5	+1	24	0
6	+2	33	+2
14	+2	40	+2
18	+1	43	+1
19	+1	46	+1
21	0	50	0
22	+1		

Using that list, we can add up our score and see that we received a score of +14 on the problem. Let's see how we might have done even better. Below is an answer sheet with every single choice exposed.

Sample Problem
Answer Sheet

	#	Response		#	Response		#	Response		#	Response		#	Response
A	1	GO TO G		11	151		21	183		31	GO TO G		41	182
	2	GO TO E		12	151		22	180	F	32	160	H	42	✓
	3	155		13	151		23	168		33	178		43	✓
	4	GO TO G	C	14	161		24	GO TO F		34	171		44	✓
	5	156		15	170	E	25	169		35	165		45	✓
	6	GO TO G		16	170		26	159		36	166		46	✓
B	7	151		17	170		27	167	G	37	176		47	✓
	8	151	D	18	173		28	177		38	181		48	✓
	9	151		19	153		29	174		39	179		49	✓
	10	151		20	158		30	163		40	164		50	152

We would never select every choice when taking a test but having the fully exposed answer sheet allows us to look at what response goes with every choice in the test and to see the effect of making different choices.

A general rule for getting the best score possible in a simulation test is to choose all of the positively weighted choices and choose none of the negatively weighted choices. Let's see how this rule applies to the choices we made when we took this test. In Section A, we took two of the three positively weighted choices. We did not choose choice 2. However, as we can see from the exposed answer sheet, a response to choice 2 directs candidates to go to Section E. Therefore, we could not have chosen both choice 2 and choice 6 since they have conflicting directions, and we would have been directed out of Section A after choosing either one of them. This section highlights the dangers in making more choices than are allowed by the directions, or not stopping when directed to go to a new section. A person who ignored the directions and chose both 2 and 6 would be faced with conflicting directions and would find it very difficult to continue with the problem.

In Section C, we chose choice 14. This was the only positively weighted choice in that section. Therefore, we received the maximum number of points in Section C as well. In Section D, we chose choices 18, 19, 21, 22 and 24. Choices 18, 19 and 22 were positively weighted, which added to our score. However, we did not choose choice 23. It was also positively weighted and had we chosen it, our score would have been one point higher. However, it was important that we did not choose choice 20. This was negatively weighted and would have subtracted a point from our score. Choosing choice 21 could have had an effect on our score even though that choice was assigned a weight of zero. In this section we were allowed to choose up to four and choice 21 was our fourth choice. By selecting it, we are prevented from taking any other remaining choices.

We were not directed to Section E so we were not able to make any choices in that section. In Section F, we chose choice 33 which was one of the two positively weighted choices in that section. We were only allowed to make one choice in that section, therefore +2 was the most points we could have received. Had we chosen choice 35 instead of choice 33, we would have been directed to response 165 which was essentially the same response we got for choosing choice 33. Therefore, we received the maximum points and it did not matter which of the two positively weighted choices we chose.

In Section G, we took choice 40 which was weighted +2. Had we chosen choice 41 first, we would have been directed to response 182 and allowed to make another choice in the section. We could then have chosen choice 40 second and received +1 for choice 41 and +2 for choice 40 for a total score of +3. However, had we chosen choice 37 first, we would have been directed to response 176 which would have sent us directly to Section D and we would not have had the opportunity to choose either choice 40 or choice 41. Then the maximum we could have received in that section would have been +1. This section demonstrates the dangers in not following the directions carefully. Candidates who violated the directions and chose choices 37 and 40 would have received only the +1 credit for choice 37. They would not have been given credit for choice 40. Again, this points out that you should not go back and make any extra choices after you have been directed out of a section.

In Section H, we took choices 43 and 46; two of the four positive choices. Had we also taken choices 44 and 45 we would have received two more points. It's also worth noting that no matter what choices we had taken, at the end we would have been directed to response 152. This response has Mike indicating that he thinks he knows what went wrong and then directs all candidates out of the section.

In summary, we could have improved our score by choosing a few more positive choices in the **Choose AS MANY** or **Choose UP TO** sections. However, it is important to note that most of the choices we did take were positive choices, and as a result we got a very good score. While it is important to choose as many positive choices as possible, automatically choosing all the choices will not result in improving your score. Section H illustrates that. We chose two positive choices and had a score of +2 for that section. Had we chosen the other two positive choices, we could have had a score of +4. However, if we had chosen all 8 of the choices we would have made 4 positive choices and 4 negative choices and our net score would have been zero, two points less than what we received when we made only two choices. It is important to choose wisely in a **Choose AS MANY** or **Choose UP TO** section. You will **NOT** get the best score by exposing all the responses.

There were two sections in this problem that we did not make any choices from: Section B and Section E. Section B is a section that no candidates should ever go to if they follow the directions carefully. This section is placed in the simulation problem after Section A to redirect candidates who are not following directions and are simply going alphabetically through the sections. In all cases, candidates who make a choice in Section B are directed to response 151 which reads as follows.

151.	**There are no instructions in this problem that direct you to this section. You may have made an error in following the directions from the box on the answer sheet or from the response; or you may not have completely exposed a direction in the choice box. Go back over your choices, the directions in the responses, and any notes you have made to determine where you should be in the problem. You will not be penalized for exposing this box on your answer sheet.**

All choices in Section B have a weight of zero, so candidates are not penalized for making choices in that section. The section exists only to remind candidates to carefully follow the directions in determining which section to answer next.

We also did not make any choices in Section E. Section E could only be entered by choosing response 2 in Section A. Because we did not choose response 2, we were not directed to Section E. We will not necessarily be directed to every section in the simulation problem and should not be concerned if there are sections in which we did not make any choices.

Also, if we were to go through the exposed answer sheet and check which responses were exposed, we would see that five response numbers were not listed on the exposed answer sheet. Responses 154, 157, 162, 172 and 175 are nowhere on the exposed answer sheet. The introductory note to the responses warns candidates that there may be responses listed that are not part of the problem. Candidates who tried to figure out this problem by reading all of the responses would have seen responses suggesting that a disagreement exists between Mike and Joan and would have received misinformation. It is important to read only the responses to which you have been directed from the answer sheet.

AN ILLUSTRATIVE PROBLEM

Taking the Illustrative Problem

On the next several pages is an actual simulation problem that has been used to assess managerial and supervisory ability. Like the Sample Problem presented earlier in this Guide, this illustrative problem is presented in parts. The first part is the Test Booklet, which contains the various sections of the problem and the options from which candidates must choose. The second part is the Answer Sheet. In this case, all of the answers are "exposed" although in an actual test you would use a special developer pen to expose the boxes next to each of the choices you made. The third part is the Response Booklet which provides feedback on your choices and directions for proceeding through the problem. The fourth and final part is the Scoring Instructions. This information would normally only be available at a computational review, but is included here to enable you to see how different choices have been valued and allow you to compute your own score on this problem.

We suggest you approach the problem as if you were taking an actual test. In taking the problem as a test, you should highlight or otherwise mark on the answer sheet each of the choices you select. This will enable you to compute your score when you are finished. After you have done that, you can go back and read the remaining choices and responses that you did not originally select if you wish.

Illustrative Problem Test Booklet

BACKGROUND FOR THE PROBLEM

To answer this problem, you are to place yourself in the role of a manager in the fictional agency described on this and the following pages. You are not expected to know anything about the technical aspects of what this agency does. The test will not assess your knowledge of the program functions that the staff perform, but rather your organization and management of the work effort. The problem begins on page 52.

The Organization

Assume that a new bureau has just been organized within the Department of Regulation Coordination. This Bureau of Public and Internal Communications has as its principal objective the efficient and effective flow of communication and information both within and among divisions and between the Department and its publics.

The Bureau of Public and Internal Communications is comprised of three groups:

The Public Relations Group serves as the liaison between the Department's Commissioner and Executive Office and the public -- primarily the media.

The Freedom of Information Group maintains and processes requests from individuals and groups for information under the Freedom of Information Laws and Regulations.

The Central Communications Group serves as an information and communication center for Department management and the general public.

An organizational chart which displays the bureau's position and reporting relationship within the Department of Regulation Coordination is attached.

You have recently been appointed as head of the Central Communications Group within the Public and Internal Communications Bureau. The principal functions and activities of your group are as follows:

- Make and coordinate presentations on Department issues to the public and other interest groups.

- Respond to letters and telephone inquiries on general issues pertinent to Department operations.

- Serve as liaison between the Department and Legislative staff.

- Produce Departmental publications.

- Design forms for public and internal use.

- Prepare Department annual report and other reports as assigned.

- Assist Public Relations Group staff with publicity issues.

- Review communication flow within the Department and recommend necessary improvements.

- Assist in drafting and disseminating policies and procedures.

Rita Meyers

> Your supervisor, Rita Meyers, is the Director of the bureau. Throughout her long career within the Department she has worked in responsible positions in several divisions. She is known to be very competent and for running a "tight ship." She is both task and results oriented. She is also extraordinarily busy. In fact, much of her time is spent "on the road" conducting hearings at the request of the Commissioner.

The Staff

Frank Williams

> Frank Williams has been an employee with the Department for almost 20 years. He has worked in several divisions in the Department and has a wide breadth of experience with Department programs. He produces work of acceptable quality, particularly in preparing correspondence; however, sometimes not on a timely basis.

Mary Walters

> Mary Walters is an employee with close to 10 years of experience. She is pleasant and easy to deal with and has very strong interpersonal skills. Mary is a very popular speaker and enjoys addressing groups. Her day-to-day work is completed on time; however, since she is not a good writer, her written work frequently requires extensive supervisory review. She volunteered to join this group since she thought it would increase her opportunities to speak to and deal with the public.

General Background Continued

Bill Richards

> Bill Richards is a recent college graduate with a master's degree in Public Administration. He has recently been assigned to your group after spending the first 18 months of his two-year traineeship in one of the line divisions. It is expected he will remain in your group when his traineeship is completed. He produces a substantial volume of work, is always eager and willing to accept assignments, and has repeatedly asked to do "more important" work. A review of the correspondence Bill has prepared shows it to be timely and written with good tone and style, if not always correct. Bill can be abrasive. On several occasions he has offended colleagues in the Department. In the short time he has been assigned to the group he has already had one argument with your secretary, Sally Majors, who also provides secretarial support to the rest of the group.

Sally Majors

> Sally is a Secretary 1 and is regarded as bright, capable, easygoing and eager to work. In addition to working as your secretary, she also provides word processing support to Frank, Mary and Bill.

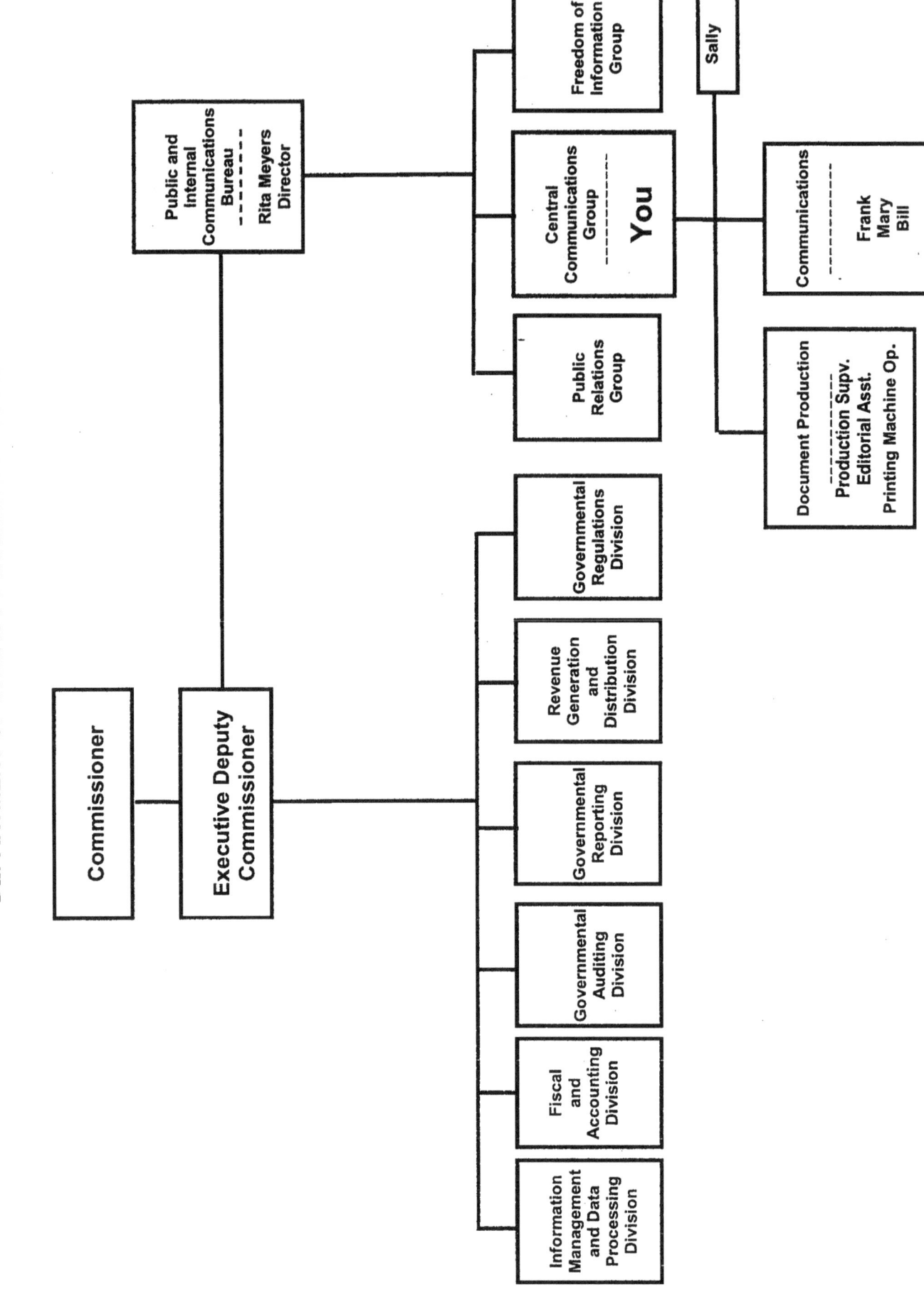

PROBLEM

Before beginning this problem, be sure you have read the Background on pages 48 through 51.

Assume today is Monday, December 16 and you have been head of the Central Communications Group for just under two months. You return from three days away from the office and find the following items pertaining to Bill Richards in your in-basket:

- a memo from Bill to Rita concerning an "Ethical Decision Making" training course

- a memo from Bill to you concerning his workload

- a memo from Sally to you complaining about Bill

**READ THE IN-BASKET MATERIALS
ON PAGES 53 THROUGH 55.**

MEMORANDUM

TO: Rita Meyers

FROM: Bill Richards

SUBJECT: What this Department needs . . .

DATE: December 10

. . . is a new training course on "Ethical Decision Making."

From my experience in working with public inquiries and Department correspondence it strikes me that our decisions are difficult, and the "best" solutions are seldom without costs. Yet we need to make these decisions without undue delay.

In one of my graduate courses, we studied F. Mosher, who emphasized the need for flexibility and value priorities in public decision-making. There is a high ethical content in governmental decisions - often they do not succumb neatly to factual analysis. Rarely are they totally right or totally wrong. And the public character of this Department's decisions adds complicating dimensions to ethical behavior.

Anyway, I have lots of ideas that would be useful for this course. I'd like to present it to interested Department employees in general and bureau staff in particular (they need it!).

I'm available to discuss this further in detail if you want at your convenience.

TO: *You*
December 12
What's with this?
Rita

MEMORANDUM

TO: You

FROM: Bill Richards

SUBJECT: Workload

DATE: December 11

I'm pleased to be assigned to this group, since the work involves critical activities occurring throughout the Department. I enjoy most of the work I have had to date, and am always eager for more.

However, I get the impression that you think some of my work is "incomplete" or has "erroneous" information. Let me point out that I probably produce more than Frank and Mary combined. Maybe if they did more of their share of the work I would feel less rushed.

So far all of my assignments involve gathering information or preparing letters or reports under very tight deadlines. I would like to get some assignments that involve longer range planning or project development as well as get a chance to do some public speaking. Also, there are some divisions I am not familiar with. If I knew more about the work of these divisions, I'm sure my work would be even better.

I would appreciate the opportunity to discuss better ways of scheduling the workload with you as soon as possible. I had a course in workload scheduling if that will be of any help.

MEMORANDUM

TO: You

FROM: Sally

DATE: December 13

Bill Richards has insulted me again and it's just not fair! I'm trying to type everybody's work around here and he keeps insisting that his is "top priority" and should be done first. He told me I'm just too slow!

I don't need this.

I'm going to ask for a transfer if he doesn't stop.

CONTINUE NOW WITH SECTION A

SECTION A

To address the most urgent of these three items you would first deal with: **(Choose ONLY ONE, unless otherwise directed.)**

1. Rita's and Bill's memos concerning the proposed training course

2. Bill's comments about the group's workload

3. Sally's complaint about Bill

SECTION B

You would now: **(Choose ONLY ONE, unless otherwise directed.)**

4. Send a copy of Bill's memo to Rita.

5. Send a copy of Frank's memo to Rita.

6. Send a copy of Mary's memo to Rita.

7. Send a copy of Sally's memo to Rita.

SECTION C

You would now: **(Choose AS MANY as are appropriate.)**

8. Ask him what aspects of his work concern him the most.

9. Ask him in what ways he feels the work isn't distributed equitably.

10. Ask him how he thinks Frank and Mary feel about their assignments.

11. Ask him why he feels he is always so rushed and under so much pressure.

12. Ask him what changes he would make in Frank's and Mary's work to make the workload more equal.

13. Review Frank's and Mary's current assignments with him.

14. Review his current assignments and his overall workload with him.

15. Explain to him that because of Mary's strong interpersonal and communication skills you've had to give her most of the group's speaking assignments and they are very time consuming.

16. Ask him what gave him the impression that you view some of his work as being incomplete and erroneous.

17. Tell him that although he had the most assignments, Frank's and Mary's are more long-range and complex and require a great deal of thought and experience.

18. Acknowledge that he is a hard worker and that you appreciate the work he does.

19. Tell him that some of the elements in the memo he sent to you seemed patronizing and he should try and avoid that tone in the future.

20. Ask for his suggestions on ways in which he could improve his knowledge of other divisions.

21. **After you have chosen AS MANY as are appropriate, have marked your choices on the answer sheet, and have read the responses, EXPOSE 21 ON THE ANSWER SHEET.**

SECTION D

At this point, a reasonable assessment of the situation is that: **(Choose AS MANY as are appropriate.)**

22. Bill's main focus is on his work, not his relationships with others.

23. Bill seems unaware of how his interpersonal relationships can affect his effectiveness.

24. There is a pattern of occasional interpersonal conflicts between Bill and other employees.

25. Overall group morale is poor.

26. Bill feels he's under a lot of pressure.

27. Sally reacted inappropriately to the most recent incident.

28. Noting this episode in Bill's personnel file will improve his behavior.

29. You should pay closer attention to Bill's interpersonal behavior.

30. Sally's workload priorities may be unclear to your staff.

31. Sally needs to make better use of her time.

32. Completing assignments on time is important to Bill.

33. Bill's tendency to give Sally work at the last minute contributes to the tension between them.

34. **After you have chosen AS MANY as are appropriate and have marked your choices on the answer sheet, EXPOSE 34 ON THE ANSWER SHEET.**

SECTION E

In bringing the discussion about the incident with Sally to a close, you would now say: **(Choose AS MANY as are appropriate.)**

35. "Bill, we need to have things going smoothly around here. I feel you owe Sally an apology."

36. "How can we best put this incident behind us and improve your working relationship with Sally?"

37. "If the group is going to be effective, it is important that we maintain good working relationships both within and outside the group. We can't tolerate any more incidents like this."

38. "Bill, you have to realize that trying to resolve these kinds of problems takes a lot of my time and energy. Please try to avoid them in the future."

39. "I know you're trying to do a good job and I value your work; your work would be even better if we could find ways to avoid interpersonal conflicts."

40. "You know, Bill, interpersonal skills are reflected in the performance appraisal process."

41. "I am going to schedule a meeting to discuss approaches to prioritizing the work we give Sally."

42. "Quite frankly, I haven't seen any of the problems with Sally's work that you've mentioned."

43. "Bill, you do the best work in the group and I don't want situations like this to hurt your reputation."

44. **After you have chosen AS MANY as are appropriate, have marked your choices on the answer sheet, and have read the responses, EXPOSE 44 ON THE ANSWER SHEET.**

SECTION F

You would now: **(Choose AS MANY as are appropriate.)**

45. Ask her why she wasn't able to resolve this problem with Bill.

46. Ask her for additional details about the complaint.

47. Ask her how well she and Bill got along before this recent argument.

48. Ask her to file a formal complaint against Bill.

49. Ask her if she also has interpersonal problems with Mary and Frank.

50. Suggest to her that she work with Bill to resolve their differences.

51. Ask her if she gets a lot of pressure to do "top priority" work right away from everyone or primarily from Bill.

52. Ask how she sets priorities for her work.

53. Ask her for ideas on how she could improve her productivity.

54. Apologize to her for Bill's behavior.

55. **After you have chosen AS MANY as are appropriate, have marked your choices on the answer sheet, and have read the responses, EXPOSE 55 ON THE ANSWER SHEET.**

SECTION G

Over the course of the next few months you would: **(Choose AS MANY as are appropriate.)**

56. Give Bill a greater variety of assignments.

57. Make sure that Bill understands that since he's a new employee you don't expect excellence in the work he produces.

58. Assign more of the work involving tight deadlines to Mary and Frank.

59. Note the recent incident with Sally in Bill's personnel file.

60. Periodically check with Sally about her working relationship with Bill.

61. Set up periodic meetings with Rita to discuss Bill's progress.

62. Increase the number of assignments which will help Bill learn more about other divisions.

63. Ask Sally, Mary and Frank to let you know as soon as possible if they have any problems with Bill.

64. Set up regularly scheduled meetings with Bill to discuss the status of his work in progress.

65. Meet with Bill before any new major assignments to discuss approaches to the work and clarify your expectations.

66. Give Bill more feedback as to your rationale for revisions to his work and let him know it's part of the normal supervisory review process.

67. **After you have chosen AS MANY as are appropriate and have marked your choices on the answer sheet, EXPOSE 67 ON THE ANSWER SHEET.**

SECTION H

You would now: **(Choose AS MANY as are appropriate.)**

68. Review Bill's trainee plan and prior evaluations.

69. Ask Frank and Mary if they have had any personal problems working with Bill.

70. Check informally with others in the Department and see how they view Bill.

71. Briefly review Frank's, Mary's and Bill's assignments and overall workload.

72. **After you have chosen AS MANY as are appropriate, have marked your choices on the answer sheet, and have read the responses, EXPOSE 72 ON THE ANSWER SHEET.**

SECTION J

In continuing your discussion, you would say: **(Choose AS MANY as are appropriate.)**

73. "Sally does the work for several people and at any given point in time your work is not necessarily her highest priority."

74. "Your way of dealing with people is starting to become a real problem."

75. "Did Sally give you any reason why she wouldn't do your work?"

76. "In what ways do you think Sally's performance could improve?"

77. "Don't you think your behavior toward Sally was unjustified?"

78. "Even if your concerns are correct, the way you expressed them caused problems with Sally."

79. "If you have any more of these problems with people, I may have to make note of them in your personnel file."

80. "Why did you insult Sally?"

81. "Sally feels that you often give her work at the last minute and want it done right away."

82. "Are you unhappy working here?"

83. "You've been in the Department less than two years and you already have had a number of incidents like this."

84. **After you have chosen AS MANY as are appropriate, have marked your choices on the answer sheet, and have read the responses, EXPOSE 84 ON THE ANSWER SHEET.**

SECTION K

As a follow up to your discussion, you would, over the next few days: **(Choose AS MANY as are appropriate.)**

85. Summarize Sally's complaints for Rita.

86. Meet individually with Frank and Mary to discuss their workload and any concerns they may have with their assignments.

87. Meet with Frank and Mary individually to discuss Bill's complaints about the inequitable distribution of workload.

88. Tell Frank and Mary about Bill's problems with deadlines and shift some of the more urgent work to them.

89. Ask Frank and Mary if they would be willing to accept some changes in workload and assignment.

90. Tell Frank and Mary individually that a review of the work assignments shows that Frank handles most of the long-term assignments; Mary has most of the speaking engagements; and Bill has the majority of the work with short deadlines. Tell them you would like to establish a more varied distribution of work among the staff.

91. Tell Frank and Mary how you see each of them benefiting from more varied assignments.

92. Tell Bill to issue a revised work plan for the entire staff.

93. Meet with Sally and tell her you discussed her complaint with Bill and, without going into specifics, indicate that she shouldn't have any more problems with him.

94. Let Sally know that you talked with Bill and explain that his assignments put him under a lot of pressure. Tell her you're going to make some changes and you expect things to improve.

95. Set up a meeting to discuss approaches to prioritizing Sally's work.

96. **After you have chosen AS MANY as are appropriate and have marked your choices on the answer sheet, EXPOSE 96 ON THE ANSWER SHEET.**

SECTION L

In continuing your discussion, you would now: **(Choose UP TO THREE.)**

97. Ask Bill to describe for you reasons why Sally may have reacted the way she did.

98. Advise Bill that Sally does not waste time.

99. Ask Bill if he can think of anything that he is doing that might cause situations like the one with Sally to occur.

100. Remind Bill that his behavior has offended others before he came to the group, and describe how this could impair his career.

101. Tell Bill he must be reasonable and give Sally more lead time to do his work.

102. Ask Bill if he agrees that conflicts with others can detract from the effectiveness of his work.

103. Ask Bill why he expects Sally to type his work right away.

104. **After you have chosen UP TO THREE, have marked your choices on the answer sheet, and have read the responses, EXPOSE 104 ON THE ANSWER SHEET.**

SECTION M

You would now: **(Choose ONLY ONE, unless otherwise directed.)**

105. Ask him if there are any problems he'd like to discuss.

106. Tell him of Sally's complaint and ask him what happened.

107. Ask him what he likes about working in the group.

108. Praise the overall quality and quantity of his work.

109. Ask him if he is aware of the effect of his interpersonal style on others.

SECTION N

In concluding your discussion, you would now: **(Choose AS MANY as are appropriate.)**

110. Tell him not to worry about deadlines but to focus on the accuracy of his work.

111. Suggest that if he organized his work better there would be less pressure.

112. Tell him you plan to look further into the issue of the mix of assignments among staff and will talk to Frank and Mary.

113. Tell him you will try to assign the work more equitably in the future.

114. Ask him if he would like to be relieved of certain assignments.

115. Tell him that since the workload is balanced, you are not going to change any assignments.

116. Tell him that perhaps the degree of urgency he places on the completion of his assignments may sometimes exceed your actual expectations.

117. Ask him if he would like a short-term rotation to another division so he can learn more about the operations of that division.

118. Tell him that, in general, suggestions and revisions pertaining to his written work are not meant to imply that his work is unsatisfactory.

119. Advise him that his suggestion that the Department needs an "Ethical Decision Making" course may be interpreted that the Department is not making ethical decisions. Suggest it would be better if he did not pursue it any further.

120. Tell him that you noticed he sent his memo on the "Ethical Decision Making" course directly to Rita rather than through you, and in the future, it is important to route these kinds of memos through you so that you are informed and can respond appropriately.

121. Suggest that perhaps you could reduce some of the pressure on him by reassigning some of his current work to Frank or Mary.

122. **After you have chosen AS MANY as are appropriate, have marked your choices on the answer sheet, and have read the responses, EXPOSE 122 ON THE ANSWER SHEET.**

Illustrative Problem Answer Sheet

EXAM DATE	CITY	IDENTIFICATION NO.	EXAM NO(S).	TITLE
ROOM	BUILDING			
XXX-X Illustrative Problem	TIME BEGAN			
	TIME ENDED			

Use ONLY the developer pen to expose the boxes on these answer sheets. You may not change your answers.

A	1	214		26	✓		51	212		76	207		101	247
	2	230		27	✓		52	208		77	246		102	259
	3	251		28	✓		53	279		78	258		103	266
B	4	201		29	✓		54	284		79	265		104	GO TO E
	5	201		30	✓		55	269		80	275	M	105	218
	6	201		31	✓	G	56	✓		81	280		106	227
	7	201		32	✓		57	✓		82	285		107	204
C	8	244		33	✓		58	✓		83	270		108	237
	9	231		34	GO TO L		59	✓		84	GO TO D		109	248
	10	240	E	35	222		60	✓	K	85	✓	N	110	219
	11	252		36	232		61	✓		86	✓		111	228
	12	262		37	242		62	✓		87	✓		112	238
	13	277		38	254		63	✓		88	✓		113	249
	14	282		39	263		64	✓		89	✓		114	260
	15	287		40	211		65	✓		90	✓		115	267
	16	213		41	278		66	✓		91	✓		116	276
	17	272		42	283		67	256		92	✓		117	281
	18	253		43	273	H	68	215		93	✓		118	286
	19	241		44	268		69	224		94	✓		119	203
	20	289	F	45	223		70	234		95	✓		120	288
	21	GO TO N		46	233		71	245		96	GO TO G		121	271
D	22	✓		47	243		72	257	L	97	217		122	GO TO K
	23	✓		48	255	J	73	225		98	226			
	24	✓		49	264		74	216		99	206			
	25	✓		50	274		75	235		100	236			

Illustrative Problem Response Booklet

PLEASE BE AWARE: Not all of the responses are actually a part of the problem you are working on. They may state accurate names and plausible events, but the information they present is misleading. These responses have been included to keep you from being able to piece the problem together by reading only the responses. The best course of action for you to take is to pay close attention ONLY to the responses to which you have been directed.

RESPONSES

201. There are no instructions in this problem that direct you to this section. You may have made an error in following the directions from the box on the answer sheet or from the response; or you may not have completely exposed a direction in the choice box. Go back over your choices, the directions in the responses, and any notes you have made to determine where you should be in the problem. You will not be penalized for exposing this box on your answer sheet.

202. They both say that they believe that their assignments should stay the way they are. **Return to the section you are working in and continue.**

203. He responds, "My professors advocated this for all bureaucracies. It seemed like a good idea to me." **Return to the section you are working in and continue.**

204. He says the work is challenging and interesting. **Make another choice in the same section.**

205. Their work currently includes a variety of assignments, ranging from general letters to several publications, reports, seminars, and presentations. Generally, work has been assigned to staff as follows:

    Frank:
    - Prepare Annual Report
    - Lead project to review and improve Departmental communication flow
    - Develop seminar projects
    - Handle policy coordination with divisions

    Mary:
    - Conduct numerous presentations
    - Coordinate presentations conducted by Department staff for groups outside the agency
    - Prepare governmental innovations publication
    - Coordinate forms review

    Bill:
    - Coordinate responses to Legislative staff inquiries for Department management
    - Research material to respond to Executive Office and Legislative inquiries
    - Draft responses to correspondence for Commissioner and Department management
    - Handle most of group telephone inquiries

    The workload for all three employees is generally equal. They all include both short and long term projects along with some public speaking.

    Return to the section you are working in and continue.

This page contains responses 201 to 205

206. He says, "I hadn't really seen this as an issue before but I guess I do tend to get abrupt and harsh when I'm under a lot of pressure." **Return to the section you are working in and continue.**

207. He responds, "I could show her how to better use her time and schedule her work." **Return to the section you are working in and continue.**

208. She responds, "I generally do your work first unless something else is an emergency. The rest generally depends upon when I get it and how soon it's due." **Return to the section you are working in and continue.**

209. A review of Bill's assignments shows that they are similar to Frank's and Mary's and include short and long term projects along with some public speaking. **Return to the section you are working in and continue.**

210. Rita asks why you didn't tell her sooner. **Return to the section you are working in and continue.**

211. He responds, "I realize that." **Return to the section you are working in and continue.**

212. She says, "No. Everyone is pretty reasonable except Bill. He always seems to want his work done first." **Return to the section you are working in and continue.**

213. He responds, "Sometimes when I've given you work you have asked me to get additional information and expand on various concepts. Also, on a lot of my work you make an awful lot of editorial revisions." **Return to the section you are working in and continue.**

214. As you are considering your approach, Rita calls and says she has heard that Sally is unhappy about Bill. She says that she herself is concerned about the way Bill deals with people and she wants you to deal with this right away. Bill is not in the office today and you leave a note on his desk asking him to come to your office when he comes in tomorrow. **GO TO SECTION H.**

215. Bill's prior supervisor notes that Bill has excellent work skills but occasional interpersonal clashes. The trainee plan indicates he needs a variety of assignments to become familiar with overall Department functions, and also indicates that his assignments should be broadened to include more public speaking and project development activities. **Return to the section you are working in and continue.**

This page contains responses 206 to 215

216. He responds, "If people want to be treated like professionals they should act that way." **Return to the section you are working in and continue.**

217. He says, "I guess I leaned on her pretty hard. I suppose she has pressures on her too." **Return to the section you are working in and continue.**

218. He says, "At some point I'd like to talk about my workload." **Make another choice in the same section.**

219. He responds, "I agree that my work should be accurate, but I think it is important to get it done quickly." **Return to the section you are working in and continue.**

220. He says, "I like tight deadlines. It's a challenge to get work done quickly." **Return to the section you are working in and continue.**

221. Frank and Mary say that they are under a lot more pressure than Bill. **Return to the section you are working in and continue.**

222. He says, "OK. I'll apologize if you say so." **Return to the section you are working in and continue.**

223. She says, "Bill doesn't see this as a problem and he doesn't listen to me." **Return to the section you are working in and continue.**

224. They say, "He is sometimes a little abrasive but we can deal with him." **Return to the section you are working in and continue.**

225. He responds, "I know that, but if I'm to complete my work on time, it's critical that Sally types it as soon as possible." **Return to the section you are working in and continue.**

226. He says, "It appears that way to me." **Return to the section you are working in and continue.**

227. He says, "I didn't mean to offend her. I had something I needed typed right away and she wouldn't do it." **GO TO SECTION J.**

228. He responds, "I don't think it is as much a question of how I organize my work as it is of too much work and too many deadlines." **Return to the section you are working in and continue.**

This page contains responses 216 to 228

229. He says, "It looks like people are jealous of me." **Return to the section you are working in and continue.**

230. As you are considering your approach, Rita calls and says she has heard that Sally is unhappy about Bill. She says that she herself is concerned about the way Bill deals with people and she wants you to deal with this right away. Bill is not in the office today and you leave a note on his desk asking him to come to your office when he comes in tomorrow. **GO TO SECTION H.**

231. He says, "I do most of the work that requires a quick turnaround and Frank and Mary don't seem to be as busy as I am; they seem to be under less urgent time constraints." **Return to the section you are working in and continue.**

232. He replies, "Perhaps it will help if I apologize to her." **Return to the section you are working in and continue.**

233. She states, "Bill treats me in a condescending manner, believes all his work is urgent and has a higher priority than anyone else's. He also said I'd get more done if I worked harder." **Return to the section you are working in and continue.**

234. They say they have heard his work is good but he seems abrasive. **Return to the section you are working in and continue.**

235. He says, "She said, 'I have something of Frank's I have to finish up first.' " **Return to the section you are working in and continue.**

236. He becomes defensive and says, "I thought my career would be determined by the quality and quantity of work that I do." **Return to the section you are working in and continue.**

237. He thanks you and says he tries to work hard. **Make another choice in the same section.**

238. He says, "Good idea. I would like to see a better mix in the variety of assignments among the staff so I don't have all the tight deadline work." **Return to the section you are working in and continue.**

239. He says, "I don't think I have done anything wrong." **Return to the section you are working in and continue.**

240. He replies, "I'm sure they're content; their assignments are a 'piece of cake.' " **Return to the section you are working in and continue.**

This page contains responses 229 to 240

241. He says, "I'm sorry if it came across that way. I'm just trying to share the knowledge I've picked up in my course work." **Return to the section you are working in and continue.**

242. He responds, "You're right, but some conflicts are unavoidable if we're going to get our work done properly." **Return to the section you are working in and continue.**

243. She says, "We've only had one other argument but he's been hard to work with ever since he came into the group." **Return to the section you are working in and continue.**

244. He responds, "I always feel rushed because I'm doing so much and it seems that Frank and Mary are doing a lot less than I am." **Return to the section you are working in and continue.**

245. Their work currently includes a variety of assignments, ranging from general letters to several publications, reports, seminars, and presentations. Generally, work has been assigned to staff as follows:

    Frank:
    - Prepare Annual Report
    - Lead project to review and improve Departmental communication flow
    - Develop seminar projects
    - Handle policy coordination with divisions

    Mary:
    - Conduct numerous presentations
    - Coordinate presentations conducted by Department staff for groups outside the agency
    - Prepare governmental innovations publication
    - Coordinate forms review

    Bill:
    - Coordinate responses to Legislative staff inquiries for Department management
    - Research material to respond to Executive Office and Legislative inquiries
    - Draft responses to correspondence for Commissioner and Department management
    - Handle most of group telephone inquiries

    The workload for all three employees is generally equal. However, most of Bill's assignments have short deadlines while Frank and Mary are engaged in planning oriented activities with long range schedules.

    Return to the section you are working in and continue.

This page contains responses 241 to 245

246. He responds, "No. I had to get my work done and she wouldn't do it." **Return to the section you are working in and continue.**

247. He says, "I can try but I'm already giving her the work as soon as I can." **Return to the section you are working in and continue.**

248. He says he is not aware of any problems. **Make another choice in the same section.**

249. He says, "Thanks. What I'd like is a better mix in the variety of assignments." **Return to the section you are working in and continue.**

250. Sally says that she doesn't see how your suggestion will help. **Return to the section you are working in and continue.**

251. As you are considering your approach, Rita calls and says she has heard that Sally is unhappy about Bill. She says that she herself is concerned about the way Bill deals with people and she wants you to deal with this right away. Bill is not in the office today and you leave a note on his desk asking him to come to your office when he comes in tomorrow. **GO TO SECTION H.**

252. He responds, "A lot of the assignments I get -- like draft letters for the Commissioner -- have tight deadlines. When you give me something like that with a date due to you, I want to get it to you before that date so you have plenty of time for review." **Return to the section you are working in and continue.**

253. He says, "I appreciate that word of recognition but it doesn't change the inequities in the workload." **Return to the section you are working in and continue.**

254. He says, "I will if I can." **Return to the section you are working in and continue.**

255. She indicates she has already sent you a memo and would prefer not to go any further than that. **Return to the section you are working in and continue.**

256. **THIS IS THE END OF THIS PROBLEM.** You should proceed to the Illustrative Problem Scoring Instructions on the page following response 289.

257. A short time later, Sally comes into your office and asks if she can talk to you about the problem she is having with Bill. **GO TO SECTION F.**

This page contains responses 246 to 257

258. He responds, "Maybe I was a little harsh, but she was giving me a hard time about typing my work right away." **Return to the section you are working in and continue.**

259. He says, "I hadn't really thought of it that way before, but I guess you're right." **Return to the section you are working in and continue.**

260. He says, "I would like to do less of the tight deadline work." **Return to the section you are working in and continue.**

261. Bill tells you that he will ask for a transfer if you do that. **Return to the section you are working in and continue.**

262. He says, "Let me give that some thought." **Return to the section you are working in and continue.**

263. He responds, "Thanks. I'm glad you think I do good work and I'm always anxious to improve." **Return to the section you are working in and continue.**

264. She says, "No. We get along fine." **Return to the section you are working in and continue.**

265. He responds, "It's not my fault. If there have been any conflicts it is because I'm trying to get my work done." **Return to the section you are working in and continue.**

266. He says, "It's important to me to get my work in to you on time and a lot of my work has short deadlines." **Return to the section you are working in and continue.**

267. He says, "You've got the final say, but it still leaves me with a lot of pressure." **Return to the section you are working in and continue.**

268. At this point in your discussion with Bill, you decide to address the concerns he has raised about his workload. **GO TO SECTION C.**

269. Your meeting with Sally concludes. It is now tomorrow morning and Bill is in your office. **GO TO SECTION M.**

270. He responds, "That's the nature of bureaucracy. To get work done there's always going to be some conflict." **Return to the section you are working in and continue.**

This page contains responses 258 to 270

271. He responds, "Maybe, but I like to finish what I start." **Return to the section you are working in and continue.**

272. He responds, "I think I could handle that kind of work." **Return to the section you are working in and continue.**

273. He says, "I appreciate your support and concern." **Return to the section you are working in and continue.**

274. She says, "I've tried, but I need your help." **Return to the section you are working in and continue.**

275. He responds, "I didn't mean to insult her. I just wanted her to work on my assignments right away." **Return to the section you are working in and continue.**

276. He responds, "You might be right. I know you have real high standards and I want to be sure I measure up to them." **Return to the section you are working in and continue.**

277. Bill reiterates the points he made in his December 11 memo. **Return to the section you are working in and continue.**

278. Bill responds, "That seems like a good idea." **Return to the section you are working in and continue.**

279. She says, "I think my productivity is good. I work hard and get a lot done." **Return to the section you are working in and continue.**

280. He responds, "I have so much work to do and so much pressure on me, that I often can't get it to Sally until the last minute." **Return to the section you are working in and continue.**

281. He responds, "I'd like to be here a little longer." **Return to the section you are working in and continue.**

This page contains responses 271 to 281

282. A review of Bill's assignments shows that he handles almost all of the group's telephone inquiries -- many of which require additional background research and work. He also is currently drafting responses to numerous letters for the Commissioner's signature and doing research for Department management in response to inquiries from the Legislative staff. His share of the workload is comparable to Frank's and Mary's but is different in that it requires much tighter turnaround time. Bill consistently completes his work on tight deadline assignments a few to several days before the deadline date that you set for him. He has no speaking/presentation work scheduled for the immediate future. **Return to the section you are working in and continue.**

283. He responds, "I don't understand that because I have problems getting my work done." **Return to the section you are working in and continue.**

284. She says, "Thanks, but that doesn't help." **Return to the section you are working in and continue.**

285. He responds, "I like the work." **Return to the section you are working in and continue.**

286. He replies, "I don't mind when you change a few words here and there, but when it goes beyond that I feel you think the work isn't any good." **Return to the section you are working in and continue.**

287. He replies, "I'd like more of that kind of assignment myself." **Return to the section you are working in and continue.**

288. He responds, "OK, I have no problem with that." **Return to the section you are working in and continue.**

289. He says, "It's in my trainee plan that I need this experience; I'd like the opportunity to increase my understanding of the work that other divisions do." **Return to the section you are working in and continue.**

This page contains responses 282 to 289

Illustrative Problem Scoring Instructions

The scoring key on the following two pages lists all the choices and their values for the illustrative simulation problem. Use this list to help compute your problem score. In an actual computational review, you would have a photocopy of your answer sheet which would indicate which choices you exposed. For this illustrative problem, consider any choice that you marked on the answer sheet on page 68 to be an "exposed" choice.

- Locate the choices you exposed on your answer sheet.

- Follow the directions that are in each of the sections of the scoring key. They will tell you which choices to mark on the scoring key. Mark only the choices you are directed to mark. Special instructions appear in Sections A, L and M to help you to mark your choices correctly. BE ALERT to those places where these special instructions appear.

- Sum the values of all your marked choices. Be sure to **subtract** negatively valued choices from the positive total, rather than adding them to it.

Depending on the choices you made in this problem, you could have a score as low as –51 or as high as +51. When this problem was actually used, the average score was between 28 and 29. If this problem were part of the Promotion Test Battery for Supervisors and Specialists, the scores would be placed on a 25 point scale. If it were part of the Promotion Test Battery for Mid- and High-Level Managers and Administrators, the scores would be placed on a 40 point scale.

Scoring Key for the Illustrative Problem

Section	Choice	Value
A	Mark **Only One** (the lowest value exposed choice) Among:	
	1.	-2
	2.	-1
	3.	+2

Section	Choice	Value
B	All Choices Are Valued At 0.	

Section	Choice	Value
C	Mark **All** Exposed Choices.	
	8.	+1
	9.	+1
	10.	-1
	11.	+1
	12.	-1
	13.	-1
	14.	+1
	15.	-1
	16.	+1
	17.	-1
	18.	+1
	19.	-1
	20.	+1
	21.	0

Section	Choice	Value
D	Mark **All** Exposed Choices.	
	22.	+1
	23.	+1
	24.	+1
	25.	-1
	26.	+1
	27.	-1
	28.	-1
	29.	+1
	30.	+1
	31.	-1
	32.	+1
	33.	+1
	34.	0

Section	Choice	Value
E	Mark **All** Exposed Choices.	
	35.	-1
	36.	+1
	37.	-1
	38.	-1
	39.	+1
	40.	-1
	41.	+1
	42.	-1
	43.	-1
	44.	0

Section	Choice	Value
F	Mark **All** Exposed Choices.	
	45.	-1
	46.	+1
	47.	+1
	48.	-1
	49.	-1
	50.	-1
	51.	+1
	52.	+1
	53.	-1
	54.	-1
	55.	0

Section	Choice	Value
G	Mark **All** Exposed Choices.	
	56.	+1
	57.	-1
	58.	+1
	59.	-1
	60.	+1
	61.	-1
	62.	+1
	63.	-1
	64.	+1
	65.	+1
	66.	+1
	67.	0

Section	Choice	Value
H	Mark **All** Exposed Choices.	
	68.	+1
	69.	0
	70.	-1
	71.	+1
	72.	0

Section	Choice	Value
J	Mark **All** Exposed Choices.	
	73.	+1
	74.	-1
	75.	+1
	76.	-1
	77.	-1
	78.	+1
	79.	-1
	80.	-1
	81.	+1
	82.	-1
	83.	-1
	84.	0

Section	Choice	Value
K	Mark **All** Exposed Choices.	
	85.	-1
	86.	+1
	87.	-1
	88.	-1
	89.	0
	90.	+1
	91.	+1
	92.	-1
	93.	-1
	94.	+1
	95.	+1
	96.	0

Scoring Key for the Illustrative Problem (cont.)

Section	Choice	Value
L	Mark **Up To Four** (the lowest value exposed choices) Among:	
	97.	+1
	98.	-1
	99.	+1
	100.	-1
	101.	0
	102.	+1
	103.	0
	Mark **All** Exposed Choices Among:	
	104.	0

Section	Choice	Value
M	Mark **All** Exposed Choices Among:	
	105.	-1
	107.	-1
	108.	0
	109.	-1
	Mark **Only One** (the lowest value exposed choice) Among:	
	106.	+2

Section	Choice	Value
N	Mark **All** Exposed Choices.	
	110.	-1
	111.	-1
	112.	+1
	113.	-1
	114.	-1
	115.	-1
	116.	+1
	117.	0
	118.	+1
	119.	-1
	120.	+1
	121.	-1
	122.	0

Add the values of all your marked choices and write the sum in the box. This is your **RAW SCORE** for the Illustrative Problem.

EXAMINATION SECTION

TEST 1

DIRECTIONS: Each question or incomplete statement is followed by several suggested answers or completions. Select the one that BEST answers the question or completes the statement. *PRINT THE LETTER OF THE CORRECT ANSWER IN THE SPACE AT THE RIGHT.*

1. The one of the following which has had GREATEST effect upon size of the budget of large cities in the last twenty years is
   A. change in the organization of the city resulting from new charters
   B. increase in services rendered by the city
   C. development of independent authorities
   D. increase in the city's ability to borrow money
   E. increase in the size of the city

   1.____

2. The one of the following services for which cities receive the LEAST amount of direct financial assistance from state governments is
   A. education   B. welfare   C. housing
   D. roads   E. museums

   2.____

3. Major problems which face most large cities, including New York, arise from the vertical sandwiching of governments in a single area and from the many independent governments that crowd the boundaries of the central city.
   Of the following methods of solving these problems, the one which has been MOST successful in the past has been to
   A. decentralize the administration of the central city
   B. create various supra-municipal authorities which tend to integrate the activities of the metropolitan area
   C. bring the metropolitan population under a single local government
   D. set up intermunicipal coordinating agencies to solve area administrative and economic problems
   E. allow each government element in the metropolitan area to work out its own solution

   3.____

4. By means of the *debt limit*, the states regulate many facets of the debt of the cities.
   The one of the following factors which is NOT regulated in this manner is the
   A. purpose for which the debt is incurred
   B. amount of debt which may be incurred
   C. terms of the notes or bonds issued by the city
   D. forms of debts which may be incurred
   E. source from which the money may be borrowed

   4.____

5. The one of the following which is a characteristic of NEITHER the state nor the federal governments, but which is a characteristic of the government of cities is that the latter
   A. is not sovereign but an agent
   B. does not have the power to raise taxes
   C. cannot enter into contracts
   D. may not make treaties with foreign countries
   E. may not coin money

Questions 6-8.

DIRECTIONS: Questions 6 through 8 are to be answered on the basis of the following paragraph.

The regressive uses of discipline is ubiquitous. Administrative architects who seek the optimum balance between structure and morale must accordingly look toward the identification and isolation of disciplinary elements. The whole range of disciplinary sanctions, from the reprimand to the dismissal presents opportunities for reciprocity and accommodation of institutional interests. When rightly seized upon, these opportunities may provide the moment and the means for fruitful exercise of leadership and collaboration.

6. The one of the following ways of reworking the ideas presented in this paragraph in order to be BEST suited for presentation in an in-service training course in supervision is:
   A. When one of your men does something wrong, talk it over with him. Tell him what he should have done. This is a chance for you to show the man that you are on his side and that you would welcome him on your side.
   B. It is not necessary to reprimand or to dismiss an employee because he needs disciplining. The alert foreman will lead and collaborate with his subordinates making discipline unnecessary.
   C. A good way to lead the men you supervise is to take those opportunities which present themselves to use the whole range of disciplinary sanctions from reprimand to dismissal as a means for enforcing collaboration.
   D. Chances to punish a man in your squad should be welcomed as opportunities to show that you are a "*good guy*" who does not bear a grudge.
   E. Before you talk to a man or have him report to the office for something he has done wrong, attempt to lead him and get him to work with you. Tell him that his actions were wrong, that you expect him not to repeat the same wrong act, and that you will take a firmer stand if the act is repeated.

7. Of the following, the PRINCIPAL point made in the paragraph is that
   A. discipline is frequently used improperly
   B. it is possible to isolate the factors entering into a disciplinary situation
   C. identification of the disciplinary elements is desirable

D. disciplinary situations may be used to the advantage of the organization
E. obtaining the best relationship between organizational form and spirit, depend upon the ability to label disciplinary elements

8. The MOST novel idea presented in the paragraph is that 8.____
   A. discipline is rarely necessary
   B. discipline may be a joint action of man and supervisor
   C. there are disciplinary elements which may be identified
   D. a range of disciplinary sanctions exist
   E. it is desirable to seek for balance between structure and morale

9. When, in the process of developing a classification plan, it has been decided that certain positions all have distinguishing characteristics sufficiently similar to justify treating them alike in the process of selecting appointees and establishing pay rates or scales, then the kind of employment represented by such positions will be called a "class." 9.____
   According to this paragraph, a group of positions is called a class if they
   A. have distinguishing characteristics
   B. represent a kind of employment
   C. can be treated in the same manner for some functions
   D. all have the same pay rates
   E. are treated in the same manner in the development of a classification plan

Questions 10-12.

DIRECTIONS: Questions 10 through 12 are to be answered on the basis of the following paragraph.

The fundamental characteristic of the type of remote control which management needs to bridge the gap between itself and actual operations is the more effective use of records and reports—more specifically, the gathering and interpretation of the facts contained in records and reports. Facts, for management purposes, are those data (narrative and quantitative) which express in simple terms the current standing of the agency's program, work and resources in relation to the plans and policies formulated by management. They are those facts or measures (1) which permit management to compare current status with past performance and with its forecasts for the immediate future, and (2) which provide management with a reliable basis for long-range forecasting.

10. According to the above statement, a characteristic of a type of management control 10.____
    A. is the kind of facts contained in records and reports
    B. is narrative and quantitative data
    C. is its remoteness from actual operations
    D. is the use of records
    E. which expresses in simple terms the current standing of the agency's program, provides management with a reliable basis for long-range forecasting

11. For management purposes, facts are, according to the paragraph, 11.____
    A. forecasts which can be compared to current status
    B. data which can be used for certain control purposes
    C. a fundamental characteristic of a type of remote control
    D. the data contained in records and reports
    E. data (narrative and quantitative) which describe the plans and policies formulated by management

12. An inference which can be drawn from this statement is that 12.____
    A. management which has a reliable basis for long-range forecasting has at its disposal a type of remote control which is needed to bridge the gap between itself and actual operations
    B. data which do not express in simple terms the current standing of the agency's program, work and resources in relationship to the plans and policies formulated by management, may still be facts for management purposes
    C. data which express relationships among the agency's program, work, and resources are management facts
    D. the gap between management and actual operations can only be bridged by characteristics which are fundamentally a type of remote control
    E. management compares current status with past performance in order to obtain a reliable basis for long-range forecasting

Questions 13-14.

DIRECTIONS: Questions 13 and 14 are to be answered on the basis of the following paragraph.

People must be selected to do the tasks involved and must be placed on a payroll in jobs fairly priced. Each of these people must be assigned those tasks which he can perform best: the work of each must be appraised, and good and poor work singled out appropriately. Skill in performing assigned tasks must be developed, and the total work situation must be conducive to sustained high performance. Finally, employees must be separated from the work force either voluntarily or involuntarily because of inefficient or unsatisfactory performance or because of curtailment of organizational activities.

13. A personnel function which is NOT included in the above description is 13.____
    A. classification   B. training   C. placement
    D. severance   E. service rating

14. The underlying implied purpose of the policy enunciated in the above paragraph is 14.____
    A. to plan for the curtailment of the organizational program when it becomes necessary
    B. to single out appropriate skill in performing assigned tasks
    C. to develop and maintain a high level of performance by employees

D. that training employees in relation to the total work situation is essential if good and poor work are to be singled out
E. that equal money for equal work results in a total work situation which insures proper appraisal

15. Changes in program must be quickly and effectively translated into organizational adjustments if the administrative machinery is to be fully adapted to current operating needs. Continuous administrative planning is indispensable to the successful and expeditious accomplishment of such organization changes. According to this statement,
    A. the absence of continuous administrative planning must result in out-moded administrative machinery
    B. continuous administrative planning is necessary for changes in program
    C. if changes in program are quickly and effectively translated into organizational adjustments, the administrative machinery is fully adapted to current operating needs
    D. continuous administrative planning results in successful and expeditious accomplishment of organization changes
    E. if administrative machinery is not fully adapted to current operating needs, then continuous administrative planning is absent

15.____

16. The first-line supervisor executes policy as elsewhere formulated. He does not make policy. He is the element of the administrative structure closest to the employee group.
    From this point of view, it follows that a MAJOR function of the first-line supervisor is to
    A. suggest desirable changes in procedure to top management
    B. prepare time schedules showing when his unit will complete a piece of work so that it will dovetail with the requirements of other units
    C. humanize policy so as to respect employee needs and interests
    D. report danger points to top management in order to forestall possible bottlenecks
    E. discipline employees who continuously break departmental rules

16.____

17. During a supervisory staff meeting, the department head said to the first-line supervisors, "*The most important job you have is to get across to the employees in your units the desirability of achieving our department's aims and the importance of the jobs they are performing toward reaching our goals.*"
    In general, adoption of this point of view would tend to result in an organization
    A. in which supervisors would be faced by many disciplinary problems caused by employee reaction to the program
    B. in which less supervision is required of the work of the average employee
    C. having more clearly defined avenues of communication
    D. lacking definition; supervisors would tend to forget their primary mission of getting the assigned work completed as efficiently as possible
    E. in which most employees would be capable of taking over a supervisory position when necessary

17.____

18. A supervisor, in assigning a man to a job, generally followed the policy of fitting the man to the job.
    This procedure is
    A. *undesirable*; the job should be fitted to the man
    B. *desirable*; primary emphasis should be on the work to be accomplished
    C. *undesirable*; the policy does not consider human values
    D. *desirable*; setting up a definite policy and following it permits careful analysis
    E. *undesirable*; it is not always possible to fit the available man to the job

18.____

19. Assume that one of the units under your jurisdiction has 40 typists. Their skill range from 15 to 80 words a minute.
    The MOST feasible of the following methods to increase the typing output of this unit is to
    A. study the various typing jobs to determine the skill requirements for each type of work and assign to each typist tasks commensurate with her skill
    B. assign the slow typists to clerical work and hire new typists
    C. assign such tasks as typing straight copy to the slower typists
    D. reduce the skill requirements necessary to produce a satisfactory quantity of work
    E. simplify procedures and keep records, memoranda, and letters short and concise

19.____

20. In a division of a department, private secretaries were assigned to members of the technical staff since each required a secretary who was familiar with his particular field and who could handle various routine matters without referring to anyone. Other members of the staff depended for their dictation and typing work upon a small pool consisting of two stenographers and two typists. Because of turnover and the difficulty of recruiting new stenographers and typists, the pool had to be discontinued.
    Of the following, the MOST satisfactory way to provide stenographic and typing service for the division is to
    A. organize the private secretaries into a decentralized pool under the direction of a supervisor to whom nontechnical staff members would send requests for stenographic and typing assistance
    B. organize the private secretaries into a central pool under the direction of a supervisor to whom all staff members would send requests for stenographic and typing assistance
    C. train clerks as typists and typists as stenographers
    D. relieve stenographers and typists of jobs that can be done by messengers or clerks
    E. conserve time by using such devices as indicating minor corrections on a final draft in such a way that they can be erased and by using duplicating machines to eliminate typing many copies

20.____

21. Even under perfect organizational conditions, the relationships between the line units and the units charged with budget planning and personnel management may be precarious at times.
 The one of the following which is a MAJOR reason for this is that
 A. service units assist the head of the agency in formulating and executing policies
 B. line units frequently find lines of communication to the agency head blocked by service units
 C. there is a natural antagonism between planners and doers
 D. service units tend to become line in attitude and emphasis, and to conflict with operating units
 E. service units tend to function apart from the operating units

22. The one of the following which is the CHIEF reason for training supervisors is that
 A. untrained supervisors find it difficult to train their subordinates
 B. most persons do not start as supervisors and consequently are in need of supervisory training
 C. training permits a higher degree of decentralization of the decision-making process
 D. training permits a higher degree of centralization of the decision-making process
 E. coordinated actions on the part of many persons pre-supposes familiarity with the procedures to be employed

23. The problem of determining the type of organization which should exist is inextricably interwoven with the problem of recruitment.
 In general, this statement is
 A. *correct*; since organizations are man-made, they can be changed
 B. *incorrect*; the organizational form which is most desirable is independent of the persons involved
 C. *correct*; the problem of organization cannot be considered apart from employee qualifications
 D. *incorrect*; organizational problems can be separated into many parts and recruitment is important in only few of these
 E. *correct*; a good recruitment program will reduce the problems of organization

24. The conference as an administrative tool is MOST valuable for solving problems which
 A. are simple and within a familiar frame of reference
 B. are of long standing
 C. are novel and complex
 D. are not solvable
 E. require immediate solution

25. Of the following, a recognized procedure for avoiding conflicts in the delegation of authority is to 25.____
    A. delegate authority so as to preserve control by top management
    B. provide for a workable span of control
    C. preview all assignments periodically
    D. assign all related work to the same control
    E. use the linear method of assignment

KEY (CORRECT ANSWERS)

1.	B	11.	B
2.	E	12.	A
3.	C	13.	A
4.	E	14.	C
5.	A	15.	A
6.	A	16.	C
7.	D	17.	B
8.	B	18.	B
9.	C	19.	A
10.	D	20.	A

21.	D
22.	C
23.	C
24.	C
25.	D

TEST 2

DIRECTIONS: Each question or incomplete statement is followed by several suggested answers or completions. Select the one that BEST answers the question or completes the statement. *PRINT THE LETTER OF THE CORRECT ANSWER IN THE SPACE AT THE RIGHT.*

1. A danger which exists in any organization as complex as that required for administration of a large city is that each department comes to believe that it exists for its own sake.
   The one of the following which has been attempted in some organizations as a cure for this condition is to
   A. build up the departmental esprit de corps
   B. expand the functions and jurisdictions of the various departments so that better integration is possible
   C. develop a body of specialists in the various subject matter fields which cut across departmental lines
   D. delegate authority to the lowest possible echelon
   E. systematically transfer administrative personnel from one department to another

   1.____

2. At best, the organization chart is ordinarily and necessarily an idealized picture of the intent of top management, a reflection of hopes and aims rather than a photograph of the operating facts within an organization.
   The one of the following which is the BASIC reason for this is that the organization chart
   A. does not show the flow of work within the organization
   B. speaks in terms of positions rather than of live employees
   C. frequently contains unresolved internal ambiguities
   D. is a record of past organization or of proposed future organization and never a photograph of the living organization
   E. does not label the jurisdiction assigned to each component unit

   2.____

3. The drag of inadequacy is always downward. The need in administration is always for the reverse; for a department head to project his thinking to the city level, for the unit chief to try to see the problems of the department.
   The inability of a city administration to recruit administrators who can satisfy this need usually results in departments characterized by
   A. disorganization   B. poor supervision
   C. circumscribed viewpoints   D. poor public relations
   E. a lack of programs

   3.____

4. When, as a result of a shift in public sentiment, the elective officers of a city are changed, is it desirable for career administrators to shift ground without performing any illegal or dishonest act in order to conform to the policies of the new elective officers?
   A. *No;* the opinions and beliefs of the career officials are the result of long experience in administration and are more reliable than those of politicians.

   4.____

B. *Yes*; only in this way can citizens, political officials, and career administrators alike have confidence in the performance of their respective functions.
C. *No*; a top career official who is so spineless as to change his views or procedures as a result of public opinion is of little value to the public service.
D. *Yes*; legal or illegal, it is necessary that a city employee carry out the orders of his superior officers
E. *No*; shifting ground with every change in administration will preclude the use of a constant overall policy.

5. Participation in developing plans which will affect levels in the organization in addition to his own, will contribute to an individual's understanding of the entire system. When possible, this should be encouraged.
This policy is, in general,
   A. *desirable*; the maintenance of any organization depends upon individual understanding
   B. *undesirable*; employees should participate only in those activities which affect their own level, otherwise conflicts in authority may arise
   C. *desirable*; an employee's will to contribute to the maintenance of an organization depends to a great extent on the level which he occupies
   D. *undesirable*; employees can be trained more efficiently and economically in an organized training program than by participating in plan development
   E. *desirable*; it will enable the employee to make intelligent suggestions for adjustment of the plan in the future

5.____

6. Constant study should be made of the information contained in reports to isolate those elements of experience which are static, those which are variable and repetitive, and those which are variable and due to chance.
Knowledge of those elements of experience in his organization which are static or constant will enable the operating official to
   A. fix responsibility for their supervision at a lower level
   B. revise the procedure in order to make the elements variable
   C. arrange for follow-up and periodic adjustment
   D. bring related data together
   E. provide a frame of reference within which detailed standards for measuremeant can be installed

6.____

7. A chief staff officer, serving as one of the immediate advisors to the department head, has demonstrated a special capacity for achieving internal agreements and for sound judgment. As a result he has been used more and more as a source of counsel and assistance by the department head. Other staff officers and line officials as well have discovered that it is wise for them to check with this colleague in advance on all problematical matters handed up to the department head.
Developments such as this are
   A. *undesirable*; they disrupt the normal lines for flow of work in an organization

7.____

B. *desirable*; they allow an organization to make the most of its strength wherever such strength resides
C. *undesirable*; they tend to undermine the authority of the department head and put it in the hands of a staff officer who does not have the responsibility
D. *desirable*; they tend to resolve internal ambiguities in organization
E. *undesirable*; they make for bad morale by causing *cut throat* competition

8. A common difference among executives is that some are not content unless they are out in front of everything that concerns their organization, while others prefer to run things by pulling strings, by putting others out in front and by stepping into the breach only when necessary.
Generally speaking, an advantage this latter method of operation has over the former is that it
    A. results in a higher level of morale over a sustained period of time
    B. gets results by exhortation and direct stimulus
    C. makes it necessary to calculate integrated moves
    D. makes the personality of the executive felt further down the line
    E. results in the executive getting the reputation for being a good fellow

8.____

9. Administrators frequently have to get facts by interviewing people. Although the interview is a legitimate fact-gathering technique, it has definite limitations which should not be overlooked.
The one of the following which is an important limitation is that
    A. people who are interviewed frequently answer questions with guesses rather than admit their ignorance
    B. it is a poor way to discover the general attitude and thinking of supervisors interviewed
    C. people sometimes hesitate to give information during an interview which they will submit in written form
    D. it is a poor way to discover how well employees understand departmental policies
    E. the material obtained from the interview can usually be obtained at lower cost from existing records

9.____

10. It is desirable and advantageous to leave a maximum measure of planning responsibility to operating agencies or units, rather than to remove the responsibility to a central planning staff agency.
Adoption of the former policy (decentralized planning) would lead to
    A. *less effective* planning; operating personnel do not have the time to make long-term plans
    B. *more effective* planning; operating units are usually better equipped technically than any staff agency and consequently are in a better position to set up valid plans
    C. *less effective* planning; a central planning agency has a more objective point of view than any operating agency can achieve
    D. *more effective* planning; plans are conceived in terms of the existing situation and their execution is carried out with the will to succeed

10.____

E. *less effective* planning; there is little or no opportunity to check deviation from plans in the proposed set-up

Questions 11-15.

DIRECTIONS: The following sections appeared in a report on the work production of two bureaus of a department. Questions 10 through 12 are to be answered on the basis of the following information. Throughout the report, assume that each month has 4 weeks.

Each of the two bureaus maintains a chronological file. In Bureau A, every 9 months on the average, this material fills a standard legal size file cabinet sufficient for 12,000 work units. In Bureau B, the same type of cabinet is filled in 18 months. Each bureau maintains three complete years of information plus a current file. When the current file cabinet is filled, the cabinet containing the oldest material is emptied, the contents disposed of and the cabinet used for current material. The similarity of these operations makes it possible to consolidate these files with little effort.

Study of the practice of using typists as filing clerks for periods when there is no typing work showed (1) Bureau A has for the past 6 months completed a total of 1,500 filing work units a week using on the average 200 man-hours of trained file clerk time and 20 man-hours of typist time, (2) Bureau B has in the same period completed a total of 2,000 filing work units a week using on the average 125 man-hours of trained file clerk time and 60 hours of typist time. This includes all work in chronological files. Assuming that all clerks work at the same speed and that all typists work at the same speed, this indicates that work other than filing should be found for typists or that they should be given some training in the filing procedures used. It should be noted that Bureau A has not been producing the 1,600 units of technical (not filing) work per 30 day period required by Schedule K, but is at present 200 units behind. The Bureau should be allowed 3 working days to get on schedule.

11. What percentage (approximate) of the total number of filing work units completed in both units consists of the work involved in the maintenance of the chronological files?
    A. 5%   B. 10%   C. 15%   D. 20%   E. 25%

12. If the two chronological files are consolidated, the number of months which should be allowed for filling a cabinet is
    A. 2   B. 4   C. 6   D. 8   E. 14

13. The MAXIMUM number of file cabinets which can be released for other uses as a result of the consolidation recommended is
    A. 0
    B. 1
    C. 2
    D. 3
    E. not determinable on the basis of the data given

14. If all the filing work for both units is consolidated without any diminution in the amount to be done and all filing work is done by trained file clerks, the number of clerks required (35-hour work week) is
 A. 4 B. 5 C. 6 D. 7 E. 8

14.____

15. In order to comply with the recommendation with respect to Schedule K, the present work production of Bureau A must be increased by
   A. 50%
   B. 100%
   C. 150%
   D. 200%
   E. an amount which is not determinable on the basis of the data given

15.____

16. A certain training program during World War II resulted in training of thousands of supervisors in industry. The methods of this program were later successfully applied in various governmental agencies. The program was based upon the assumption that there is an irreducible minimum of three supervisory skills. The one of these skills among the following is
   A. to know how to perform the job at hand well
   B. to be able to deal personally with workers, especially face-to-face
   C. to be able to imbue workers with the will to perform the job well
   D. to know the kind of work that is done by one's unit and the policies and procedures of one's agency
   E. the "know-how" of administrative and supervisory processes

16.____

17. A comment made by an employee about a training course was, *We never have any idea how we are getting along in that course."*
   The fundamental error in training methods to which this criticism points is
   A. insufficient student participation
   B. failure to develop a feeling of need or active want for the material being presented
   C. the training sessions may be too long
   D. no attempt may have been made to connect the new material with what was already known
   E. no goals have been set for the students

17.____

18. Assume that you are attending a departmental conference on efficiency ratings at which it is proposed that a man-to-man rating scale be introduced.
   You should point out that, of the following, the CHIEF weakness of the man-to-man rating scale is that
   A. it involves abstract numbers rather than concrete employee characteristics
   B. judges are unable to select their own standards for comparison
   C. the standard for comparison shifts from man to man for each person rated
   D. not every person rated is given the opportunity to serve as a standard for comparison
   E. standards for comparison will vary from judge to judge

18.____

19. Assume that you are conferring with a supervisor who has assigned to his subordinates efficiency ratings which you believe to be generally too low. The supervisor argues that his ratings are generally low because his subordinates are generally inferior.
    Of the following, the evidence MOST relevant to the point at issue can be secured by comparing efficiency ratings assigned by this supervisor
    A. with ratings assigned by other supervisors in the same agency
    B. this year with ratings assigned by him in previous years
    C. to men recently transferred to his unit with ratings previously earned by these men
    D. with the general city average of ratings assigned by all supervisors to all employees
    E. with the relative order of merit of his employees as determined independently by promotion test marks

20. The one of the following which is NOT among the most common of the compensable factors used in wage evaluation studies is
    A. initiative and ingenuity required
    B. physical demand
    C. responsibility for the safety of others
    D. working conditions
    E. presence of avoidable hazards

21. If independent functions are separated, there is an immediate gain in conserving special skills. If we are to make optimum use of the abilities of our employees, these skills must be conserved.
    Assuming the correctness of this statement, it follows that
    A. if we are not making optimum use of employee abilities, independent functions have not been separated
    B. we are making optimum use of employee abilities if we conserve special skills
    C. we are making optimum use of employee abilities if independent functions have been separated
    D. we are not making optimum use of employee abilities if we do not conserve special skills
    E. if special skills are being conserved, independent functions need not be separated

22. A reorganization of the bureau to provide for a stenographic pool instead of individual unit stenographer will result in more stenographic help being available too each unit when it is required, and consequently will result in greater productivity for each unit. An analysis of the space requirements shows that setting up a stenographic pool will require a minimum of 400 square feet of good space. In order to obtain this space, it will be necessary to reduce the space available for technical personnel, resulting in lesser productivity for each unit.
    On the basis of the above discussion, it can be stated that in order to obtain greater productivity for each unit,

A. a stenographic pool should be set up
B. further analysis of the space requirement should be made
C. it is not certain as to whether or not a stenographic pool should be set up
D. the space available for each technician should be increased in order to compensate for the absence of a stenographic pool
E. a stenographic pool should not be set up

23. The adoption of a single consolidated form will mean that most of the form will not be used in any one operation. This would create waste and confusion. This conclusion is based upon the unstated hypothesis that
    A. if waste and confusion are to be avoided, a single consolidated form should be used
    B. if a single consolidated form is constructed, most of it can be used in each operation
    C. if waste and confusion are to be avoided, most of the form employed should be used
    D. most of a single consolidated form is not used
    E. a single consolidated form should not be used

23.____

24. Assume that you are studying the results of mechanizing several hand operations.
    The type of data which would be MOST useful in proving that an increase in mechanization is followed by a lower cost of operation is data which show that in
    A. some cases a lower cost of operation was not preceded by an increase in mechanization
    B. no case was a higher cost of operation preceded by a decrease in mechanization
    C. some cases a lower cost of operation was preceded by a decrease in mechanization
    D no case was a higher cost of operation preceded by an increase in mechanization
    E. some cases an increase in mechanization was followed by a decrease in cost of operation

24.____

25. The type of data which would be MOST useful in determining if an increase in the length of rest periods is followed by an increased rate of production is data which would indicate that _____ in the length of the rest period.

    A. *decrease* in the total production never follows an increase in
    B. *increase* in the total production never follows an increase
    C. *increase* in the rate of production never follows a decrease
    D. *decrease* in the total production may follow a decrease
    E. *increase* in the total production sometimes follows an increase

25.____

KEY (CORRECT ANSWERS)

1. E
2. B
3. C
4. B
5. E

6. A
7. B
8. A
9. A
10. D

11. C
12. C
13. B
14. D
15. E

16. B
17. E
18. E
19. C
20. E

21. D
22. C
23. C
24. D
25. A

TEST 3

DIRECTIONS: Each question or incomplete statement is followed by several suggested answers or completions. Select the one that BEST answers the question or completes the statement. *PRINT THE LETTER OF THE CORRECT ANSWER IN THE SPACE AT THE RIGHT.*

1. You have been asked to answer a request from a citizen of the city. After giving the request careful consideration, you find that it cannot be granted.
   In answering the letter, you should begin by
   A. saying that the request cannot be granted
   B. discussing in detail the consideration you have to the request
   C. quoting the laws relating to the request
   D. explaining in detail why the request cannot be granted
   E. indicating an alternative method of achieving the end desired

   1._____

2. Reports submitted to the department head should be complete to the last detail. A far as possible, summaries should be avoided.
   This statement is, in general,
   A. *correct*; only on the basis of complete information can a proper decision be reached
   B. *incorrect*; if all reports submitted were of this character, a department head would never complete his work
   C. *correct*; the decision as to what is important and what is not can only be made by the person who is responsible for the action
   D. *incorrect*; preliminary reports, obviously, cannot be complete to the last detail
   E. *correct*; summaries tend to conceal the actual state of affairs and to encourage generalizations which would not be made if the details were known; consequently, they should be avoided if possible

   2._____

3. The supervisor of a large bureau, who was required in the course of business to answer a large number of letters from the public, completely formalized his responses, that is, the form and vocabulary of every letter he prepared were the same as far as possible.
   This method of solving the problem of how to handle correspondence is, in general
   A. *good*; it reduces the time and thought necessary for a response
   B. *bad*; the time required to develop a satisfactory standard form and vocabulary is usually not available in an active organization
   C. *good*; the use of standard forms causes similar requests to be answered in a similar way
   D. *bad*; the use of standard forms and vocabulary to the extent indicated results in letters in *officialese* hindering unambiguous explanation and clear understanding
   E. *good*; if this method were applied to an entire department, the answering of letters could be left to clerks and the administrators would be free for more constructive work

   3._____

4. Of the following systems of designating the pages in a looseleaf manual subject to constant revision and addition, the MOST practicable one is to use _____ for main divisions and _____ for subdivisions.
   A. decimals; integers
   B. integers; letters
   C. integers; decimals
   D. letters; integers
   E. integers; integers

5. A subordinate submits a proposed draft of a form which is being revised to facilitate filling in the form on a typewriter. The draft shows that the captions for each space will be printed below the space to be filled in.
   This proposal is
   A. *undesirable*; it decreases visibility
   B. *desirable*; it makes the form easy to understand
   C. *undesirable*; it makes the form more difficult to understand
   D. *desirable*; it increases visibility
   E. *undesirable*; it is less compact than other layouts

6. The one of the following which is NOT an essential element of an integrated reporting system for work-measurement is a
   A. uniform record form for accumulating data and instructions for its maintenance
   B. procedure for routing reports upward through the organization and routing summaries downward
   C. standard report form for summarizing basic records and instructions for its preparation
   D. method for summarizing, analyzing and presenting data from several reports
   E. looseleaf revisable manual which contains all procedural materials that are reasonably permanent and have a substantial reference value

7. Forms control only accomplishes the elimination, consolidation, and simplification of forms. It contributes little to the elimination, consolidation, and simplification of procedures.
   This statement is
   A. *correct*; the form is static while the procedure is dynamic; consequently, control of one does not necessarily result in control of the other
   B. *incorrect*; forms frequently dictate the way work is laid out; consequently, control of one frequently results in control of the other
   C. *correct*; the procedure is primary and the form secondary; consequently, control of procedure will also control form
   D. *incorrect*; the form and procedure are identical from the viewpoint of work control; consequently, control of one means control of the other
   E. *correct*; the assurance that forms are produced and distributed economically has little relationship to the consolidation and simplification of procedures

8. Governmental agencies frequently attempt to avoid special interest group pressures by referring them to the predetermined legislative policy, or to the necessity for rules and regulations applying generally to all groups and situations.
Of the following, the MOST important weakness of this formally correct position is that
   A. it is not tenable in the face of determined opposition
   B. it tends to legalize and formalize the informal relationships between citizen groups and the government
   C. the achievement of an agency's aims is in large measure dependent upon its ability to secure the cooperation and support of special interest groups
   D. independent groups which participate in the formulation of policy in their sphere of interest tend to criticize openly and to press for changes in the direction of their policy
   E. agencies following this policy find it difficult to decentralize their public relation activities as subdivisions can only refer to the agency's overall policy

8.____

9. One of the primary purposes of the performance budget is to improve the ability to examine budgetary requirement by groups who have not been engaged in the construction of the budget.
This is accomplished by
   A. making line by line appropriations
   B. making lump sum appropriations by department
   C. enumerating authorization for all expenditures
   D. standardizing the language used and the kinds of authorizations permitted
   E. permitting examination on the level of accomplishment

9.____

10. When engaged in budget construction or budget analysis, there is no point in trying to determine the total or average benefits to be obtained from total expenditures for a particular commodity or function.
The validity of this argument is USUALLY based upon the
   A. viewpoint that it is not possible to construct a functional budget
   B. theory (or phenomenon) of diminishing utility
   C. hypothesis that as governmental budgets provide in theory for minimum requirements, there is no need to determine total benefits
   D. assumption that such determinations are not possible
   E. false hypothesis that a comparison between expected and achieved results does not aid in budget construction

10.____

Questions 11-12.

DIRECTIONS: Questions 11 and 12 are to be answered on the basis of the following paragraph.

Production planning is mainly a process of synthesis. As a basis for the positive act of bringing complex production elements properly together, however, analysis is necessary, especially if improvement is to be made in an existing organization. The necessary analysis requires customary means of orientation and preliminary fact gathering with emphasis, however, on the recognition of administrative goals and of the relationship among work steps.

11. The entire process described is PRIMARILY one of
    A. taking apart, examining, and recombining
    B. deciding what changes are necessary, making the changes and checking on their value
    C. fact finding so as to provide the necessary orientation
    D. discovering just where the emphasis in production should be placed and then modifying the existing procedure so that it is placed properly
    E. recognizing administrative goals and the relationship among work steps

12. In production planning according to the above paragraph, analysis is used PRIMARILY as
    A. a means of making important changes in an organization
    B. the customary means of orientation and preliminary fact finding
    C. a development of the relationship among work steps
    D. a means for holding the entire process intact by providing a logical basis
    E. a method to obtain the facts upon which a theory can be built

Questions 13-15.

DIRECTIONS: Questions 13 through 15 are to be answered on the basis of the following paragraph.

Public administration is policy-making. But it is not autonomous, exclusive or isolated policy-making. It is policy-making on a field where mighty forces contend, forces engendered in and by society. It is policy-making subject to still other and various policy makers. Public administration is one of a number of basic political processes by which these people achieves and controls government.

13. From the point of view expressed in the above paragraph, public administration is
    A. becoming a technical field with completely objective processes
    B. the primary force in modern society
    C. a technical field which should be divorced from the actual decision-making function
    D. basically anti-democratic
    E. intimately related to politics

14. According to the above paragraph, public administration is NOT entirely
    A. a force generated in and by society
    B. subject at times to controlling influences
    C. a social process
    D. policy-making relating to administrative practices
    E. related to policy-making at lower levels

15. The above paragraph asserts that public administration 15.____
    A. develops the basic and controlling policies
    B. is the result of policies made by many different forces
    C. should attempt to break through its isolated policy-making and engage on a broader field
    D. is a means of directing government
    E. is subject to the political processes by which acts are controlled

Questions 16-18.

DIRECTIONS: Questions 16 through 18 are to be answered on the basis of the following chart.

In order to understand completely the source of an employee's insecurity on his job, it is necessary to understand how he came to be, who he is and what kind of person he is away from his job. This would necessitate an understanding of those personal assets and liabilities which the employee brings to the job situation. These arise from his individual characteristics and his past experiences and established patterns of interpersonal relations. This whole area is of tremendous scope, encompassing everything included within the study of psychiatry and interpersonal relations. Therefore, it has been impracticable to consider it in detail. Attention has been focused on the relatively circumscribed area of the actual occupational situation. The factors considered those which the employee brings to the job situation and which arise from his individual characteristics and his past experience and established patterns of interpersonal relations are: intellectual-level or capacity, specific aptitudes, education, work experience, health, social and economic background, patterns of interpersonal relations and resultant personality characteristics.

16. According to the above paragraph, the one of the following fields of study which would be of LEAST importance in the study of the problem is the 16.____
    A. relationships existing among employees
    B. causes of employee insecurity in the job situation
    C. conflict, if it exists, between intellectual level and work experience
    D. distribution of intellectual achievement
    E. relationship between employee characteristics and the established pattern of interpersonal relations in the work situation

17. According to the above paragraph, in order to make a thoroughgoing and comprehensive study of the sources of employee insecurity, the field of study should include 17.____
    A. only such circumscribed areas as are involved in extra-occupational situations
    B. a study of the dominant mores of the period
    C. all branches of the science of psychology
    D. a determination of the characteristics, such as intellectual capacity, which an employee should bring to the job situation
    E. employee personality characteristics arising from previous relationships with other people

18. It is implied by this paragraph that it would be of GREATEST advantage to bring   18.____
    to this problem a comprehensive knowledge of
    A. all established patterns of interpersonal relations
    B. the milieu in which the employee group is located
    C. what assets and liabilities are presented in the job situation
    D. methods of focusing attention on relatively circumscribed regions
    E. the sources of an employee's insecurity on his job

Questions 19-20.

DIRECTIONS: Questions 19 and 20 are to be answered on the basis of the following paragraph.

If, during a study, some hundreds of values of a variable (such as annual number of latenesses for each employee in a department) have been noted merely in the arbitrary order in which they happen to occur, the mind cannot properly grasp the significance of the record, the observations must be ranked or classified in some way before the characteristics of the series can be comprehended, and those comparisons, on which arguments as to causation depend, can be made with other series. A dichotomous classification is too crude; if the values are merely classified according to whether they exceed or fall short of some fixed value, a large part of the information given by the original record is lost. Numerical measurements lend themselves with peculiar readiness to a manifold classification.

19. According to the above paragraph, if the values of a variable which are gathered   19.____
    during a study are classified in a few subdivisions, the MOST likely result will be
    A. an inability to grasp the signification of the record
    B. an inability to relate the series with other series
    C. a loss of much of the information in the original data
    D. a loss of the readiness with which numerical measurements lend
       themselves to a manifold classification
    E. that the order in which they happen to occur will be arbitrary

20. The above paragraph advocates, with respect to numerical data, the use of   20.____
    A. arbitrary order   B. comparisons with other series
    C. a two-value classification D. a many value classification
    E. all values of a variable

Questions 21-25.

DIRECTIONS: Questions 21 through 25 are to be answered on the basis of the following chart.

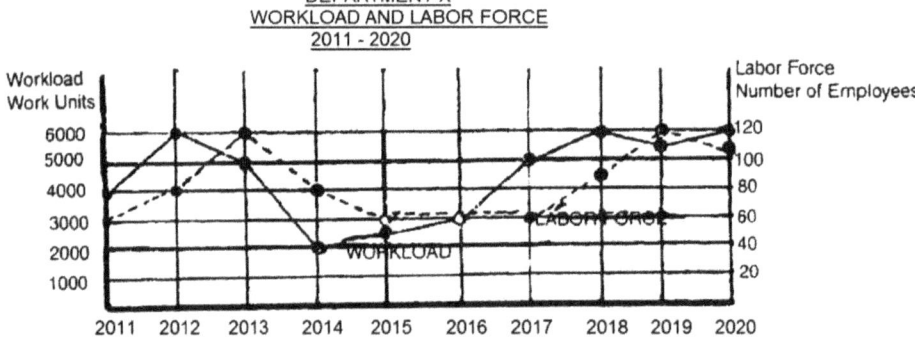

7 (#3)

21. The one of the following years for which average employee production was LOWEST was 21._____
    A. 2012   B. 2014   C. 2016   D. 2018   E. 2020

22. The average annual employee production for the ten-year period was, in terms of work units, MOST NEARLY 22._____
    A. 30   B. 50   C. 70   D. 80   E. 90

23. On the basis of the chart, it can be deduced that personnel needs for the coming year are budgeted on the basis of 23._____
    A. workload for the current year
    B. expected workload for the coming year
    C. no set plan
    D. average workload over the five years immediately preceding the period
    E. expected workload for the five coming years

24. The chart indicates that the operation is carefully programmed and that the labor force has been used properly. 24._____
    This opinion is
    A. *supported* by the chart; the organization has been able to meet emergency situations requiring much additional work without commensurate increase in staff
    B. *not supported* by the chart; the irregular workload shows a complete absence of planning
    C. *supported* by the chart; the similar shapes of the workload and labor force curves show that these important factors are closely related
    D. *not supported* by the chart; poor planning with respect to labor requirements is obvious from the chart
    E. *supported* by the chart; the average number of units of work performed in any 5-year period during the 10 years shows sufficient regularity to indicate a definite trend

25. The chart indicates that the department may be organized in such a way as to require a permanent minimum staff which is too large for the type of operation indicated. 25._____
    This opinion is
    A. *supported* by the chart; there is indication that the operation calls for an irreducible minimum number of employees and application of the most favorable work production records shows this to be too high for normal operation
    B. *not supported* by the chart; the absence of any sort of regularity makes it impossible to express any opinion with any degree of certainty
    C. *supported* by the chart; the expected close relationship between workload and labor force is displaced somewhat, a phenomenon which usually occurs as a result of a fixed minimum requirement
    D. *not supported* by the chart; the violent movement of the labor force curve makes it evident that no minimum requirements are in effect

E. *supported* by the chart; calculation shows that the average number of employees was 84 with an average variation of 17.8, thus indicating that the minimum number of 60 persons was too high for efficient operation

---

KEY (CORRECT ANSWERS)

1. A
2. B
3. D
4. C
5. A

6. E
7. B
8. C
9. E
10. B

11. A
12. E
13. E
14. D
15. D

16. D
17. E
18. B
19. C
20. D

21. B
22. B
23. A
24. D
25. A

EXAMINATION SECTION
TEST 1

DIRECTIONS: Each question or incomplete statement is followed by several suggested answers or completions. Select the one that BEST answers the question or completes the statement. *PRINT THE LETTER OF THE CORRECT ANSWER IN THE SPACE AT THE RIGHT.*

1. Assume that a manager is preparing a list of reasons to justify making a major change in methods and procedures in his agency.
   Which of the following reasons would be LEAST appropriate on such a list?
   A. Improve the means for satisfying needs and wants of agency personnel
   B. Increase efficiency
   C. Intensify competition and stimulate loyalty to separate work groups
   D. Contribute to the individual and group satisfaction of agency personnel

   1.____

2. Many managers recognize the benefits of decentralization but are concerned about the danger of over-relaxation of control as a result of increased delegation.
   Of the following, the MOST appropriate means of establishing proper control under decentralization is for the manager to
   A. establish detailed standards for all phases of operation
   B. shift his attention from operating details to appraisal of results
   C. keep himself informed by decreasing the time span covered by reports
   D. make unilateral decisions on difficult situations that arise in decentralized locations

   2.____

3. In some agencies, the counsel to the agency head is given the right to bypass the chain of command and issue orders directly to the staff concerning matters that involve certain specific processes and practices.
   This situation MOST NEARLY illustrates the principle of _____ authority.
   A. the acceptance theory of   B. multiple-linear
   C. splintered   D. functional

   3.____

4. Assume that a manager is writing a brief report to his superior outlining the advantages of matrix organization.
   Of the following, it would be INCORRECT to state that
   A. in matrix organization, a project is emphasized by designating one individual as the focal point for all matters pertaining to it
   B. utilization of manpower can be flexible in matrix organization because a reservoir of specialists is maintained in the line operations
   C. the usual line staff arrangement is generally reversed in matrix organization
   D. in matrix organization, responsiveness to project needs is generally faster due to establishing needed communication lines and decision points

   4.____

5. It is commonly understood that communication is an important part of the administrative process.
   Which of the following is NOT a valid principle of the communication process in administration?
   A. The channels of communication should be spontaneous.
   B. The lines of communication should be as direct and as short as possible.
   C. Communications should be authenticated.
   D. The persons serving in communications centers should be competent.

6. The PRIMARY purpose of the quantitative approach in management is to
   A. identify better alternatives for management decision-making
   B. substitute data for judgment
   C. match opinions to data
   D. match data to opinions

7. If an executive wants to make a strong case for running his agency as a flat type of structure, he should point out that the PRIMARY advantage of doing so is to
   A. provide less experience in decision-making for agency personnel
   B. facilitate frequent contact between each superior and his immediate subordinates
   C. improve communication and unify attitudes
   D. improve communication and diversify attitudes

8. In deciding how detailed his delegation of authority to a subordinate should be, a manager should follow the general principle that
   A. delegation of authority is more detailed at the top of the organizational structure
   B. detailed delegation of authority is associated with detailed work assignments
   C. delegation of authority should be in sufficient detail to prevent overlapping assignments
   D. detailed delegation of authority is associated with broad work assignments

9. In recent years, newer and more fluid types of organizational forms have been developed. One of these is a type of free-form organization.
   Another name for this type of organization is the
   A. project organization   B. semimix organization
   C. naturalistic structure   D. semipermanent structure

10. Which of the following is the MAJOR objective of operational or management systems audits?
    A. Determining the number of personnel needed
    B. Recommending opportunities for improving operating and management practices
    C. Detecting fraud
    D. Determining organization problems

11. Assume that a manager observes that conflict exists between his agency and another operating agency of government.
    Which of the following statements is the LEAST probable cause of this conflict?
    A. Incompatibility between the agencies' goals but similarity in their resource allocations
    B. Compatibility between agencies' goals and resources
    C. Status differences between agency personnel
    D. Differences in perceptions of each other's policies

12. Of the following, a MAJOR purpose of brainstorming as a problem-solving technique is to
    A. develop the ability to concentrate
    B. encourage creative thinking
    C. evaluate employees' ideas
    D. develop critical ability

13. The one of the following requirements which is LEAST likely to accompany regular delegation of work from a manager to a subordinate is a(n)
    A. need to review the organization's workload
    B. indication of what work the subordinate is to do
    C. need to grant authority to the subordinate
    D. obligation for the subordinate who accepts the work to try to complete it

14. Of the following, the one factor which is generally considered LEAST essential to successful committee operation is
    A. stating a clear definition of the authority and scope of the committee
    B. selecting the committee chairman carefully
    C. limiting the size of the committee to four persons
    D. limiting the subject matter to that which can be handled in group discussion

15. In using the program evaluation and review technique, the *critical path* is the path that
    A. requires the shortest time
    B. requires the longest time
    C. focuses most attention on social constraints
    D. focuses most attention to repetitious jobs

16. Which one of the following is LEAST characteristic of the management-by-objectives approach?
    A. The scope within which the employee may exercise decision-making is broadened.
    B. The employee starts with a self-appraisal of his performances, abilities, and potential.
    C. Emphasis is placed on activities performed; activities orientation is maximized.
    D. Each employee participates in determining his own objectives.

17. The function of management which puts into effect the decisions, plans, and programs that have previously been worked out for achieving the goals of the group is MOST appropriately called
    A. scheduling   B. classifying   C. budgeting   D. directing

18. In the establishment of a plan to improve office productive efficiency, which of the following guidelines is LEAST helpful in setting sound work standards?
    A. Employees must accept the plan's objectives.
    B. Current production averages must be promulgated as work standards for a group.
    C. The work flow must generally be fairly constant.
    D. The operation of the plan must be expressed in terms understandable to the worker.

19. The one of the following activities which, generally speaking, is of *relatively* MAJOR importance at the lower-management level and of *somewhat* LESSER importance at higher-management levels is
    A. actuating   B. forecasting   C. organizing   D. planning

20. Three styles of leadership exist: democratic, authoritarian, and laissez-faire. Of the following work situations, the one in which a democratic approach would normally be the MOST effective is when the work is
    A. routine and moderately complex   B. repetitious and simple
    C. complex and not routine   D. simple and not routine

21. Governmental and business organizations *generally* encounter the GREATEST difficulties in developing tangible measures of which one of the following?
    A. The level of expenditures   B. Contributions to social welfare
    C. Retention rates   D. Causes of labor unrest

22. Of the following, a *management-by-objectives* program is BEST described as
    A. a new comprehensive plan of organization
    B. introduction of budgets and financial controls
    C. introduction of long-range planning
    D. development of future goals with supporting and related progress reviews

23. Research and analysis is probably the most widely used technique for selecting alternatives when major planning decisions are involved.
    Of the following, a VALUABLE characteristic of research and analysis is that this technique
    A. places the problem in a meaningful conceptual framework
    B. involves practical application of the various alternatives
    C. accurately analyzes all important tangibles
    D. is much less expensive than other problem-solving methods

24. If a manager were assigned the task of using a systems approach to designing a new work unit, which of the following should he consider FIRST in carrying out his design?
    A. Networks
    B. Work flows and information processes
    C. Linkages and relationships
    D. Decision points and control loops

25. The MAIN distinction between Theory X and Theory Y approaches to organization, in accordance with Douglas McGregor's view, is that Theory Y
    A. considers that work is natural to people; Theory X assumes that people are lazy and avoid work
    B. leads to a tall, narrow organization structure, while Theory X leads to one that is flat
    C. organizations motivate people with money; Theory X organizations motivate people with good working conditions
    D. represents authoritarian management, while Theory X management is participative

KEY (CORRECT ANSWERS)

1.	C		11.	B
2.	B		12.	B
3.	D		13.	A
4.	C		14.	C
5.	A		15.	B
6.	A		16.	C
7.	C		17.	D
8.	B		18.	B
9.	A		19.	A
10.	B		20.	C

21. B
22. D
23. A
24. B
25. A

TEST 2

DIRECTIONS: Each question or incomplete statement is followed by several suggested answers or completions. Select the one that BEST answers the question or completes the statement. *PRINT THE LETTER OF THE CORRECT ANSWER IN THE SPACE AT THE RIGHT.*

1. Of the following, the stage in decision-making which is usually MOST difficult is
   A. stating the alternatives
   B. predicting the possible outcome of each alternative
   C. evaluating the relative merits of each alternative
   D. minimizing the undesirable aspects of the alternative selected

   1.____

2. In a department where a clerk is reporting both to a senior clerk in charge of the mail room and also to a supervising clerk in charge of the duplicating section, there may be a breakdown of the management principle called
   A. horizontal specialization B. job enrichment
   C. unity of command D. Graicunas' Law

   2.____

3. Of the following, the failure by line managers to accept and appreciate the benefits and limitations of a new program or system VERY frequently can be traced to the
   A. budgetary problems involved
   B. resultant need to reduce staff
   C. lack of controls it engenders
   D. failure of top management to support its implementation

   3.____

4. Although there is general agreement that *management-by-objectives* has made a major contribution to modern management of large organizations, criticisms of the system during the past few years have resulted in
   A. mounting pressure for relaxation of management goals
   B. renewed concern with human values and the manager's personal needs
   C. over-mechanistic application of the perceptions of the behavioral scientists
   D. disillusionment with *management-by-objectives* on the part of a majority of managers

   4.____

5. Of the following, which is usually considered to be a MAJOR obstacle to the systematic analysis of potential problems by managers?
   A. Managers have a tendency to think that all the implications of some proposed step cannot be fully understood.
   B. Rewards rarely go to those managers who are most successful at resolving current problems in management.
   C. There is a common conviction of manages that their goals are difficult to achieve.
   D. Managers are far more concerned about correcting today's problems than with preventing tomorrow's.

   5.____

2 (#2)

6. Which of the following should generally have the MOST influence on the selection of supervisors?
   A. Experience within the work unit where the vacancies exist
   B. Amount of money needed to effect the promotion
   C. Personal preferences of the administration
   D. Evaluation of capacity to exercise supervisory responsibilities

6.____

7. In questioning a potential administrator for selection purposes, the one of the following practices which is MOST desirable is to
   A. encourage the job applicant to give primarily *yes* or *no* replies
   B. get the applicant to talk freely and in detail about his background
   C. let the job applicant speak most of the time
   D. probe the applicant's attitudes, motivation, and willingness to accept responsibility

7.____

8. In implementing the managerial function of training subordinates, it is USEFUL to know that a widely agreed-upon definition of human learning is that learning
   A. is a relatively permanent change in behavior that results from reinforced practice or experience
   B. involves an improvement, but not necessarily a change in behavior
   C. involves a change in behavior, but not necessarily an improvement
   D. is a temporary change in behavior which must be subject to practice or experience

8.____

9. If a manager were thinking about using a committee of subordinates to solve an operating problem, which of the following would generally NOT be an advantage of such use of the committee approach?
   A. Improved coordination   B. Low cost
   C. Increased motivation   D. Integrated judgment

9.____

10. Which one of the following management approaches MOST often uses model-building techniques to solve management problems?
    _____ approach.
    A. Behavioral   B. Fiscal   C. Quantitative   D. Process

10.____

11. Of the following, the MOST serious risk in using budgets as a tool for management control is the
    A. probable neglect of other good management practices
    B. likelihood of guesswork because of the need to plan far in advance
    C. possibility of undue emphasis on factors that are easiest to measure
    D. danger of making qualitative rather than quantitative assessments of performance

11.____

12. In government budgeting, the problem of relating financial transactions to the fiscal year in which they are budgeted is BEST met by
    A. determining the cash balance by comparing how much money has been received and how much has been paid out
    B. applying net revenue to the fiscal year in which they are collected as offset by relevant expenses

12.____

C. adopting a system whereby appropriations are entered when they are received and expenditures are entered when they are paid out
D. entering expenditures on the books when the obligation to make the expenditure is made

13. If the agency's bookkeeping system records income when it is received and expenditures when the money is paid out this system is USUALLY known as a _____ system.
    A. cash
    B. flow-payment
    C. deferred
    D. fiscal year income

14. An audit, as the term applies to budget execution, is MOST NEARLY a
    A. procedure based on the budget estimates
    B. control exercised by the executive on the legislature in the establishment of program priorities
    C. check on the legality of expenditures and is based on the appropriations act
    D. requirement which must be met before funds can be spent

15. In government budgeting, there is a procedure known as *allotment*.
    Of the following statements which relate to allotment, select the one that is MOST generally considered to be correct.
    Allotment
    A. increases the practice of budget units coming back to the legislature branch for supplemental appropriations
    B. is simply an example of red tape
    C. eliminates the requirement of timing of expenditures
    D. is designed to prevent waste

16. In government budgeting, the establishment of the schedules of allotments is MOST generally the responsibility of the
    A. budget unit and the legislature
    B. budget unit and the executive
    C. budget unit only
    D. executive and the legislature

17. Of the following statements relating to preparation of an organization's budget request, which is the MOST generally valid precaution?
    A. Give specific instructions on the format or budget requests and required supporting data
    B. Because of the complexity of preparing a budget request, avoid argumentation to support the requests
    C. Put requests in whatever format is desirable
    D. Consider that final approval will be given to initial estimates

18. Of the following statements which relate to the budget process in a well-organized government, select the one that is MOST NEARLY correct.
    A. The budget cycle is the step-by-step process which is repeated each and every fiscal year.
    B. Securing approval of the budget does not take place within the budget cycle.

C. The development of a new budget and putting it into effect is a two-step process known as the budget cycle.
D. The fiscal period, usually a fiscal year, has no relation to the budget cycle.

19. If a manager were asked what PPBS stands for, he would be RIGHT if he said _____ budgeting system.
    A. public planning
    B. planning programming
    C. planning projections
    D. programming procedures

Questions 20-21.

DIRECTIONS: Questions 20 and 21 are to be answered on the basis of the following information.

Sample Budget

Refuse Collection	Amount
Personal Services	$30,000
Contractual Services	5,000
Supplies and Materials	5,000
Capital Outlay	10,000
	$50,000

Residential Collections	
Dwellings – 1 pickup per week	1,000
Tons of refuse collected per year	375
Cost of collections per ton	$ 8
Cost per dwelling pickup per year	$ 3
Total annual cost	$3,000

20. The sample budget shown is a simplified example of a _____ budget.
    A. factorial   B. performance   C. qualitative   D. rational

21. The budget shown in the sample differs CHIEFLY from line-item and program budgets in that it includes
    A. objects of expenditure but not activities or functions
    B. only activities, functions, and control
    C. activities and functions but not objects of expenditures
    D. levels of service

Question 22.

DIRECTIONS: Question 22 is to be answered on the basis of the following information.

Sample Budget

Environmental Safety
Air Pollution Protection
Personal Services	$20,000,000	
Contractual Services	4,000,000	
Supplies and Materials	4,000,000	
Capital Outlay	2,000,000	
Total Air Pollution Protection		$30,000,000

Water Pollution Protection
Personal Services	$23,000,000	
Supplies and Materials	4,500,000	
Capital Outlay	20,500,000	
Total Water Pollution Protection		$48,000,000

Total Environmental Safety $78,000,000

22. Based on the above budget, which is the MOST valid statement?
    A. Environmental Safety, Air Pollution Protection, and Water Pollution Protection could all be considered program elements.
    B. The object listings included water pollution protection and capital outlay.
    C. Examples of the program element listings in the above are personal services and supplies and materials
    D. Contractual Services and Environmental Safety were the program element listings.

23. Which of the following is NOT an advantage of a program budget over a line-item budget?
    A program budget
    A. allows us to set up priority lists in deciding what activities we will spend our money on
    B. gives us more control over expenditures than a line-item budget
    C. is more informative in that we know the broad purposes of spending money
    D. enables us to see if one program is getting much less money than the others

24. If a manager were trying to explain the fundamental difference between traditional accounting theory and practice and the newer practice of managerial accounting, he would be MOST accurate if he said that
    A. traditional accounting practice focused on providing information for persons outside organizations, while managerial accounting focuses on providing information for people inside organizations
    B. traditional accounting practice focused on providing information for persons inside organizations while managerial accounting focuses on providing information for persons outside organizations

C. managerial accounting is exclusively concerned with historical facts while traditional accounting stresses future projections exclusively
D. traditional accounting practice is more budget-focused than managerial accounting

25. Which of the following formulas is used to determine the number of days required to process work?
_____ = Days to Process Work

A. $\dfrac{\text{Employees} \times \text{Daily Output}}{\text{Volume}}$

B. $\dfrac{\text{Volume} \times \text{Daily Output}}{\text{Volume}}$

C. $\dfrac{\text{Volume}}{\text{Employees} \times \text{Daily Output}}$

D. $\dfrac{\text{Employees} \times \text{Volume}}{\text{Daily Output}}$

KEY (CORRECT ANSWERS)

1.	C	11.	C
2.	C	12.	D
3.	D	13.	A
4.	B	14.	C
5.	D	15.	D
6.	D	16.	C
7.	D	17.	A
8.	A	18.	A
9.	B	19.	B
10.	C	20.	B

21. D
22. A
23. B
24. A
25. C

TEST 3

DIRECTIONS: Each question or incomplete statement is followed by several suggested answers or completions. Select the one that BEST answers the question or completes the statement. *PRINT THE LETTER OF THE CORRECT ANSWER IN THE SPACE AT THE RIGHT.*

1. Electronic data processing equipment can produce more information faster than can be generated by any other means.
   In view of this, the MOST important problem faced by management at present is to
   A. keep computers fully occupied
   B. find enough computer personnel
   C. assimilate and properly evaluate the information
   D. obtain funds to establish appropriate information systems

2. A well-designed management information system ESSENTIALLY provides each executive and manager the information he needs for
   A. determining computer time requirements
   B. planning and measuring results
   C. drawing a new organization chart
   D. developing a new office layout

3. It is generally agreed that management policies should be periodically reappraised and restated in accordance with current conditions.
   Of the following, the approach which would be MOST effective in determining whether a policy should be revised is to
   A. conduct interviews with staff members at all levels in order to ascertain the relationship between the policy and actual practice
   B. make proposed revisions in the policy and apply it to current problems
   C. make up hypothetical situations using both the old policy and a revised version in order to make comparisons
   D. call a meeting of top level staff in order to discuss ways of revising the policy

4. Every manager has many occasions to lead a conference or participate in a conference of some sort.
   Of the following statements that pertain to conferences and conference leadership, which is generally considered to be MOST valid?
   A. Since World War II, the trend has been toward fewer shared decisions and more conferences.
   B. The most important part of a conference leader's job is to direct discussion.
   C. In providing opportunities for group interaction, management should avoid consideration of its past management philosophy.
   D. A good administrator cannot lead a good conference if he is a poor public speaker.

5. Of the following, it is usually LEAST desirable for a conference leader to
   A. turn the question to the person who asked it
   B. summarize proceedings periodically
   C. make a practice of not repeating questions
   D. ask a question without indicating who is to reply

6. The behavioral school of management thought bases its beliefs on certain assumptions.
   Which of the following is NOT a belief of this school of thought?
   A. People tend to seek and accept responsibility.
   B. Most people can be creative in solving problems.
   C. People prefer security above all else.
   D. Commitment is the most important factor in motivating people.

7. The one of the following objectives which would be LEAST appropriate as a major goal of research in the field of human resources management is to
   A. predict future conditions, events, and manpower needs
   B. evaluate established policies, programs, and practices
   C. evaluate proposed policies, programs, and practices
   D. identify deficient organizational units and apply suitable penalties

8. Of the following general interviewing methods or techniques, the one that is USUALLY considered to be effective in counseling, grievances, and appraisal interviews is the _____ interview.
   A. directed   B. non-directed   C. panel   D. patterned

9. The ESSENTIAL first phase of decision-making is
   A. finding alternative solutions
   B. making a diagnosis of the problem
   C. selecting the plan to follow
   D. analyzing and comparing alternative solutions

10. Assume that, in a certain organization, a situation has developed in which there is little difference in status or authority between individuals.
    Which of the following would be the MOST likely result with regard to communication in this organization?
    A. Both the accuracy and flow of communication will be improved.
    B. Both the accuracy and flow of communication will substantially decrease.
    C. Employees will seek more formal lines of communication.
    D. Neither the flow nor the accuracy of communication will be improved over the former hierarchical structure.

11. The main function of many agency administrative offices is *information management*. Information that is received by an administrative officer may be classified as active or passive, depending upon whether or not it requires the recipient to take some action.

Of the following, the item received which is clearly the MOST active information is
- A. an appointment of a new staff member
- B. a payment voucher for a new desk
- C. a press release concerning a past city event
- D. the minutes of a staff meeting

12. Which one of the following sets BEST describes the general order in which to teach an operation to a new employee?
    - A. Prepare, present, tryout, follow-up
    - B. Prepare, test, tryout, re-test
    - C. Present, test, tryout, follow-up
    - D. Test, present, follow-up, re-test

13. Of the following, public employees may be separated from public service
    - A. for the same reasons which are generally acceptable for discharging employees in private industry
    - B. only under the most trying circumstances
    - C. under procedures that are neither formalized nor subject to review
    - D. solely in extreme cases involving offenses of gravest character

14. Of the following, the one LEAST considered to be a communication barrier is
    - A. group feedback
    - B. charged words
    - C. selective perception
    - D. symbolic meanings

15. Of the following ways for a manager to handle his appointments, the BEST way, according to experts in administration, generally is to
    - A. schedule his own appointments and inform his secretary not to reserve his time without his approval
    - B. encourage everyone to make appointments through his secretary and tell her when he makes his own appointments
    - C. see no one who has not made a previous appointment
    - D. permit anyone to see him without an appointment

16. Assume that a manager decides to examine closely one of five units under his supervision to uncover problems common to all five.
    His research technique is MOST closely related to the method called
    - A. experimentation
    - B. simulation
    - C. linear analysis
    - D. sampling

17. If one views the process of management as a dynamic process, which one of the following functions is NOT a legitimate part of that process?
    - A. Communication
    - B. Decision-making
    - C. Organizational slack
    - D. Motivation

18. Which of the following would be the BEST statement of a budget-oriented purpose for a government administrator? To
    A. provide 200 hours of instruction in basic reading for 3,500 adult illiterates at a cost of $1 million in the next fiscal year
    B. inform the public of adult educational programs
    C. facilitate the transfer to a city agency of certain functions of a federally-funded program which is being phased out
    D. improve the reading skills of the adult citizens in the city

19. Modern management philosophy and practices are changing to accommodate the expectations and motivations of organization personnel.
    Which of the following terms INCORRECTLY describes these newer managerial approaches?
    A. Rational management
    B. Participative management
    C. Decentralization
    D. Democratic supervision

20. Management studies support the hypothesis that, in spite of the tendency of employees to censor the information communicated to their supervisor, subordinates are MORE likely to communicate problem-oriented information upward when they have
    A. a long period of service in the organization
    B. a high degree of trust in the supervisor
    C. a high educational level
    D. low status on the organizational ladder

KEY (CORRECT ANSWERS)

1.	C	11.	A
2.	B	12.	A
3.	A	13.	A
4.	B	14.	A
5.	A	15.	B
6.	C	16.	D
7.	D	17.	C
8.	B	18.	A
9.	B	19.	A
10.	D	20.	B

EXAMINATION SECTION
TEST 1

DIRECTIONS: Each question or incomplete statement is followed by several suggested answers or completions. Select the one that BEST answers the question or completes the statement. *PRINT THE LETTER OF THE CORRECT ANSWER IN THE SPACE AT THE RIGHT.*

1. You are assigned to form a new unit to compile data which is to facilitate an executive in decision-making.
   In planning the organization of this unit, the question to be answered FIRST is:

   A. What interpretations are likely to be made of the data by the executive in making a decision?
   B. At what point in the decision-making process will the data be most usefully introduced?
   C. What type of data is needed by the executive in his area of decision-making?
   D. What criteria will the executive use to evaluate the data?

   1.____

2. The extent of effective decentralization within an organization is INVERSELY related to the

   A. size of the organization
   B. availability of sufficient competent personnel
   C. physical dispersion of the organization's activities
   D. effectiveness of communication within the organization

   2.____

3. *The tasks of coordination, supervision, and control are likely to become more complicated as the specialization of an organization increases.*
   This statement is GENERALLY

   A. *false;* better performance of these tasks is likely to follow from the detailed attention given to particular problems
   B. *false;* the proportion of specialized personnel is small in proportion to total personnel
   C. *true;* the increased interrelationships arising from increased specialization are sources of potential friction
   D. *true;* the specialist tends to resent direction from superiors who are not specialists

   3.____

4. The distinctive feature between a method and a procedure may BEST be illustrated by a

   A. series of procedures comprising a method
   B. series of related methods performed usually by one person constituting a procedure
   C. procedure comprised of a series of related methods
   D. procedure encompassing a range more limited than that of a method

   4.____

5. As part of your duties to analyze operating practices, you make a tour of a unit during which you talk to the employees about work methods, problems, and other pertinent topics. Such informal data gathering is often incomplete or inaccurate. At a later meeting with the unit supervisor, you question him about the information you have gathered, but he is unable to answer the questions immediately. He asks to accompany you on another tour of his unit and answer the questions on the spot. Explaining that employees will be reluctant to speak up in the presence of a supervisor, you refuse.
The situation you have created may BEST be described as a violation of the principle of organization called

   A. delegation of authority
   B. specialization of work
   C. span of control
   D. unity of command

6. A person desiring greater status and income in municipal government must, with few exceptions, move into the supervisory ranks. When he does, he will encounter certain changes in attitudes and relationships to which he must make satisfactory adjustments. His rise will create a degree of hostility and natural jealousy among his colleagues who have not tried to improve their situation or who have tried and failed. In a sense, too, he is forced upon the group he will supervise because under normal civil service practice, the group has little to say in his appointment.
A subtle change takes place also in his social situation; he must be in contact with his subordinates but he cannot be part of them, otherwise he yields a basic obligation to management, of which he is a part.
The MOST important conclusion to be made from this statement is that

   A. a manager should limit his contacts with subordinates to a minimum
   B. he must plan to advance himself further
   C. he should isolate himself from the work of the supervised group
   D. he must subordinate personnel popularity to the interest of the organization

7. A budget that itemizes expenditure estimates by detailing materials to be purchased, equipment to be maintained, salaries to be paid, etcetera, is known as a _____ budget.

   A. performance
   B. capital
   C. line-item
   D. program

8. Organizational activities for which there are no allocated funds available are financed from the _____ funds.

   A. special revenue
   B. sinking
   C. general
   D. special assessment

9. One of the real revolutions in public administration during the last half-century is the growth in importance of the budget as a planning and control instrument. Several trends account for this growing importance. Which of the following is NOT one of these trends?

   A. Rapid growth of the urban population
   B. The cheapening of the dollar
   C. The improved standards of living
   D. Full employment

10. The position classifying bureau of the personnel agency is normally NOT responsible for

    A. allocating individuals to classes
    B. assigning titles to classes of positions
    C. establishing minimum qualifications for positions
    D. determining which positions are necessary

11. Which of the following statements concerning a job analysis for position classification is FALSE?

    A. It is a study of the person who is to occupy the job.
    B. Time and motion studies may be used.
    C. It may be used in establishing rates of compensation.
    D. It is often done by staff authority.

12. Which of the following is considered to be an ESSENTIAL element of classifying a position?

    A. Number of positions similar to the one being classified
    B. Determination of salary to be paid for position
    C. Comparison of the position with similar and related positions
    D. Evaluation of the skills demanded by the position

13. The LEAST important objective of devising a service rating system is

    A. validating selection procedures
    B. improving quality of supervision
    C. encouraging the development of employee performance
    D. furnishing the basis of formulating a position classification plan

Questions 14-15.

DIRECTIONS: Questions 14 and 15 are to be answered in accordance with the following statement.

The process of validating a factual proposition is quite distinct from the process of validating a value judgment. The former is validated by its agreement with the facts, the latter by human authority.

14. According to the above statement, the one of the following methods which is MOST acceptable for determining whether or not a proposition is factually correct is to

    A. prove that a related proposition is factually correct
    B. derive it logically from accepted assumptions
    C. show that it will lead to desired results
    D. compare it with experience

15. Assuming that the above statement is correct, the theory that the correctness of all ethical propositions can be tested empirically is

    A. *correct;* testing empirically is validating by agreement with facts
    B. *incorrect;* ethical propositions are value judgments
    C. *correct;* ethical propositions are based on rational hypotheses
    D. *incorrect;* a factual proposition is validated by its agreement with facts

16. The rejection of the theory of inverse probability was, for a time, wrongly taken to imply that we cannot draw, from knowledge of a sample, inferences respecting the corresponding population. Such a view would entirely deny validity to all experimental science.
According to the above statement,

    A. the theory of inverse probability cannot be applied to an entire population
    B. making deductions from a sample is consistent with experimental science
    C. making deductions from a sample is inconsistent with experimental science
    D. the theory of Inverse probability is based on the study of samples

17. May I point out that if technical employees are given assignments only in their special fields, there will be an immediate gain in conserving special skills. And, if we are to make optimum use of the abilities of the technical employees, it is necessary that these skills be conserved.
Assuming that this analysis is correct, it follows that

    A. if we are not making optimum use of the abilities of technical employees, we have been giving technical employees assignments outside of their special fields
    B. we are making optimum use of the abilities of technical employees if we conserve special skills
    C. we are making optimum use of the abilities of technical employees if we give them assignments only in their special fields
    D. we are not making optimum use of the abilities of technical employees if we give them assignments outside of their special fields

18. *It is less costly to replace old equipment than to repair it.*
Which of the following statements tends to prove this hypothesis MOST conclusively?

    A. The repair of old equipment is frequently as costly as the purchase of new equipment.
    B. Continuance in service of old equipment is at least as costly as its replacement by new equipment.
    C. The replacement of old equipment is more desirable than its repair.
    D. The cost for repairing old equipment is not a one-time cost, while the cost of new equipment is a one-time cost.

19. *An increasing birth rate will be followed by an increased school registration.*
On the basis of this statement *only*, it would be MOST accurate to state that

    A. school registration does not change during a period with a level birth rate
    B. an increasing school registration is preceded by a period with an increasing birth rate
    C. a period with an increasing birth rate is sometimes followed by a decreasing school registration
    D. a period with a decreasing birth rate is sometimes followed by a decreasing school registration

20. It is generally agreed that the *face-to-face* method of communicating is the most effective from a supervisor's standpoint.
    This is true PRIMARILY because   20.____

    A. the attitude of the recipient can be accurately appraised
    B. it provides a two-way channel of expression which results in clarification of ideas
    C. it is illustrative of the extremely desirable supervisory technique known as the *democratic approach*
    D. it brings the supervisor closer to the actual level of operation

Questions 21-25.

DIRECTIONS: Questions 21 through 25 contain incorrectly used words which change the meaning of the statement. Identify the word in the statement that is incorrect and select the choice that would make the sentence correct.

21. Lack of employee input in the case of training often exists, but is frequently dealt with in evaluation of the training effort. Failure to deal with as important a factor as this can be ruinous to the training effort.   21.____

    A. Seldom   B. Margin   C. Ancillary   D. Contributory

22. It is a fallacy that policies generated at the top of the hierarchy are often not acceptable to those on the lower levels, particularly in the case of blue-collar workers among whom the rewards and sanctions of the union or members of the immediate social group are more impelling than the rewards or sanctions available to management.   22.____

    A. Parologism   B. Truism
    C. Commands   D. Undetermined

23. Basically, an organization develops when employees in it have rather free control over their behavior within the organization, when the philosophy of the organization is that maximum interpersonal interplay through a minimum number of hierarchical levels is desirable, and when a person traditionally called a *trainer* performs an integrating function.   23.____

    A. Instinctively   B. Total
    C. Flat   D. Strong

24. In gaining cooperation in human relations, the one who would influence must often foster his own ego and fertilize and feed that of the one who is to be influenced.   24.____

    A. Lassitude   B. Emulate   C. Suppress   D. Implant

25. In the United States, in general, we have been criticized for our emphasis upon physical, materialistic, and economic goals. These are still important, but the trends point toward the more complex, or appreciation of the beautiful, as for example in the architecture of our new factories and colors in the workplaces.   25.____

    A. Ephemeral   B. Concrete   C. Prosaic   D. Aesthetic

KEY (CORRECT ANSWERS)

1.	C	11.	A
2.	D	12.	C
3.	C	13.	D
4.	C	14.	D
5.	D	15.	B
6.	D	16.	B
7.	C	17.	D
8.	C	18.	B
9.	D	19.	B
10.	D	20.	B

21. A
22. B
23. D
24. C
25. D

TEST 2

DIRECTIONS: Each question or incomplete statement is followed by several suggested answers or completions. Select the one that BEST answers the question or completes the statement. *PRINT THE LETTER OF THE CORRECT ANSWER IN THE SPACE AT THE RIGHT.*

1. In the communications process, a formal communication should contain a multiplicity of ideas and several related objectives in order to provide for time-saving economy and to enhance the prospects of eventual compliance by subordinates.
This statement is GENERALLY

   A. *true*, since it reduces to a minimum the need for issuance of frequent communications from policy-making levels
   B. *false*, since the number of ideas and objectives contained in a single communication operates in inverse ratio to the degree of compliance
   C. *true*, since continuity and cohesiveness of plans are developed by infrequent but elaborate formal communications
   D. *false*, since time-saving devices are not the concern of superiors engaged in developing an effective communications process

2. Experts in supervisory practices have been emphasizing the importance of the art of listening on the part of supervisors. A recently published text devotes over three hundred pages to a discussion on how managers and supervisors can improve their ability to listen.
Which one of the following is NOT considered an important rule to follow in developing the skill of listening?

   A. Be attentive and concentrate on what is being said.
   B. Concentrate on the spoken word without concern for implied meanings.
   C. Ask an occasional question when appropriate to the discussion.
   D. Make sure you understand fully what is being said.

3. A supervisor who is to direct a team of senior clerks and clerks in a complex project calls them together beforehand to inform them of the tasks each employee will perform on this job.
Of the following, the CHIEF value of this action by the supervisor is that each member of this team will be able to

   A. work independently in the absence of the supervisor
   B. understand what he will do and how this will fit into the total picture
   C. share in the process of decision-making as an equal participant
   D. judge how well the plans for this assignment have been made

4. A supervisor who has both younger and older employees under his supervision may sometimes find that employee absenteeism seriously interferes with accomplishment of goals.
Studies of such employee absenteeism have shown that the absences of employees

   A. under 35 years of age are usually unexpected and the absences of employees over 45 years are usually unnecessary
   B. of all age groups show the same characteristics as to length of absence

219

C. under 35 years of age are for frequent, short periods while the absences of employees over 45 years of age are less frequent but of longer duration
D. under 35 years of age are for periods of long duration and the absences of employees over 45 years of age are for periods of short duration

5. A long-standing procedure for getting a certain job done by subordinates is apparently a good procedure. Changes in some steps of the procedure are made from time to time to handle special problems that come up.
Reviewing this procedure periodically is *desirable* MAINLY because

   A. the system is working well
   B. checking routines periodically is a supervisor"s chief responsibility
   C. subordinates may be confused as to how the procedure operates as a result of the changes made
   D. it is necessary to determine whether the procedure has become outdated or is in need of improvement

6. In conducting an interview, the BEST type of questions with which to begin the interview are those which the person interviewed is _____ to answer.

   A. willing and able
   B. willing but unable
   C. able to, but unwilling
   D. unable and unwilling

7. In order to determine accurately a child's age, it is BEST for an interviewer to rely on

   A. the child's grade in school
   B. what the mother says
   C. birth records
   D. a library card

8. In his first interview with a new employee, it would be LEAST appropriate for a unit supervisor to

   A. find out the employee's preference for the several types of jobs to which he is able to assign him
   B. determine whether the employee will make good promotion material
   C. inform the employee of what his basic job responsibilities will be
   D. inquire about the employee's education and previous employment

9. If an interviewer takes care to phrase his questions carefully and precisely, the result will MOST probably be that

   A. he will be able to determine whether the person interviewed is being truthful
   B. the free flow of the interview will be lost
   C. he will get the information he wants
   D. he will ask stereotyped questions and narrow the scope of the interview

10. During an interview, the person interviewed is LEAST likely to be cautious about what he tells the interviewer

    A. shortly after the beginning when the questions normally suggest pleasant associations to the person interviewed
    B. as long as the interviewer keeps the questions to the point

C. at the point where the person interviewed gains a clear insight into the area being discussed
D. when the interview appears formally ended and good-byes are being said

11. In an interview held for the purpose of getting information from the person interviewed, it is sometimes desirable for the interviewer to repeat the answer he has received to a question.
For the interviewer to rephrase such an answer in his own words is good practice MAINLY because it

   A. gives the interviewer time to make up his next question
   B. gives the person interviewed a chance to correct any possible misunderstanding
   C. gives the person interviewed the feeling that the interviewer considers his answer important
   D. prevents the person interviewed from changing his answer

12. There are several methods of formulating questions during an interview. The particular method used should be adapted to the interview problems presented by the person being questioned.
Of the following methods of formulating questions during an interview, the ACCEPTABLE one is for the interviewer to ask questions which

   A. incorporate several items in order to allow a cooperative interviewee freedom to organize his statements
   B. are ambiguous in order to foil a distrustful inter-viewee
   C. suggest the correct answer in order to assist an interviewee who appears confused
   D. would help an otherwise unresponsive interviewee to become more responsive

13. An interviewer permits the person being interviewed to read the data the interviewer writes as he records the person's responses on a routine departmental form. This practice is

   A. *desirable,* because it serves to assure the person interviewed that his responses are being recorded accurately
   B. *undesirable,* because it prevents the interviewer from clarifying uncertain points by asking additional questions
   C. *desirable,* because it makes the time that the person interviewed must wait while the answer is written seem shorter
   D. *undesirable,* because it destroys the confidentiality of the interview

14. Suppose that a stranger enters the office of which you are in charge and asks for the address and telephone number of one of your employees.
The MOST appropriate reaction would be to

   A. find out why he needs the information and release it if his reason is a good one
   B. explain that you are not permitted to release such information to unauthorized persons
   C. give him the information but tell him it must be kept confidential
   D. ask him to leave the office immediately

15. A member of the public approaches an employee who is at work at his desk. The employee cannot interrupt his work in order to take care of this person.
The BEST and MOST courteous way of handling this situation is for the employee to

   A. avoid looking up from his work until he is finished with what he is doing
   B. tell this person that he will not be able to take care of him for quite a while
   C. refer the individual to another employee who can take care of him right away
   D. chat with the individual while he continues with his work

16. Some organizations, as a matter of policy, transfer their administrative staff personnel from one unit to another after stated periods of service in the unit.
The MAIN advantage of such a policy is that it

   A. helps keep the staff members abreast of the technical developments in their fields
   B. impedes the formation of personal cliques among staff members
   C. helps develop wider outlook and loyalty to the organization as a whole rather than to the unit assigned
   D. permits the more effective utilization of the individual talents of staff members

17. Leaders generally are somewhat more intelligent than their followers.
The CHIEF difficulty of the leader who is markedly more intelligent than his followers is that a leader has difficulty in

   A. overcoming the suspicion and distrust of intellectuals on the part of the group
   B. understanding the thought processes of persons who are intellectually inferior
   C. accepting the irrational and emotional basis of much of human conduct
   D. making himself understood by the group

18. A psychological study of leadership found that it is possible to predict the behavior of a new man in a leadership position more accurately on the basis of the behavior of his predecessor in the position than on the behavior of the man himself in his previous job.
The BEST explanation of this observation is that there is a tendency

   A. to select similar types of personalities to fill the same type of position
   B. for a newly appointed man to avoid instituting basic changes in operational procedures
   C. for a given organizational structure and set of duties to produce similar patterns of behavior
   D. for increased responsibility to impose more mature patterns of behavior on an incumbent

19. An administrative official finds that the reports reaching him from his subordinates tend to exaggerate the favorable and minimize the unfavorable aspects of situations existing within the unit.
The MOST valid conclusion to draw is that

   A. the administrative official has been overly severe with subordinates and has instilled fear in them
   B. there is a normal tendency for persons to represent themselves and their actions in the best possible light
   C. members of the department tend to be optimists
   D. the administrative official has not been sufficiently critical of previous reports and has not been alert to conditions in the unit

20. A special unit of a department is rife with rumors concerning plans for its future and the possibility of its abolition. As a result, morale and productivity of members assigned to it have suffered. To handle this situation, the administrative official in charge of the unit adopts a policy of promptly corroborating factual rumors and denying false ones.
    This method of dealing with the problem will achieve some good results, but its CHIEF weakness is that

    A. it gives status to the rumors by the attention paid to them
    B. the administrative official may not have the necessary information at hand to dispose promptly of all rumors
    C. it *chases* the rumors rather than forestalling them by giving information concerning the unit's future
    D. the administrative official may have confidential information which he should not divulge

21. An administrative official, realizing the importance of harmonious relationships within his unit, made a practice of unobtrusively intervening in any conflict situation between subordinates. Whenever friction seemed to be developing, he would attempt to soothe ruffled feelings, remove the source of difficulty by rescheduling activities or reassigning personnel, et cetera. His efforts were always behind-the-scenes and unknown to the employees involved. Although this method of operation produces some good results, its CHIEF drawback is that it

    A. violates the chain of command principle
    B. involves the administrative official in personal relationships which are not properly his concern
    C. requires confidential sources of information about relationships within the unit, which borders on spying
    D. permits subordinates to engage in unacceptable practices without correction

22. At a division conference at which a basic change in the department's procedure was to be announced, the conference leader started the discussion by asking the group for criticisms of the existing procedures. He then described the new procedures to be employed and explained the improvements in operations that were anticipated.
    The conference leader's method of introducing the change was

    A. *good,* mainly because the conference members would be more receptive to the new procedure if they understood the inadequacies of the old
    B. *bad,* mainly because the conference members would realize that the decision for change had been made before the discussion and without consideration of their comments
    C. *good,* mainly because the comments and criticisms of the old procedure would provide the basis for evaluating the feasibility of the new method
    D. *bad,* mainly because the focus of the discussion was on the procedure being replaced rather than on the procedure being introduced

23. A section chief in charge of a specialized unit calls a staff conference to discuss a proposed modification of some procedures. After making some introductory remarks, the chief wants the comments of the members of the staff. The staff consists of eight subordinates ranging in rank from office aide to principal administrative assistant III, each subordinate having responsibility for a different aspect of the program. Of the following, the BEST procedure for the chief to follow is to call upon each subordinate in

A. descending order of rank, mainly because the employees with the highest rank are likely to have the most experience and ability
B. ascending order of rank, mainly because the junior employees are more likely to be freer in their comments if they give their views before the senior employees speak
C. order of their specialized knowledge and competence in the subjects under discussion mainly because those with most knowledge and competence can best lead the discussion
D. order of seating around the table, mainly because informality of procedure and democrative leadership is obtained

24. As a supervisor assigned to a public relations unit in a city agency, you find a certain program under severe attack by a citizen's, group.
To be of GREATEST value to your supervisor, you should

    A. present the department side of the story to all meetings or to all groups whether hostile or not
    B. attempt to get another citizen's group to defend the department program
    C. get greater support from the general public and the press to effectuate the program
    D. ignore group opinions; rather, strive to affect individuals and let them persuade their groups

25. The commission has assigned you to present the department side to a group of citizens well-disposed to government programs.
You should present

    A. *only* the department side
    B. both sides of the story, but present the department side last
    C. both sides of the story, but present the department side first
    D. the facts and let the audience draw its own conclusion

KEY (CORRECT ANSWERS)

1.	B	11.	B
2.	B	12.	D
3.	B	13.	A
4.	C	14.	B
5.	D	15.	C
6.	A	16.	C
7.	C	17.	D
8.	B	18.	C
9.	C	19.	B
10.	D	20.	C

21. D
22. B
23. C
24. B
25. A

———

TEST 3

DIRECTIONS: Each question or incomplete statement is followed by several suggested answers or completions. Select the one that BEST answers the question or completes the statement. *PRINT THE LETTER OF THE CORRECT ANSWER IN THE SPACE AT THE RIGHT.*

1. Supervisor X, as a representative of the Commissioner, has been ordered to present the department arguments in reference to a new program of inspections and to emphasize such presentation by stressing the enforcement that will follow.
   In this instance,

   A. a mild threat is less of a deterrent than a strong threat
   B. any form of threat should be avoided since you are seeking cooperation
   C. an overly strong threat is less of a deterrent than a mild threat
   D. the mere statement that enforcement will follow is sufficient to effect cooperation

2. If, after an investigation and further consultation with central authorities, wholesale bribe-taking has been confirmed within a certain unit, the agency involved should

   A. withhold information from the public until a more secure image can be created
   B. break the story since such agency can present the least damaging picture
   C. arrange a compromise solution and present it to the public as an accomplished fact
   D. permit the central authorities to break the story since it presents a more efficient picture

3. The characteristic of flexibility versus stability of a policy seems contradictory to subordinate A.
   The difference can BEST be explained by the administrative manager if he points out that

   A. policies are decision guides and definite formulae for specific actions; therefore, stability must outweigh flexibility
   B. changing events and materials force a change in policy; therefore, flexibility refers to the ability to change policy when it becomes outmoded
   C. policy should be as stable as possible but sufficiently flexible to handle problems that vary from the normal; policy's true purpose must be understood as a guide for decisions, not an inflexible formula for action
   D. most policy at unit level is based on precedent and tradition and, therefore, subject always to the discretion of the supervisor

4. When an administrative manager devotes too much time to telling his subordinates how to handle their job problems, then he

   A. is spending too little time in formulating policies for the guidance of his subordinates
   B. is neglecting to delegate sufficient authority to his subordinates
   C. should immediately begin to plan for better use of his time
   D. should evaluate his approach to the administration of his section and establish better controls

5. Since the policies of a department are well established, an administrator does not need to formulate section policy. This statement is

   A. *true;* it is difficult for an administrator to establish a policy which will not in some way coincide or contradict established, overall policies
   B. *false;* department policies have to be broad enough to cover the whole organization; they are seldom detailed enough to guide a section in its internal organization
   C. *true;* the administrator's responsibility in this area is to formulate procedure to implement department policy
   D. *false;* uniformity of enforcement is essential, and this is impossible when the administrator does not establish his own section policy

6. Manager X, when giving a decision on a controversial item, reminds the subordinates of the policy under which such a decision was made.
   This reminder is

   A. *good;* the subordinates will be aware that he is not being arbitrary, operating by whim, or playing favorites
   B. *unnecessary;* policies have been explained over and over again to subordinates
   C. a form of buck-passing since the manager is blaming a policy for his unfavorable decision
   D. *bad;* policy commits management to specific decisions and, as such, should not be given unfavorable publicity

7. After objectives and policies have been stated, the next step should be to

   A. develop plans and procedures
   B. make forecasts
   C. examine conditions; gather data
   D. consider a budget

8. After establishing objectives and identifying problems and opportunities, the planning should be

   A. turned over to the controller. You can alter his plan if you do not agree.
   B. assigned to the division heads. Each will work out a plan for his own division
   C. a joint effort of the controller and other division heads. You and any staff experts available will cooperate and assist as planning progresses.
   D. a joint effort of all supervisors and subordinates

9. The MOST; accurate statement concerning plans and planning is:

   A. In the absence of an agency-wide plan, it is better to avoid planning in the individual work unit
   B. Every manager or supervisor must plan if he is to carry out his managerial functions
   C. Every manager should make a preliminary plan and then await the agency-wide plan
   D. The agency-wide plan should precede the preliminary plan

10. Objectives, programs, policies, budgets, and procedures are all _____ planning.

    A. elements of overall   B. guides for
    C. alternates to   D. methods of

11. Developing and understanding objectives, establishing policies, collecting data, developing alternative action proposals, and deciding on action are all

    A. steps in planning
    B. guidelines to consider in planning
    C. the action motif ascribed to planning
    D. alternatives to planning

12. Work measurement can be applied to operations where workload can be related to

    A. available personnel for the implementation of assigned tasks
    B. follow-up programs for continued progress
    C. cost abatement and optimum efficiency
    D. man-hour utilization on assigned tasks

13. If you ask for additional historical information on costs, caseloads, et cetera, you will be

    A. refining the forecast process
    B. developing the groundwork for forecasting
    C. estimating the future
    D. evaluating your research department's efficiency

14. Suppose that the majority of mathematical projections predicts a serious downturn in new cases, while you and your advisors believe that a mild upturn is approaching. In this situation, the BEST procedure is to

    A. follow the course dictated by the mathematical projections because that is what they are there for
    B. follow your own ideas and those of your advisors; management is an art, not a science
    C. modify the course dictated by the mathematical projections so as to reflect both management and specialist judgment
    D. consult another advisor

15. The director of a personnel bureau with 100 employees would probably operate MOST efficiently if he had under his immediate supervision approximately _____ subordinates.

    A. 5   B. 25   C. 50   D. 100

16. A worker is *usually* MOST productive when he is assigned to work which

    A. he is able to do best
    B. involves a variety of skills
    C. is under close supervision
    D. requires little skill

17. It is desirable for all staff specialists to have some knowledge of line activities PRIMARILY in order that they may

    A. direct line activities when necessary
    B. have a proper framework for research
    C. know how to deal with all types of personnel
    D. take cognizance of the agency's needs and problems

18. When a supervisor delegates an assignment, he should 18.____

    A. delegate his responsibility for the assignment
    B. make certain that the assignment is properly performed
    C. participate in the beginning and final stages of the assignment
    D. retain all authority needed to complete the assignment

19. Which one of the following is LEAST important in the management of a suggestion program? 19.____

    A. Giving awards which are of sufficient value to encourage competition
    B. Securing full support from the department's officers and executives
    C. Publicizing the program and the awards given
    D. Providing suggestion boxes in numerous locations

20. The MOST certain means to *decrease* morale is to 20.____

    A. insist on strict adherence to safety rules
    B. make each employee responsible for the tidiness of his work area
    C. overlook evidence of hostility between groups of employees
    D. provide strong, aggressive leadership

KEY (CORRECT ANSWERS)

1.	C	11.	A
2.	B	12.	D
3.	C	13.	B
4.	A	14.	C
5.	B	15.	A
6.	A	16.	A
7.	C	17.	D
8.	C	18.	B
9.	B	19.	D
10.	A	20.	C

SUPERVISION, ADMINISTRATION, MANAGEMENT, AND ORGANIZATION

EXAMINATION SECTION

TEST 1

DIRECTIONS: Each question or incomplete statement is followed by several suggested answers or completions. Select the one that BEST answers the question or completes the statement. *PRINT THE LETTER OF THE CORRECT ANSWER IN THE SPACE AT THE RIGHT.*

1. In coaching a subordinate on the nature of decision-making, an executive would be right if he stated that the one of the following which is general the BEST definition of decision-making is:
   A. Choosing between alternatives
   B. Making diagnoses of feasible ends
   C. Making diagnoses of feasible means
   D. Comparing alternatives

2. Of the following, which one would be LEAST valid as a purpose of an organizational policy statement?
   To
   A. keep personnel from performing improper actions and functions on routine matters
   B. prevent the mishandling of non-routine matters
   C. provide management personnel with a tool that precludes the need for their use of judgment
   D. provide standard decisions and approaches in handling problems of a recurrent nature

3. Much has been written criticizing bureaucratic organizations. Current thinking on the subject is GENERALLY that
   A. bureaucracy is on the way out
   B. bureaucracy, though not perfect, is unlikely to be replaced
   C. bureaucratic organizations are most effective in dealing with constant change
   D. bureaucratic organizations are most effective when dealing with sophisticated customers or clients

4. The development of alternate plans as a major step in planning will normally result in the planner having several possible courses of action available.
   GENERALLY, this is
   A. *desirable*, since such development helps to determine the most suitable alternative and to provide for the unexpected
   B. *desirable*, since such development makes the use of planning premises and constraints unnecessary

C. *undesirable*, since the planners should formulate only one way of achieving given goals at a given time
D. *undesirable*, since such action restricts efforts to modify the planning to take advantage of opportunities

5. The technique of departmentation by task force includes the assigning of a team or task force to a definite project or block of work which extends from the beginning to the completing of a wanted and definite type and quantity of work.
Of the following, the MOST important actor aiding the successful use of this technique *normally* is
   A. having the task force relatively large, at least one hundred members
   B. having a definite project termination date established
   C. telling each task force member what his next assignment will be only after the current project ends
   D. utilizing it only for projects that are regularly recurring

6. With respect to communication in small group settings such as may occur in business, government, and the military, it is generally TRUE that people usually derive more satisfaction and are usually more productive under conditions which
   A. permit communication only with superiors
   B. permit the minimum intragroup communication possible
   C. are generally restricted by management
   D. allow open communication among all group members

7. If an executive were asked to list some outstanding features of decentralization, which one of the following would NOT be such a feature?
Decentralization
   A. provides decision-making experience for lower level managers
   B. promotes uniformity of policy
   C. is a relatively new concept in management
   D. is similar to the belief in encouragement of free enterprise

8. Modern management experts have emphasized the importance of the informal organization in motivating employees to increase productivity.
Of the following, the characteristic which would have the MOST direct influence on employee motivation is the tendency of members of the informal organization to
   A. resist change
   B. establish their own norms
   C. have similar outside interests
   D. set substantially higher goals than those of management

9. According to leading management experts, the decision-making process contains separate and distinct steps that must be taken in an orderly sequence.
Of the following arrangements, which one is in CORRECT order?

A. I. Search for alternatives; II. diagnosis; III. comparison; IV. choice
B. I. Diagnose; II. comparison; III. search for alternatives; IV. choice
C. I. Diagnose; II. search for alternatives; III. comparison; IV. choice
D. I. Diagnose; II. search for alternatives; III. choice; IV. comparison

10. Of the following, the growth of professionalism in large organizations can PRIMARILY be expected to result in
    A. greater equalization of power
    B. increased authoritarianism
    C. greater organizational disloyalty
    D. increased promotion opportunities

10.____

11. Assume an executive carries out his responsibilities to his staff according to what is now known about managerial leadership.
    Which of the following statements would MOST accurately reflect his assumptions about proper management?
    A. Efficiency in operations results from allowing the human element to participate in a minimal way.
    B. Efficient operation result from balancing work considerations with personnel considerations.
    C. Efficient operation results from a workforce committed to its self-interest.
    D. Efficient operation results from staff relationships that produce a friendly work climate.

11.____

12. Assume that an executive is called upon to conduct a management audit. To do this properly, he would have to take certain steps in a specific sequence.
    Of the following steps, which step should this manager take FIRST?
    A. Managerial performance must be surveyed.
    B. A method of reporting must be established.
    C. Management auditing procedures and documentation must be developed.
    D. Criteria for the audit must be considered.

12.____

13. If a manager is required to conduct a scientific investigation of an organizational problem, the FIRST step he should take is to
    A. state his assumptions about the problem
    B. carry out a search for background information
    C. choose the right approach to investigate the validity of his assumptions
    D. define and state the problem

13.____

14. An executive would be right to assert that the principle of delegation states that decisions should be made PRIMARILY
    A. by persons in an executive capacity qualified to make them
    B. by persons in a non-executive capacity
    C. at as low an organization level of authority as practicable
    D. by the next lower level of authority

14.____

15. Of the following, which one is NOT regarded by management authorities as a FUNDAMENTAL characteristic of an *ideal* bureaucracy?
    A. Division of labor and specialization
    B. An established hierarchy
    C. Decentralization of authority
    D. A set of operating rules and regulations

16. As the number of subordinates in a manager's span of control increases, the ACTUAL number of possible relationships
    A. increases disproportionately to the number of subordinates
    B. increases in equal number to the number of subordinates
    C. reaches a stable level
    D. will first increase then slowly decrease

17. An executive's approach to controlling the activities of his subordinates concentrated on ends rather than means, and was diagnostic rather than punitive.
    This manager may MOST properly be characterized as using the managerial technique of management-by-
    A. exception   B. objectives   C. crisis   D. default

18. In conducting a training session on the administrative control process, which of the following statements would be LEAST valid for an executive to make? Controlling
    A. requires checking upon assignments to see what is being done
    B. involves comparing what is being done to what ought to be done
    C. requires corrective action when what is being done does not meet expectations
    D. occurs after all the other managerial processes have been performed

19. The "brainstorming" technique for creative solutions of management problems MOST generally consists of
    A. bringing staff together in an exchange of a quantity of freewheeling ideas
    B. isolating individual staff members to encourage thought
    C. developing improved office procedures
    D. preparation of written reports on complex problems

20. Computer systems hardware MOST often operates in relation to which one of the following steps in solving a data-processing problem?
    A. Determining the problem
    B. Defining and stating the problem
    C. Implementing the programmed solution
    D. Completing the documentation of every unexplored solution

21. There is a tendency in management to upgrade objectives.
    This trend is generally regarded as
    A. *desirable*; the urge to improve is demonstrated by adopting objectives that have been adjusted to provide improved service

B. *undesirable*; the typical manager searches for problems which obstruct his objectives
C. *desirable*; it is common for a manager to find that the details of an immediate operation have occupied so much of his time that he has lost sight of the basic overall objective
D. *undesirable*; efforts are wasted when they are expended on a mass of uncertain objectives, since the primary need of most organizations is a single target or several major ones

22. Of the following, it is generally LEAST effective for an executive to delegate authority where working conditions involve
    A. rules establishing normal operating procedures
    B. consistent methods of operation
    C. rapidly changing work standards
    D. complex technology

23. If an executive was explaining the difficulty of making decisions under *risk* conditions, he would be MOST accurate if he said that such decisions would be difficult to make when the decision maker has _____ information and experience and can expect _____ outcomes for each action.
    A. limited; many
    B. much; many
    C. much; few
    D. limited; few

24. If an executive were asked to list some outstanding features of centralized organization, which one of the following would be INCORRECT?
    Centralized organization
    A. lessens risks of errors by unskilled subordinates
    B. utilizes the skills of specialized experts at a central location
    C. produces uniformity of policy and non-uniformity of action
    D. enables closer control of operations than a decentralized set-up

25. It is possible for an organization's management to test whether or not the organization has a sound structure.
    Of the following, which one is NOT a test of soundness in an organization's structure?
    The
    A. ability to replace key personnel with minimum loss of effectiveness
    B. ability of information and decisions to flow more freely through the *grapevine* than through formal channels
    C. provision for orderly organizational growth with the ability to handle change as the need arises.

KEY (CORRECT ANSWERS)

1.	A	11.	B
2.	C	12.	D
3.	B	13.	D
4.	A	14.	C
5.	B	15.	C
6.	D	16.	A
7.	B	17.	B
8.	B	18.	D
9.	C	19.	A
10.	A	20.	C

21. A
22. C
23. A
24. C
25. B

TEST 2

DIRECTIONS: Each question or incomplete statement is followed by several suggested answers or completions. Select the one that BEST answers the question or completes the statement. *PRINT THE LETTER OF THE CORRECT ANSWER IN THE SPACE AT THE RIGHT.*

1. Management experts generally believe that computer-based management information systems (MIS) have greater potential for improving the process of management than any other development in recent decades.
   The one of the following which MOST accurately describes the objectives of MIS is to
   A. provide information for decision-making on planning, initiating, and controlling the operations of the various units of the organization
   B. establish mechanization of routine functions such as clerical records, payroll, inventory, and accounts receivable in order to promote economy and efficiency
   C. computerize decision-making on planning, initiative, organizing, and controlling the operations of an organization
   D. provide accurate facts and figures on the various programs of the organization to be used for purposes of planning and research

   1.____

2. The one of the following which is the BEST application on the *management-by-exception* principle is that this principle
   A. stimulates communication and aids in management of crisis situations, thus reducing the frequency of decision-making
   B. saves time and reserves top-management decisions only for crisis situations, thus reducing the frequency of decision-making
   C. stimulates communication, saves time, and reduces the frequency of decision-making
   D. is limited to crisis-management situations

   2.____

3. It is generally recognized that each organization is dependent upon availability of qualified personnel.
   Of the following, the MOST important factor affecting the availability of qualified people to each organization is
   A. innovations in technology and science
   B. the general decline in the educational levels of our population
   C. the rise of sentiment against racial discrimination
   D. pressure by organized community groups

   3.____

4. A fundamental responsibility of all managers is to decide what physical facilities and equipment are needed to help attain basic goals.
   Good planning for the purchase and use of equipment is seldom easy to do and is complicated MOST by the fact that
   A. organizations rarely have stable sources of supply
   B. nearly all managers tend to be better at personnel planning than at equipment planning

   4.____

C. decisions concerning physical resources are made too often on a *crash basis* rather than under carefully prepared policies
D. legal rulings relative to depreciation fluctuate very frequently

5. In attempting to reconcile managerial objectives and an individual employee's goals, it is generally LEAST desirable for management to
   A. recognize the capacity of the individual to contribute toward realization of managerial goals
   B. encourage self-development of the employee to exceed minimum job performance
   C. consider an individual employee's work separately from other employees
   D. demonstrate that an employee advances only to the extent that he contributes directly to the accomplishment of stated goals

6. As a management tool for discovering individual training needs a job analysis would generally be of LEAST assistance in determining
   A. the performance requirements of individual jobs
   B. actual employee performance on the job
   C. acceptable standards of performance
   D. training needs for individual jobs

7. One of the major concerns of organizational managers today is how the spread of automation will affect them and the status of their positions. Realistically speaking, one can say that the MOST likely effect of our newer forms of highly automated technology on managers will be to
   A. make most top-level positions superfluous or obsolete
   B. reduce the importance of managerial work in general
   C. replace the work of managers with the work of technicians
   D. increase the importance of and demand for top managerial personnel

8. Which one of the following is LEAST likely to be an area or cause of trouble in the use of staff people (e.g., assistants to the administrator)?
   A. Misunderstanding of the role the staff people are supposed to play, as a result of vagueness of definition of their duties and authority
   B. Tendency of staff personnel almost always to be older than line personnel at comparable salary levels with who they must deal
   C. Selection of staff personnel who fail to have simultaneously both competence in their specialties and skill in staff work
   D. The staff person fails to understand mixed staff and operating duties

9. The one of the following which is the BEST measure of decentralization in an agency is the
   A. amount of checking required on decisions made at lower levels in the chain of command
   B. amount of checking required on decisions made at lower levels of the chain of command and the number of functions affected thereby
   C. number of functions affected by decisions made at higher levels
   D. number of functions affected by middle echelon decision-making

10. Which of the following is generally NOT a valid statement with respect to the supervisory process?
    A. General supervision is more effective than close supervision.
    B. Employee-centered supervisors lead more effectively than do production-centered supervisors.
    C. Employee satisfaction is directly related to productivity.
    D. Low-producing supervisors use techniques that are different from high-producing supervisors.

11. The one of the following which is the MOST essential element for proper evaluation of the performance of subordinate supervisors is a
    A. careful definition of each supervisor's specific job responsibilities and of his progress in meeting mutually agreed upon work goals
    B. system of rewards and penalties based on each supervisor's progress in meeting clearly defined performance standards
    C. definition of personality traits, such as industry, initiative, dependability, and cooperativeness, required for effective job performance
    D. breakdown of each supervisor's job into separate components and a rating of his performance on each individual task

12. The one of the following which is the PRINCIPAL advantage of specialization for the operating efficiency of a public service agency is that specialization
    A. reduces the amount of red tape in coordinating the activities of mutually dependent departments
    B. simplifies the problem of developing adequate job controls
    C. provides employees with a clear understanding of the relationship of their activities to the overall objectives of the agency
    D. reduces destructive competition for power between departments

13. Of the following, the group which generally benefits MOST from supervisory training programs in public service agencies are those supervisors who have
    A. accumulated a long period of total service to the agency
    B. responsibility for a large number of subordinate personnel
    C. been in the supervisory ranks for a long period of time
    D. a high level of formalized academic training

14. A list of conditions which encourages good morale inside a work group would NOT include a
    A. high rate of agreement among group members on values and objectives
    B. tight control system to minimize the risk of individual error
    C. good possibility that joint action will accomplish goals
    D. past history of successful group accomplishment

15. Of the following, the MOST important factor to be considered in selecting a training strategy or program is the
    A. requirements of the job to be performed by the trainees
    B. educational level or prior training of the trainees
    C. size of the training group
    D. quality and competence of available training specialists

16. Of the following, the one which is considered to be LEAST characteristic of the higher ranks of management is
    A. that higher levels of management benefit from modern technology
    B. that success is measured by the extent to which objectives are achieved
    C. the number of subordinates that directly report to an executive
    D. the de-emphasis of individual and specialized performance

16.____

17. Assume that an executive is preparing a training syllabus to be used in training members of his staff.
Which of the following would NOT be a valid principle of the learning process for this manager to keep in mind in the preparation of the training syllabus?
    A. When a person has thoroughly learned a task, it takes a lot of effort to create a little more improvement.
    B. In complicated learning situations, there is a period in which an additional period of practice produces an equal amount of improvement in learning.
    C. The less a person knows about the task, the slower the initial progress.
    D. The more the person knows about the risk, the slower the initial progress.

17.____

18. Of the following, which statement BEST illustrates when collective bargaining agreements are working well?
    A. Executives strongly support subordinate managers.
    B. The management rights clause in the contract is clear and enforced.
    C. Contract provisions are competently interpreted.
    D. The provisions of the agreement are properly interpreted, communicated, and observed.

18.____

19. An executive who wishes to encourage subordinates to communicate freely with him about a job-related problem should FIRST
    A. state his own position on the problem before listening to the subordinates' ideas
    B. invite subordinates to give their own opinions on the problem
    C. ask subordinates for their reactions to his own ideas about the problem
    D. guard the confidentiality of management information about the problem

19.____

20. The ability to deal constructively with intra-organizational conflict is an essential attribute of the successful manager.
The one of the following types of conflict which would be LEAST difficult to handle constructively is a situation in which there is
    A. agreement on objectives, but disagreement as to the probable results of adopting the various alternatives
    B. agreement on objectives, disagreement on alternative courses of action, and relative certainty as to the outcome of one of the alternatives
    C. disagreement on objectives and on alternate courses of action, but relative certainty as to the outcome of the alternatives
    D. disagreement on objectives and on alternative course of action, but uncertainty as to the outcome of the alternatives

20.____

21. Which of the following statements is LEAST accurate in describing formal job evaluation and wage and salary classification plans? 21.____
    A. Parties that disagree on wage matters can examine an established system rather than unsupported opinions.
    B. The use of such plans tends to overlook the effect of age and seniority of employees on job values in the plan.
    C. Such plans can eliminate salary controversies in organizations designing and using them properly.
    D. These plans are not particularly useful in checking on executive compensation.

22. In carrying out disciplinary action, the MOST important procedure for all managers to follow is to 22.____
    A. sell all levels of management on the need for discipline from the organization's viewpoint
    B. follow up on a disciplinary action and not assume that the action has been effective
    C. convince all executives that proper discipline is a legitimate tool for their use
    D. convince all executives that they need to display confidence in the organization's rules

Questions 23-25.

DIRECTIONS: Questions 23 through 25 are to be answered on the basis of the following situation. Richard Ford, a top administrator, is responsible for output in his organization. Because productivity had been lagging for two periods in a row, Ford decided to establish a committee of his subordinate managers to investigate the reasons for the poor performance and to make recommendations for improvements. After two meetings, the committee came to the conclusions and made the recommendations that follow:

Output forecasts had been handed down from the top without prior consultation with middle management and first level supervision. Lines of authority and responsibility had been unclear. The planning and control process should be decentralized.
After receiving the committee's recommendations, Ford proceeded to take the following actions:
Ford decided he would retain final authority to establish quotas but would delegate to the middle managers the responsibility for meeting quotas.
After receiving Ford's decision, the middle managers proceeded to delegate to the first-line supervisors the authority to establish their own quotas. The middle managers eventually received and combined the first-line supervisors' quotas so that these conformed with Ford's.

23. Ford's decision to delegate responsibility for meeting quotas to the middle managers is INCONSISTENT with sound management principles because of which one of the following? 23.____
    A. Ford shouldn't have involved himself in the first place.
    B. Middle managers do not have the necessary skills.

C. Quotas should be established by the chief executive.
D. Responsibility should not be delegated.

24. The principle of co-extensiveness of responsibility and authority bears on Ford's decision.
    In this case, it IMPLIES that
    A. authority should exceed responsibility
    B. authority should be delegated to match the degree of responsibility
    C. both authority and responsibility should be retained and not delegated
    D. responsibility should be delegated but authority should be retained

25. The middle manager's decision to delegate to the first-line supervisors the authority to establish quotas was INCORRECTLY reasoned because
    A. delegation and control must go together
    B. first-line supervisors are in no position to establish quotas
    C. one cannot delegate authority that one does not possess
    D. the meeting of quotas should not be delegated

KEY (CORRECT ANSWERS)

1.	A		11.	A
2.	C		12.	B
3.	A		13.	D
4.	C		14.	B
5.	C		15.	A
6.	B		16.	C
7.	D		17.	D
8.	B		18.	D
9.	B		19.	B
10.	C		20.	B

21.	C
22.	B
23.	D
24.	B
25.	C

TEST 3

DIRECTIONS: Each question or incomplete statement is followed by several suggested answers or completions. Select the one that BEST answers the question or completes the statement. *PRINT THE LETTER OF THE CORRECT ANSWER IN THE SPACE AT THE RIGHT.*

1. A danger which exists in any organization as complex as that required for administration of a large public agency is that each department comes to believe that it exists for its own sake.
   The one of the following which has been attempted in some organizations as a cure for this condition is to
   A. build up the departmental esprit de corps
   B. expand the functions and jurisdictions of the various departments so that better integration is possible
   C. develop a body of specialists in the various subject matter fields which cut across departmental lines
   D. delegate authority to the lowest possible echelon
   E. systematically transfer administrative personnel from one department to another

   1.____

2. At best, the organization chart is ordinarily and necessarily an idealized picture of the intent of top management, a reflection of hopes and aims rather than a photograph of the operating facts within the organization.
   The one of the following which is the basic reason for this is that the organization chart
   A. does not show the flow of work within the organization
   B. speaks in terms of positions rather than of live employees
   C. frequently contains unresolved internal ambiguities
   D. is a record of past organization or proposed future organization and never a photograph of the living organization
   E. does not label the jurisdiction assigned to each component unit

   2.____

3. The drag of inadequacy is always downward. The need in administration is always for the reverse; for a department head to project his thinking to the city level, for the unit chief to try to see the problems of the department.
   The inability of a city administration to recruit administrators who can satisfy this need usually results in departments characterized by
   A. disorganization   B. poor supervision
   C. circumscribed viewpoints   D. poor public relations
   E. a lack of programs

   3.____

4. When, as a result of a shift in public sentiment, the elective officers of a city are changed, is it desirable for career administrators to shift ground without performing any illegal or dishonest act in order to conform to the policies of the new elective officers?
   A. *No*; the opinions and beliefs of the career officials are the result of long experience in administration and are more reliable than those of politicians

   4.____

B. *Yes*; only in this way can citizens, political officials, and career administrators alike have confidence in the performance of their respective functions
C. *No*; a top career official who is so spineless as to change his views or procedures as a result of public opinion is of little value to the public service
D. *Yes*; legal or illegal, it is necessary that a city employee carry out the orders of his superior officers
E. *No*; shifting ground with every change in administration will preclude the use of a constant overall policy

5. Participation in developing plans which will affect levels in the organization in addition to his own, will contribute to an individual's understanding of the entire system. When possible, this should be encouraged.
   This policy is, in general,
   A. *desirable*; the maintenance of any organization depends upon individual understanding
   B. *undesirable*; employees should participate only in these activities which affect their own level, otherwise conflicts in authority may arise
   C. *desirable*; an employee's will to contribute to the maintenance of an organization depends to a great extent on the level which he occupies
   D. *undesirable*; employees can be trained more efficiently and economically in an organized training program than by participating in plan development
   E. *desirable*; it will enable the employee to make intelligent suggestions for adjustment of the plan in the future

6. Constant study should be made of the information contained in reports to isolate those elements of experience which are static, those which are variable and repetitive, and those which are variable and due to chance.
   Knowledge of those elements of experience in his organization which are static or constant will enable the operating official to
   A. fix responsibility for their supervisor at a lower level
   B. revise the procedure in order to make the elements variable
   C. arrange for follow-up and periodic adjustment
   D. bring related data together
   E. provide a frame of reference within which detailed standards for measurement can be installed

7. A chief staff officer, serving as one of the immediate advisors to the department head, has demonstrated a special capacity for achieving internal agreements and for sound judgment. As a result he has been used more and more as a source of counsel and assistance by the department head. Other staff officers and line officials as well have discovered that it is wise for them to check with this colleague in advance on all problematical matters handed up to the department head.

Developments such as this are
- A. *undesirable*; they disrupt the normal lines for flow of work in an organization
- B. *desirable*; they allow an organization to make the most of its strength wherever such strength resides
- C. *undesirable*; they tend to undermine the authority of the department head and put it in the hands of a staff officer who does not have the responsibility
- D. *desirable*; they tend to resolve internal ambiguities in organization
- E. *undesirable*; they make for bad morale by causing *cutthroat* competition

8. A common difference among executives is that some are not content unless they are out in front of everything that concerns their organization, while others prefer to run things by pulling strings, by putting others out in front and by stepping into the breach only when necessary.
Generally speaking, an advantage this latter method of operation has over the former is that it
- A. results in a higher level of morale over a sustained period of time
- B. gets results by exhortation and direct stimulus
- C. makes it unnecessary to calculate integrated moves
- D. makes the personality of the executive felt further down the line
- E. results in the executive getting the reputation for being a good fellow

8.____

9. Administrators frequently have to get facts by interviewing people. Although the interview is a legitimate fact gathering technique, it has definite limitations which should not be overlooked.
The one of the following which is an important limitation is that
- A. people who are interviewed frequently answer questions with guesses rather than admit their ignorance
- B. it is a poor way to discover the general attitude and thinking of supervisors interviewed
- C. people sometimes hesitate to give information during an interview which they will submit in written form
- D. it is a poor way to discover how well employees understand departmental policies
- E. the material obtained from the interview can usually be obtained at lower cost from existing records

9.____

10. It is desirable and advantageous to leave a maximum measure of planning responsibility to operating agencies or units, rather than to remove the responsibility to a central planning staff agency.
Adoption of the former policy (decentralized planning) would lead to
- A. *less effective planning*; operating personnel do not have the time to make long-term plans
- B. *more effective planning*; operating units are usually better equipped technically than any staff agency and consequently are in a better position to set up valid plans
- C. *less effective planning*; a central planning agency has a more objective point of view than any operating agency can achieve

10.____

D. *more effective planning*; plans are conceived in terms of the existing situation and their execution is carried out with the will to succeed
E. *less effective planning*; there is little or no opportunity to check deviation from plans in the proposed set-up

Questions 11-15.

DIRECTIONS: The following sections appeared in a report on the work production of two bureaus of a department. Base your answers to Questions 11 through 15 on this information. Throughout the report, assume that each month has 4 weeks.

Each of the two bureaus maintains a chronological file. In Bureau A, every 9 months on the average, this material fills a standard legal size cabinet sufficient for 12,000 work units. In Bureau B the same type of cabinet is filled in 18 months. Each bureau maintains three complete years of information plus a current file. When the current file cabinet is filled, the cabinet containing the oldest material is emptied, the contents disposed of, and the cabinet used for current material. The similarity of these operations makes it possible to consolidate these files with little effort.

Study of the practice of using typists as filing clerks for periods when there is no typing work showed: (1) Bureau A has for the past 6 months completed a total of 1,500 filing work units a week using on the average 100 man-hours of trained file clerk time and 20 man-hours of typist time; (2) Bureau B has in the same period completed a total of 2,000 filing work units a week using on the average 125 man-hours of trained file clerk time and 60 hours of typist time. This includes all work in chronological files. Assuming that all clerks work at the same speed and that all typists work at the same speed, this indicates that work other than filing should be found for typists or that they should be given some training in the filing procedures used. It should be noted that Bureau A has not been producing the 1,600 units of technical (not filing) work per 30-day period required by Schedule K, but is at present 200 units behind. The Bureau should be allowed 3 working days to get on schedule.

11. What percentage (approximate) of the total number of filing work units completed in both units consists of the work involved in the maintenance of the chronological files?
   A. 5%   B. 10%   C. 15%   D. 20%   E. 25%

11._____

12. If the two chronological files are consolidated, the number of months which should be allowed for filling a cabinet is
   A. 2   B. 4   C. 6   D. 8   E. 14

12._____

13. The MAXIMUM number of file cabinets which can be released for other uses as a result of the consolidation recommended is
   A. 0
   B. 1
   C. 2
   D. 3
   E. not determinable on the basis of the data given

13._____

14. If all the filing work for both units is consolidated without diminution in the amount to be done and all filing work is done by trained file clerks, the number of clerks required (35-hour work week) is
    A. 4   B. 5   C. 6   D. 7   E. 8

14.____

15. In order to comply with the recommendation with respect to Schedule K, the present work production of Bureau A must be increased by
    A. 50%
    B. 100%
    C. 150%
    D. 200%
    E. an amount which is not determinable

15.____

16. A certain training program during World War II resulted in the training of thousands of supervisors in industry. The methods of this program were later successfully applied in various government agencies. The program was based upon the assumption that there is an irreducible minimum of three supervisory skills.
    The one of these skills among the following is
    A. to know how to perform the job at hand well
    B. to be able to deal personally with workers, especially face-to-face
    C. to be able to imbue workers with the will to perform the job well
    D. to know the kind of work that is done by one's unit and the policies and procedures of one's agency
    E. the *know-how* of administrative and supervisory processes

16.____

17. A comment made by an employee about a training course was, "*We never have any idea how we ae getting along in that course.*"
    The fundamental error in training methods to which this criticism points is
    A. insufficient student participation
    B. failure to develop a feeling of need or active want for the material being presented
    C. the training sessions may be too long
    D. no attempt may have been made to connect the new material with what was already known
    E. no goals have been set for the students

17.____

18. Assume that you are attending a departmental conference on efficiency ratings at which it is proposed that a man-to-man rating scale be introduced.
    You should point out that, of the following, the CHIEF weakness of the man-to-man rating scale is that
    A. it involves abstract numbers rather than concrete employee characteristics
    B. judges are unable to select their own standards for comparison
    C. the standard for comparison shifts from man-to-man for each person rated
    D. not every person rated is given the opportunity to serve as a standard for comparison
    E. standards for comparison will vary from judge to judge

18.____

19. Assume that you are conferring with a supervisor who has assigned to his subordinates efficiency ratings which you believe to be generally too low. The supervisor argues that his ratings are generally low because his subordinates are generally inferior.
Of the following, the evidence MOST relevant to the point at issue can be secured by comparing efficiency ratings assigned by the supervisor
    A. with ratings assigned by other supervisors in the same agency
    B. this year with ratings assigned by him in previous years
    C. to men recently transferred to his unit with ratings previously earned by these men
    D. with the general city average of ratings assigned by all supervisors to all employees
    E. with the relative order of merit of his employees as determined independently by promotion test marks

19.____

20. The one of the following which is NOT among the most common of the compensable factors used in wage evaluation studies is
    A. initiative and ingenuity required
    B. physical demand
    C. responsibility for the safety of others
    D. working conditions
    E. presence of avoidable hazards

20.____

21. If independent functions are separated, there is an immediate gain in conserving special skills. If we are to make optimum use of the abilities of our employees, these skills must be conserved.
Assuming the correctness of this statement, it follows that
    A. if we are not making optimum use of employee abilities, independent functions have not been separated
    B. we are making optimum uses of employee abilities if we conserve special skills
    C. we are making optimum use of employee abilities if independent functions have been separated
    D. we are not making optimum use of employee abilities if we do not conserve special skills
    E. if special skills are being conserved, independent functions need not be separated

21.____

22. A reorganization of the bureau to provide for a stenographic pool instead of individual unit stenographers will result in more stenographic help being available to each unit when it is required, and consequently will result in greater productivity for each unit. An analysis of the space requirements shows that setting up a stenographic pool will require a minimum of 400 square feet of good space. In order to obtain this space, it will be necessary to reduce the space available for technical personnel, resulting in lesser productivity for each unit.

22.____

On the basis of the above discussion, it can be stated that, in order to obtain greater productivity for each unit,
- A. a stenographic pool should be set up
- B. further analysis of the space requirement should be made
- C. it is not certain as to whether or not a stenographic pool should be set up
- D. the space available for each technician should be increased in order to compensate for the absence of a stenographic pool
- E. a stenographic pool should not be set up

23. The adoption of single consolidated form will mean that most of the form will not be used in any one operation. This would create waste and confusion. This conclusion is based upon the unstated hypothesis that
    - A. if waste and confusion are to be avoided, a single consolidated form should be used
    - B. if a single consolidated form is constructed, most of it can be used in each operation
    - C. if waste and confusion are to be avoided, most of the form employed should be used
    - D. most of a single consolidation form is not used
    - E. a single consolidated form should not be used

23._____

KEY (CORRECT ANSWERS)

1.	E	11.	C
2.	B	12.	C
3.	C	13.	B
4.	B	14.	D
5.	E	15.	E
6.	A	16.	B
7.	B	17.	E
8.	A	18.	E
9.	A	19.	C
10.	D	20.	E

21. D
22. C
23. C

PRINCIPLES AND PRACTICES, OF ADMINISTRATION, SUPERVISION AND MANAGEMENT

TABLE OF CONTENTS

	Page
GENERAL ADMINISTRATION	1
SEVEN BASIC FUNCTIONS OF THE SUPERVISOR	2
I. Planning	2
II. Organizing	3
III. Staffing	3
IV. Directing	3
V. Coordinating	3
VI. Reporting	3
VII. Budgeting	3
PLANNING TO MEET MANAGEMENT GOALS	4
I. What is Planning	4
II. Who Should Make Plans	4
III. What are the Results of Poor Planning	4
IV. Principles of Planning	4
MANAGEMENT PRINCIPLES	5
I. Management	5
II. Management Principles	5
III. Organization Structure	6
ORGANIZATION	8
I. Unity of Command	8
II. Span of Control	8
III. Uniformity of Assignment	9
IV. Assignment of Responsibility and Delegation of Authority	9
PRINCIPLES OF ORGANIZATION	9
I. Definition	9
II. Purpose of Organization	9
III. Basic Considerations in Organizational Planning	9
IV. Bases for Organization	10
V. Assignment of Functions	10
VI. Delegation of Authority and Responsibility	10
VII. Employee Relationships	11

DELEGATING		11
I.	WHAT IS DELEGATING:	11
II.	TO WHOM TO DELEGATE	11
REPORTS		12
I.	DEFINITION	12
II.	PURPOSE	12
III.	TYPES	12
IV.	FACTORS TO CONSIDER BEFORE WRITING REPORT	12
V.	PREPARATORY STEPS	12
VI.	OUTLINE FOR A RECOMMENDATION REPORT	12
MANAGEMENT CONTROLS		13
I.	Control	13
II.	Basis for Control	13
III.	Policy	13
IV.	Procedure	14
V.	Basis of Control	14
FRAMEWORK OF MANAGEMENT		14
I.	Elements	14
II.	Manager's Responsibility	15
III.	Control Techniques	16
IV.	Where Forecasts Fit	16
PROBLEM SOLVING		16
I.	Identify the Problem	16
II.	Gather Data	17
III.	List Possible Solutions	17
IV.	Test Possible Solutions	18
V.	Select the Best Solution	18
VI.	Put the Solution into Actual Practice	19
COMMUNICATION		19
I.	What is Communication?	19
II.	Why is Communication Needed?	19
III.	How is Communication Achieved?	20
IV.	Why Does Communication Fail?	21
V.	How to Improve Communication	21
VI.	How to Determine If You Are Getting Across	21
VII.	The Key Attitude	22
HOW ORDERS AND INSTRUCTIONS SHOULD BE GIVEN		22
I.	Characteristics of Good Orders and Instructions	22
FUNCTIONS OF A DEPARTMENT PERSONNEL OFFICE		23

SUPERVISION	23
I. Leadership	23
A. The Authoritarian Approach	23
B. The Laissez-Faire Approach	24
C. The Democratic Approach	24
II. Nine Points of Contrast Between Boss and Leader	25
EMPLOYEE MORALE	25
I. Some Ways to Develop and Maintain Good Employee Morale	25
II. Some Indicators of Good Morale	26
MOTIVATION	26
EMPLOYEE PARTICIPATION	27
I. WHAT IS PARTICIPATION	27
II. WHY IS IT IMPORTANT?	27
III. HOW MAY SUPERVISORS OBTAIN IT?	28
STEPS IN HANDLING A GRIEVANCE	28
DISCIPLINE	29
I. THE DISCIPLINARY INTERVIEW	29
II. PLANNING THE INTERVIEW	29
III. CONDUCTING THE INTERVIEW	30

PRINCIPLES AND PRACTICES, OF ADMINISTRATION, SUPERVISION AND MANAGEMENT

Most people are inclined to think of administration as something that only a few persons are responsible for in a large organization. Perhaps this is true if you are thinking of Administration with a capital A, but administration with a lower case a is a responsibility of supervisors at all levels each working day.

All of us feel we are pretty good supervisors and that we do a good job of administering the workings of our agency. By and large, this is true, but every so often it is good to check up on ourselves. Checklists appear from time to time in various publications which psychologists say tell whether or not a person will make a good wife, husband, doctor, lawyer, or supervisor.

The following questions are an excellent checklist to test yourself as a supervisor and administrator.

Remember, Administration gives direction and points the way but administration carries the ideas to fruition. Each is dependent on the other for its success. Remember, too, that no unit is too small for these departmental functions to be carried out. These statements apply equally as well to the Chief Librarian as to the Department Head with but one or two persons to supervise.

GENERAL ADMINISTRATION: General Responsibilities of Supervisors

1. Have I prepared written statements of functions, activities, and duties for my organizational unit?

2. Have I prepared procedural guides for operating activities?

3. Have I established clearly in writing, lines of authority and responsibility for my organizational unit?

4. Do I make recommendations for improvements in organization, policies, administrative and operating routines and procedures, including simplification of work and elimination of non-essential operations?

5. Have I designated and trained an understudy to function in my absence?

6. Do I supervise and train personnel within the unit to effectively perform their assignments?

7. Do I assign personnel and distribute work on such a basis as to carry out the organizational unit's assignment or mission in the most effective and efficient manner?

8. Have I established administrative controls by:

    a. Fixing responsibility and accountability on all supervisors under my direction for the proper performance of their functions and duties.

b. Preparations and submitting periodic work load and progress reports covering the operations of the unit to my immediate superior.

c. Analysis and evaluation of such reports received from subordinate units.

d. Submission of significant developments and problems arising within the organizational unit to my immediate superior.

e. Conducting conferences, inspections, etc., as to the status and efficiency of unit operations.

9. Do I maintain an adequate and competent working force?

10. Have I fostered good employee-department relations, seeing that established rules, regulations, and instructions are being carried out properly?

11. Do I collaborate and consult with other organizational units performing related functions to insure harmonious and efficient working relationships?

12. Do I maintain liaison through prescribed channels with city departments and other governmental agencies concerned with the activities of the unit?

13. Do I maintain contact with and keep abreast of the latest developments and techniques of administration (professional societies, groups, periodicals, etc.) as to their applicability to the activities of the unit?

14. Do I communicate with superiors and subordinates through prescribed organizational channels?

15. Do I notify superiors and subordinates in instances where bypassing is necessary as soon thereafter as practicable?

16. Do I keep my superior informed of significant developments and problems?

SEVEN BASIC FUNCTIONS OF THE SUPERVISOR

I. PLANNING
This means working out goals and means to obtain goals. <u>What</u> needs to be done, <u>who</u> will do it, <u>how</u>, <u>when</u>, and <u>where</u> it is to be done.

SEVEN STEPS IN PLANNING

A. Define job or problem clearly.
B. Consider priority of job.
C. Consider time-limit—starting and completing.
D. Consider minimum distraction to, or interference with, other activities.
E. Consider and provide for contingencies—possible emergencies.
F. Break job down into components.

G. Consider the 5 W's and H:
   WHY..........is it necessary to do the job? (Is the purpose clearly defined?)
   WHAT........needs to be done to accomplish the defined purpose?
   ....is needed to do the job? (Money, materials, etc.)
   WHO..........is needed to do the job?
   ....will have responsibilities?
   WHERE......is the work to be done?
   WHEN........is the job to begin and end? (Schedules, etc.)
   HOW..........is the job to bed done? (Methods, controls, records, etc.)

II. ORGANIZING

This means dividing up the work, establishing clear lines of responsibility and authority and coordinating efforts to get the job done.

III. STAFFING

The whole personnel function of bringing in and <u>training</u> staff, getting the right man and fitting him to the right job—the job to which he is best suited.

In the normal situation, the supervisor's responsibility regarding staffing normally includes providing accurate job descriptions, that is, duties of the jobs, requirements, education and experience, skills, physical, etc.; assigning the work for maximum use of skills; and proper utilization of the probationary period to weed out unsatisfactory employees.

IV. DIRECTING

Providing the necessary leadership to the group supervised. Important work gets done to the supervisor's satisfaction.

V. COORDINATING

The all-important duty of inter-relating the various parts of the work.
The supervisor is also responsible for controlling the coordinated activities. This means measuring performance according to a time schedule and setting quotas to see that the goals previously set are being reached. Reports from workers should be analyzed, evaluated, and made part of all future plans.

VI. REPORTING

This means proper and effective communication to your superiors, subordinates, and your peers (in definition of the job of the supervisor). Reports should be read and information contained therein should be used, not be filed away and forgotten. Reports should be written in such a way that the desired action recommended by the report is forthcoming.

VII. BUDGETING
This means controlling current costs and forecasting future costs. This forecast is based on past experience, future plans and programs, as well as current costs.

You will note that these seven functions can fall under three topics:

Planning) Make a plan
Organizing)

Staffing)
Directing) Get things done
Controlling)

Reporting) Watch it work
Budgeting)

PLANNING TO MEET MANAGEMENT GOALS

I. WHAT IS PLANNING?

   A. Thinking a job through before new work is done to determine the best way to do it
   B. A method of doing something
   C. Ways and means for achieving set goals
   D. A means of enabling a supervisor to deliver with a minimum of effort, all details involved in coordinating his work

II. WHO SHOULD MAKE PLANS?

   Everybody!
   All levels of supervision must plan work. (Top management, heads of divisions or bureaus, first line supervisors, and individual employees.) The higher the level, the more planning required.

III. WHAT ARE THE RESULTS OF POOR PLANNING?

   A. Failure to meet deadline
   B. Low employee morale
   C. Lack of job coordination
   D. Overtime is frequently necessary
   E. Excessive cost, waste of material and manhours

IV. PRINCIPLES OF PLANNING

   A. Getting a clear picture of your objectives. What exactly are you trying to accomplish?
   B. Plan the whole job, then the parts, in proper sequence.
   C. Delegate the planning of details to those responsible for executing them.
   D. Make your plan flexible.
   E. Coordinate your plan with the plans of others so that the work may be processed with a minimum of delay.
   F. Sell your plan before you execute it.
   G. Sell your plan to your superior, subordinate, in order to gain maximum participation and coordination.
   H. Your plan should take precedence. Use knowledge and skills that others have brought to a similar job.
   I. Your plan should take account of future contingencies; allow for future expansion.
   J. Plans should include minor details. Leave nothing to chance that can be anticipated.
   K. Your plan should be simple and provide standards and controls. Establish quality and quantity standards and set a standard method of doing the job. The controls will indicate whether the job is proceeding according to plan.
   L. Consider possible bottlenecks, breakdowns, or other difficulties that are likely to arise.

V. Q. WHAT ARE THE YARDSTICKS BY WHICH PLANNING SHOULD BE MEASURED?
   A. Any plan should:
   — Clearly state a definite course of action to be followed and goal to be achieved, with consideration for emergencies.
   — Be realistic and practical.
   — State what's to be done, when it's to be done, where, how, and by whom.
   — Establish the most efficient sequence of operating steps so that more is accomplished in less time, with the least effort, and with the best quality results.
   — Assure meeting deliveries without delays.
   — Establish the standard by which performance is to be judged.

   Q. WHAT KINDS OF PLANS DOES EFFECTIVE SUPERVISION REQUIRE?
   A. Plans should cover such factors as:
   — Manpower: right number of properly trained employees on the job
   — Materials: adequate supply of the right materials and supplies
   — Machines: full utilization of machines and equipment, with proper maintenance
   — Methods: most efficient handling of operations
   — Deliveries: making deliveries on time
   — Tools: sufficient well-conditioned tools
   — Layout: most effective use of space
   — Reports: maintaining proper records and reports
   — Supervision: planning work for employees and organizing supervisor's own time

MANAGEMENT PRINCIPLES

I. MANAGEMENT
    Q. What do we mean by management?
    A. Getting work done through others.

    Management could also be defined as planning, directing, and controlling the operations of a bureau or division so that all factors will function properly and all persons cooperate efficiently for a common objective.

II. MANAGEMENT PRINCIPLES

    A. There should be a hierarchy—wherein authority and responsibility run upward and downward through several levels—with a broad base at the bottom and a single head at the top.

    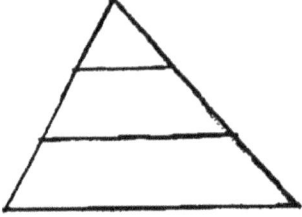

    B. Each and every unit or person in the organization should be answerable ultimately to the manager at the apex. In other words, *The buck stops here!*

C. Every necessary function involved in the bureau's objectives is assigned to a unit in that bureau.

D. Responsibilities assigned to a unit are specifically clear-cut and understood.

E. Consistent methods of organizational structure should be applied at each level of the organization.

F. Each member of the bureau from top to bottom knows: to whom he reports and who reports to him.

G. No member of one bureau reports to more than one supervisor. No dual functions.

H. Responsibility for a function is matched by authority necessary to perform that function. Weight of authority.

I. Individuals or units reporting to a supervisor do not exceed the number which can be feasibly and effectively coordinated and directed. Concept of *span of control.*

J. Channels of command (management) are not violated by staff units, although there should be staff services to facilitate and coordinate management functions.

K. Authority and responsibility should be decentralized to units and individuals who are responsible for the actual performance of operations.
Welfare – down to Welfare Centers
Hospitals – down to local hospitals

L. Management should exercise control through attention to policy problems of exceptional performance, rather than through review of routine actions of subordinates.

M. Organizations should never be permitted to grow so elaborate as to hinder work accomplishments.

III. ORGANIZATION STRUCTURE

Types of Organizations
The purest form is a leader and a few followers, such as:

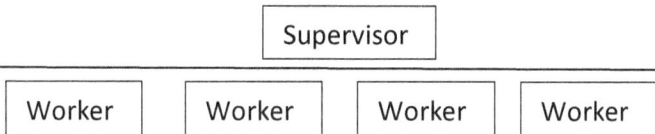

(Refer to organization chart) from supervisor to workers.

The line of authority is direct, The workers know exactly where they stand in relation to their boss, to whom they report for instructions and direction.

Unfortunately, in our present complex society, few organizations are similar to this example of a pure line organization. In this era of specialization, other people are often needed in the simplest of organizations. These specialists are known as staff. The sole purpose for their existence (staff) is to assist, advise, suggest, help or counsel line organizations. Staff has no authority to direct line people—nor do they give them direct instructions.

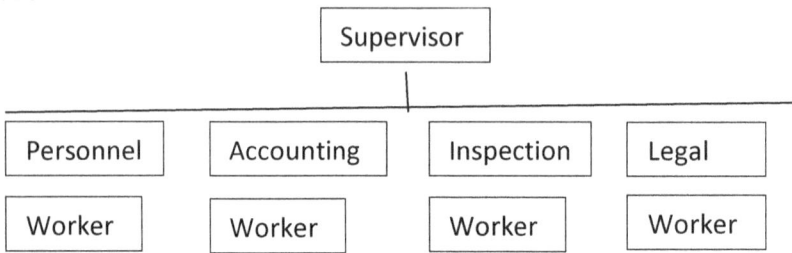

Line Functions
1. Directs
2. Orders
3. Responsibility for carrying out activities from beginning to end
4. Follows chain of command
5. Is identified with what it does
6. Decides when and how to use staff advice
7. Line executes

Staff Functions
1. Advises
2. Persuades and sells
3. Staff studies, reports, recommends but does not carry out
4. May advise across department lines
5. May find its ideas identified with others
6. Has to persuade line to want its advice
7. Staff: Conducts studies and research. Provides advice and instructions in technical matters. Serves as technical specialist to render specific services.

Types and Functions of Organization Charts
An organization chart is a picture of the arrangement and inter-relationship of the subdivisions of an organization.

A. Types of Charts:
   1. Structural: basic relationships only
   2. Functional: includes functions or duties
   3. Personnel: positions, salaries, status, etc.
   4. Process Chart: work performed
   5. Gantt Chart: actual performance against planned
   5. Flow Chart: flow and distribution of work

B. Functions of Charts:
   1. Assist in management planning and control
   2. Indicate duplication of functions
   3. Indicate incorrect stressing of functions
   4. Indicate neglect of important functions
   5. Correct unclear authority
   6. Establish proper span of control

C. Limitations of Charts:
   1. Seldom maintained on current basis
   2. Chart is oversimplified
   3. Human factors cannot adequately be charted

D. Organization Charts should be:
   1. Simple
   2. Symmetrical
   3. Indicate authority
   4. Line and staff relationship differentiated
   5. Chart should be dated and bear signature of approving officer
   6. Chart should be displayed, not hidden

ORGANIZATION

There are four basic principles of organization:
1. Unity of command
2. Span of control
3. Uniformity of assignment
4. Assignment of responsibility and delegation of authority

I. UNITY OF COMMAND

Unity of command means that each person in the organization should receive orders from one, and only one, supervisor. When a person has to take orders from two or more people, (a) the orders may be in conflict and the employee is upset because he does not know which he should obey, or (b) different orders may reach him at the same time and he does not know which he should carry out first.

Equally as bad as having two bosses is the situation where the supervisor is bypassed. Let us suppose you are a supervisor whose boss bypasses you (deals directly with people reporting to you). To the worker, it is the same as having two bosses; but to you, the supervisor, it is equally serious. Bypassing on the part of your boss will undermine your authority, and the people under you will begin looking to your boss for decisions and even for routine orders.

You can prevent bypassing by telling the people you supervise that if anyone tries to give them orders, they should direct that person to you.

II. SPAN OF CONTROL

Span of control on a given level involves:
A. The number of people being supervised
B. The distance
C The time involved in supervising the people. (One supervisor cannot supervise too many workers effectively.)

Span of control means that a supervisor has the right number (not too many and not too few) of subordinates that he can supervise well.

III. UNIFORMITY OF ASSIGNMENT

In assigning work, you as the supervisor should assign to each person jobs that are similar in nature. An employee who is assigned too many different types of jobs will waste time in going from one kind of work to another. It takes time for him to get to top production in one kind of task and, before he does so, he has to start on another.
When you assign work to people, remember that:

A. Job duties should be definite. Make it clear from the beginning <u>what</u> they are to do, <u>how</u> they are to do it, and <u>why</u> they are to do it. Let them know how much they are expected to do and how well they are expected to do it.
B. Check your assignments to be certain that there are no workers with too many unrelated duties, and that no two people have been given overlapping responsibilities. Your aim should be to have every task assigned to a specific person with the work fairly distributed and with each person doing his part.

IV. ASSIGNMENT OF RESPONSIBILITY AND DELEGATION OF AUTHORITY

A supervisor cannot delegate his final responsibility for the work of his department. The experienced supervisor knows that he gets his work done through people. He can't do it all himself. So he must assign the work and the responsibility for the work to his employees. Then they must be given the authority to carry out their responsibilities.

By assigning responsibility and delegating authority to carry out the responsibility, the supervisor builds in his workers initiative, resourcefulness, enthusiasm, and interest in their work. He is treating them as responsible adults. They can find satisfaction in their work, and they will respect the supervisor and be loyal to the supervisor.

PRINCIPLES OF ORGANIZATION

I. DEFINITION

Organization is the method of dividing up the work to provide the best channels for coordinated effort to get the agency's mission accomplished.

II. PURPOSE OF ORGANIZATION

A. To enable each employee within the organization to clearly know his responsibilities and relationships to his fellow employees and to organizational units
B. To avoid conflicts of authority and overlapping of jurisdiction.
C. To ensure teamwork.

III. BASIC CONSIDERATIONS IIN ORGANIZATIONAL PLANNING

A. The basic plans and objectives of the agency should be determined, and the organizational structure should be adapted to carry out effectively such plans and objectives.
B. The organization should be built around the major functions of the agency and not individuals or groups of individuals.

C. The organization should be sufficiently flexible to meet new and changing conditions which may be brought about from within or outside the department.
D. The organizational structure should be as simple as possible and the number of organizational units kept at a minimum.
E. The number of levels of authority should be kept at a minimum. Each additional management level lengthens the chain of authority and responsibility and increases the time for instructions to be distributed to operating levels and for decisions to be obtained from higher authority.
F. The form of organization should permit each executive to exercise maximum initiative within the limits of delegated authority.

IV. BASES FOR ORGANIZATION

A. Purpose (Examples: education, police, sanitation)
B. Process (Examples: accounting, legal, purchasing)
C. Clientele (Examples: welfare, parks, veteran)
D. Geographic (Examples: borough offices, precincts, libraries)

V. ASSIGNMENTS OF FUNCTIONS

A. Every function of the agency should be assigned to a specific organizational unit. Under normal circumstances, no single function should be assigned to more than one organizational unit.
B. There should be no overlapping, duplication, or conflict between organizational elements.
C. Line functions should be separated from staff functions, and proper emphasis should be placed on staff activities.
D. Functions which are closely related or similar should normally be assigned to a single organizational unit.
E. Functions should be properly distributed to promote balance, and to avoid overemphasis of less important functions and underemphasis of more essential functions.

VI. DELEGATION OF AUTHORITY AND RESPONSIBILITY

A. Responsibilities assigned to a specific individual or organizational unit should carry corresponding authority, and all statements of authority or limitations thereof should be as specific as possible.
B. Authority and responsibility for action should be decentralized to organizational units and individuals responsible for actual performance to the greatest extent possible, without relaxing necessary control over policy or the standardization of procedures. Delegation of authority will be consistent with decentralization of responsibility but such delegation will not divest an executive in higher authority of his overall responsibility.
C. The heads of organizational units should concern themselves with important matters and should delegate to the maximum extent details and routines performed in the ordinary course of business.
D. All responsibilities, authorities, and relationships should be stated in simple language to avoid misinterpretation.
E. Each individual or organizational unit charged with a specific responsibility will be held responsible for results.

VII. EMPLOYEE RELATIONSHIPS

    A. The employees reporting to one executive should not exceed the number which can be effectively directed and coordinated. The number will depend largely upon the scope and extent of the responsibilities of the subordinates.

    B. No person should report to more than one supervisor. Every supervisor should know who reports to him, and every employee should know to whom he reports. Channels of authority and responsibility should not be violated by staff units.

    C. Relationships between organizational units within the agency and with outside organizations and associations should be clearly stated and thoroughly understood to avoid misunderstanding.

DELEGATING

I. WHAT IS DELEGATING?
Delegating is assigning a job to an employee, giving him the authority to get that job done, and giving him the responsibility for seeing to it that the job is done.

    A. What To Delegate
       1. Routine details
       2. Jobs which may be necessary and take a lot of time, but do not have to be done by the supervisor personally (preparing reports, attending meetings, etc.)
       3. Routine decision-making (making decisions which do not require the supervisor's personal attention)

    B. What Not To Delegate
       1. Job details which are *executive functions* (setting goals, organizing employees into a good team, analyzing results so as to plan for the future)
       2. Disciplinary power (handling grievances, preparing service ratings, reprimands, etc.)
       3. Decision-making which involves large numbers of employees or other bureaus and departments
       4. Final and complete responsibility for the job done by the unit being supervised

    C. Why Delegate?
       1. To strengthen the organization by developing a greater number of skilled employees
       2. To improve the employee's performance by giving him the chance to learn more about the job, handle some responsibility, and become more interested in getting the job done
       3. To improve a supervisor's performance by relieving him of routine jobs and giving him more time for *executive functions* (planning, organizing, controlling, etc.) which cannot be delegated

II. TO WHOM TO DELEGATE
People with abilities not being used. Selection should be based on ability, not on favoritism.

REPORTS

I. **DEFINITION**
A report is an orderly presentation of factual information directed to a specific reader for a specific purpose

II. **PURPOSE**
The general purpose of a report is to bring to the reader useful and factual information about a condition or a problem. Some specific purposes of a report may be:

   A. To enable the reader to appraise the efficiency or effectiveness of a person or an operation
   B. To provide a basis for establishing standards
   C. To reflect the results of expenditures of time, effort, and money
   D. To provide a basis for developing or altering programs

III. **TYPES**

   A. Information Report: Contains facts arranged in sequence
   B. Summary (Examination) Report: Contains facts plus an analysis or discussion of the significance of the facts. Analysis may give advantages and disadvantages or give qualitative and quantitative comparisons
   C. Recommendation Report: Contains facts, analysis, and conclusion logically drawn from the facts and analysis, plus a recommendation based upon the facts, analysis, and conclusions

IV. **FACTORS TO CONSIDER BEFORE WRITING REPORT**

   A. <u>Why</u> write the report?: The purpose of the report should be clearly defined.
   B. <u>Who</u> will read the report?: What level of language should be used? Will the reader understand professional or technical language?
   C. <u>What</u> should be said?: What does the reader need or want to know about the subject?
   D. <u>How</u> should it be said?: Should the subject be presented tactfully? Convincingly? In a stimulating manner?

V. **PREPARATORY STEPS**

   A. Assemble the facts: Find out who, why, what, where, when, and how.
   B. Organize the facts: Eliminate unnecessary information
   C. Prepare an outline: Check for orderliness, logical sequence
   D. Prepare a draft: Check for correctness, clearness, completeness, conciseness, and tone
   E. Prepare it in final form: Check for grammar, punctuation, appearance

VI. **OUTLINE FOR A RECOMMENDATION REPORT**

   Is the report:
   A. Correct in information, grammar, and tone?
   B. Clear?
   C. Complete?

D. Concise?
E. Timely?
F. Worth its cost?

Will the report accomplish its purpose?

MANAGEMENT CONTROLS

I. CONTROL

What is control? What is controlled? Who controls?

The essence of control is action which adjusts operations to predetermined standards, and its basis is information in the hands of managers. Control is checking to determine whether plans are being observed and suitable progress toward stated objectives is being made, and action is taken, if necessary, to correct deviations.

We have a ready-made model for this concept of control in the automatic systems which are widely used for process control in the chemical land petroleum industries. A process control system works this way. Suppose, for example, it is desired to maintain a constant rate of flow of oil through a pipe at a predetermined or set-point value. A signal, whose strength represents the rate of flow, can be produced in a measuring device and transmitted to a control mechanism. The control mechanism, when it detects any deviation of the actual from the set-point signal, will reposition the value regulating flow rate.

II. BASIS FOR CONTROL

A process control mechanism thus acts to adjust operations to predetermined standards and does so on the basis of information it receives. In a parallel way, information reaching a manager gives him the opportunity for corrective action and is his basis for control. He cannot exercise control without such information, and he cannot do a complete job of managing without controlling.

III. POLICY

What is policy?

Policy is simply a statement of an organization's intention to act in certain ways when specified types of circumstances arise. It represents a general decision, predetermined and expressed as a principle or rule, establishing a normal pattern of conduct for dealing with given types of business events—usually recurrent. A statement is therefore useful in economizing the time of managers and in assisting them to discharge their responsibilities equitably and consistently.

Policy is not a means of control, but policy does generate the need for control.

Adherence to policies is not guaranteed nor can it be taken on faith. It has to be verified. Without verification, there is no basis for control. Policy and procedures, although closely related and interdependent to a certain extent, are not synonymous. A policy may be adopted, for example, to maintain a materials inventory not to exceed one million dollars.

A procedure for inventory control could interpret that policy and convert it into methods for keeping within that limit, with consideration, too, of possible but foreseeable expedient deviation.

IV. PROCEDURE

What is procedure?

A procedure specifically prescribes:
A. What work is to be performed by the various participants
B. Who are the respective participants
C. When and where the various steps in the different processes are to be performed
D. The sequence of operations that will insure uniform handling of recurring transactions
E. The paper that is involved, its origin, transition, and disposition

Necessary appurtenances to a procedure are:
A. Detailed organizational chart
B. Flow charts
C. Exhibits of forms, all presented in close proximity to the text of the procedure

V. BASIS OF CONTROL – INFORMATION IN THE HANDS OF MANAGERS

If the basis of control is information in the hands of managers, then reporting is elevated to a level of very considerable importance.

Types of reporting may include:
A. Special reports and routine reports
B. Written, oral, and graphic reports
C. Staff meetings
D. Conferences
E. Television screens
F. Non-receipt of information, as where management is by exception
G. Any other means whereby information is transmitted to a manager as a basis for control action

FRAMEWORK OF MANAGEMENT

I. ELEMENTS

A. Policy: It has to be verified, controlled.

B. Organization is part of the giving of an assignment. The organizational chart gives to each individual in his title, a first approximation of the nature of his assignment and orients him as being accountable to a certain individual. Organization is not in a true sense a means of control. Control is checking to ascertain whether the assignment is executed as intended and acting on the basis of that information.

C. Budgets perform three functions:
1. They present the objectives, plans, and programs of the organization in financial terms.

2. They report the progress of actual performance against these predetermined objectives, plans, and programs.
3. Like organizational charts, delegations of authority, procedures, and job descriptions, they define the assignments which have flowed from the Chief Executive. Budgets are a means of control in the respect that they report progress of actual performance against the program. They provide information which enables managers to take action directed toward bringing actual results into conformity with the program.

D. Internal Check provides in practice for the principle that the same person should not have responsibility for all phases of a transaction. This makes it clearly an aspect of organization rather than of control. Internal Check is static, or built-in.

E. Plans, Programs, Objectives
People must know what they are trying to do. Objectives fulfill this need. Without them, people may work industriously and yet, working aimlessly, accomplish little. Plans and Programs complement Objectives, since they propose how and according to what time schedule the objectives are to be reached.

F. Delegations of Authority
Among the ways we have for supplementing the titles and lines of authority of an organizational chart are delegations of authority. Delegations of authority clarify the extent of authority of individuals and in that way serve to define assignments. That they are not means of control is apparent from the very fact that wherever there has been a delegation of authority, the need for control increases. This could hardly be expected to happen if delegations of authority were themselves means of control.

II. MANAGER'S RESPONSIBILITY

Control becomes necessary whenever a manager delegates authority to a subordinate because he cannot delegate and then simply sit back and forget4 about it. A manager's accountability to his own superior has not diminished one whit as a result of delegating part of his authority to a subordinate. The manager must exercise control over actions taken under the authority so delegated. That means checking serves as a basis for possible corrective action.

Objectives, plans, programs, organizational charts, and other elements of the managerial system are not fruitfully regarded as either controls or means of control. They are pre-established standards or models of performance to which operations are adjusted by the exercise of management control. These standards or models of performance are dynamic in character for they are constantly altered, modified, or revised. Policies, organizational set-up, procedures, delegations, etc. are constantly altered but, like objectives and plans, they remain in force until they are either abandoned or revised. All of the elements (or standards or models of performance), objectives, plans, and programs, policies, organization, etc. can be regarded as a *framework of management*.

III. CONTROL TECHNIQUES

Examples of control techniques:
A. Compare against established standards
B. Compare with a similar operation
C. Compare with past operations
D. Compare with predictions of accomplishment

IV. WHERE FORECASTS FIT

Control is after-the-fact while forecasts are before. Forecasts and projections are important for setting objectives and formulating plans.

Information for aiming and planning does not have to be before-the-fact. It may be an after-the-fact analysis proving that a certain policy has been impolitic in its effect on the relation of the company or department with customer, employee, taxpayer, or stockholder; or that a certain plan is no longer practical, or that a certain procedure is unworkable.

The prescription here certainly would not be in control (in these cases, control would simply bring operations into conformity with obsolete standards) but the establishment of new standards, a new policy, a new plan, and a new procedure to be controlled too.

Information is, of course, the basis for all communication in addition to furnishing evidence to management of the need for reconstructing the framework of management.

PROBLEM SOLVING

The accepted concept in modern management for problem solving is the utilization of the following steps:

A. Identify the problem
B. Gather data
C. List possible solutions
D. Test possible solutions
E. Select the best solution
F. Put the solution into actual practice

Occasions might arise where you would have to apply the second step of gathering data before completing the first step.

You might also find that it will be necessary to work on several steps at the same time.

I. IDENTIFY THE PROBLEM

Your first step is to define as precisely as possible the problem to be solved. While this may sound easy, it is often the most difficult part of the process.

It has been said of problem solving that you are halfway to the solution when you can write out a clear statement of the problem itself.

Our job now is to get below the surface manifestations of the trouble and pinpoint the problem. This is usually accomplished by a logical analysis, by going from the general to the particular; from the obvious to the not-so-obvious cause.

Let us say that production is behind schedule. WHY? Absenteeism is high. Now, is absenteeism the basic problem to be tackled, or is it merely a symptom of low morale among the workforce? Under these circumstances, you may decide that production is not the problem; the problem is *employee morale*.

In trying to define the problem, remember there is seldom one simple reason why production is lagging, or reports are late, etc.

Analysis usually leads to the discovery that an apparent problem is really made up of several subproblems which must be attacked separately.

Another way is to limit the problem, and thereby ease the task of finding a solution, and concentrate on the elements which are within the scope of your control.

When you have gone this far, write out a tentative statement of the problem to be solved.

II. GATHER DATA

In the second step, you must set out to collect all the information that might have a bearing on the problem. Do not settle for an assumption when reasonable fact and figures are available.

If you merely go through the motions of problem-solving, you will probably shortcut the information-gathering step. Therefore, do not stack the evidence by confining your research to your own preconceived ideas.

As you collect facts, organize them in some form that helps you make sense of them and spot possible relationships between them. For example, plotting cost per unit figures on a graph can be more meaningful than a long column of figures.

Evaluate each item as you go along. Is the source material absolutely, reliable, probably reliable, or not to be trusted.

One of the best methods for gathering data is to go out and look the situation over carefully. Talk to the people on the job who are most affected by this problem.

Always keep in mind that a primary source is usually better than a secondary source of information.

III. LIST POSSIBLE SOLUTIONS

This is the creative thinking step of problem solving. This is a good time to bring into play whatever techniques of group dynamics the agency or bureau might have developed for a joint attack on problems.

Now the important thing for you to do is: Keep an open mind. Let your imagination roam freely over the facts you have collected. Jot down every possible solution that occurs to you. Resist the temptation to evaluate various proposals as you go along. List seemingly absurd ideas along with more plausible ones. The more possibilities you list during this step, the less risk you will run of settling for merely a workable, rather than the best, solution.

Keep studying the data as long as there seems to be any chance of deriving additional ideas, solutions, explanations, or patterns from it.

IV. TEST POSSIBLE SOLUTIONS

Now you begin to evaluate the possible solutions. Take pains to be objective. Up to this point, you have suspended judgment but you might be tempted to select a solution you secretly favored all along and proclaim it as the best of the lot.

The secret of objectivity in this phase is to test the possible solutions separately, measuring each against a common yardstick. To make this yardstick try to enumerate as many specific criteria as you can think of. Criteria are best phrased as questions which you ask of each possible solution. They can be drawn from these general categories:

- Suitability – Will this solution do the job?
  Will it solve the problem completely or partially?
  Is it a permanent or a stopgap solution?

- Feasibility - Will this plan work in actual practice?
  Can we afford this approach?
  How much will it cost?

- Acceptability - Will the boss go along with the changes required in the plan?
  Are we trying to drive a tack with a sledge hammer?

V. SELECT THE BEST SOLUTION

This is the area of executive decision.

Occasionally, one clearly superior solution will stand out at the conclusion of the testing process. But often it is not that simple. You may find that no one solution has come through all the tests with flying colors.

You may also find that a proposal, which flunked miserably on one of the essential tests, racked up a very high score on others.

The best solution frequently will turn out to be a combination.

Try to arrange a marriage that will bring together the strong points of one possible solution with the particular virtues of another. The more skill and imagination that you apply, the greater is the likelihood that you will come out with a solution that is not merely adequate and workable, but is the best possible under the circumstances.

VI. PUT THE SOLUTION INTO ACTUAL PRACTICE

As every executive knows, a plan which works perfectly on paper may develop all sorts of bugs when put into actual practice.

Problem-solving does not stop with selecting the solution which looks best in theory. The next step is to put the chosen solution into action and watch the results. The results may point towards modifications.

If the problem disappears when you put your solution into effect, you know you have the right solution.

If it does not disappear, even after you have adjusted your plan to cover unforeseen difficulties that turned up in practice, work your way back through the problem-solving solutions.

> Would one of them have worked better?
> Did you overlook some vital piece of data which would have given you a different slant on the whole situation? Did you apply all necessary criteria in testing solutions? If no light dawns after this much rechecking, it is a pretty good bet that you defined the problem incorrectly in the first place.

You came up with the wrong solution because you tackled the wrong problem.

Thus, step six may become step one of a new problem-solving cycle.

COMMUNICATION

I. WHAT IS COMMUNICATION?
We communicate through writing, speaking, action, or inaction. In speaking to people face-to-face, there is opportunity to judge reactions and to adjust the message. This makes the supervisory chain one of the most, and in many instances the most, important channels of communication.

In an organization, communication means keeping employees informed about the organization's objectives, policies, problems, and progress. Communication is the free interchange of information, ideas, and desirable attitudes between and among employees and between employees and management.

II. WHY IS COMMUNICATION NEEDED?

A. People have certain social needs
B. Good communication is essential in meeting those social needs
C. While people have similar basic needs, at the same time they differ from each other
D. Communication must be adapted to these individual differences

An employee cannot do his best work unless he knows why he is doing it. If he has the feeling that he is being kept in the dark about what is going on, his enthusiasm and productivity suffer.

Effective communication is needed in an organization so that employees will understand what the organization is trying to accomplish; and how the work of one unit contributes to or affects the work of other units in the organization and other organizations.

III. HOW IS COMMUNICATION ACHIEVED?

Communication flows downward, upward, sideways.

A. Communication may come from top management down to employees. This is downward communication.

   Some means of downward communication are:
   1. Training (orientation, job instruction, supervision, public relations, etc.)
   2. Conferences
   3. Staff meetings
   4. Policy statements
   5. Bulletins
   6. Newsletters
   7. Memoranda
   8. Circulation of important letters

   In downward communication, it is important that employees be informed in advance of changes that will affect them.

B. Communications should also be developed so that the ideas, suggestions, and knowledge of employees will flow upward to top management.

   Some means of upward communication are:
   1. Personal discussion conferences
   2. Committees
   3. Memoranda
   4. Employees suggestion program
   5. Questionnaires to be filled in giving comments and suggestions about proposed actions that will affect field operations.

   Upward communication requires that management be willing to listen, to accept, and to make changes when good ideas are present. Upward communication succeeds when there is no fear of punishment for speaking out or lack of interest at the top. Employees will share their knowledge and ideas with management when interest is shown and recognition is given.

C. The advantages of downward communication:
   1. It enables the passing down of orders, policies, and plans necessary to the continued operation of the station.
   2. By making information available, it diminishes the fears and suspicions which result from misinformation and misunderstanding.
   3. It fosters the pride people want to have in their work when they are told of good work.
   4. It improves the morale and stature of the individual to be *in the know*.

5. It helps employees to understand, accept, and cooperate with changes when they know about them in advance.

D. The advantages of upward communication:
1. It enables the passing upward of information, attitudes, and feelings.
2. It makes it easier to find out how ready people are to receive downward communication.
3. It reveals the degree to which the downward communication is understood and accepted.
4. It helps to satisfy the basic social needs.
5. It stimulates employees to participate in the operation of their organization.
6. It encourage employees to contribute ideas for improving the efficiency and economy of operations.
7. It helps to solve problem situations before they reach the explosion point.

IV. WHY DOES COMMUNICATION FAIL?

A. The technical difficulties of conveying information clearly
B. The emotional content of communication which prevents complete transmission
C. The fact that there is a difference between what management needs to say, what it wants to day, and what it does say
D. The fact that there is a difference between what employees would like to say, what they think is profitable or safe to say, and what they do say

V. HOW TO IMPROVE COMMUNICATION

As a supervisor, you are a key figure in communication. To improve as a communicator, you should:
A. Know: Knowing your subordinates will help you to recognize and work with individual differences.
B. Like: If you like those who work for you and those for whom you work, this will foster the kind of friendly, warm, work atmosphere that will facilitate communication.
C. Trust: Showing a sincere desire to communicate will help to develop the mutual trust and confidence which are essential to the free flow of communication.
D. Tell: Tell your subordinates and superiors *what's doing*. Tell your subordinates *why* as well as *how*.
E. Listen: By listening, you help others to talk and you create good listeners. Don't forget that listening implies action.
F. Stimulate: Communication has to be stimulated and encouraged. Be receptive to ideas and suggestions and motivate your people so that each member of the team identifies himself with the job at hand.
G. Consult: The most effective way of consulting is to let your people participate, insofar as possible, in developing determinations which affect them or their work.

VI. HOW TO DETERMINE WHETHER YOU ARE GETTING ACROSS

A. Check to see that communication is received and understood
B. Judge this understanding by actions rather than words
C. Adapt or vary communication, when necessary
D. Remember that good communication cannot cure all problems

VII. THE KEY ATTITUDE

Try to see things from the other person's point of view. By doing this, you help to develop the permissive atmosphere and the shared confidence and understanding which are essential to effective two-way communication.

Communication is a two-way process:
A. The basic purpose of any communication is to get action.
B. The only way to get action is through acceptance.
C. In order to get acceptance, communication must be humanly satisfying as well as technically efficient.

HOW ORDERS AND INSTRUCTIONS SHOULD BE GIVEN

I. CHARACTERISTICS OF GOOD ORDERS AND INSTRUCTIONS

   A. Clear
      Orders should be definite as to
      —What is to be done
      —Who is to do it
      —When it is to be done
      —Where it is to be done
      —How it is to be done

   B. Concise
      Avoid wordiness. Orders should be brief and to the point.

   C. Timely
      Instructions and orders should be sent out at the proper time and not too long in advance of expected performance.

   D. Possibility of Performance
      Orders should be feasible:
      1. Investigate before giving orders
      2. Consult those who are to carry out instructions before formulating and issuing them

   E. Properly Directed
      Give the orders to the people concerned. Do not send orders to people who are not concerned. People who continually receive instructions that are not applicable to them get in the habit of neglecting instructions generally.

   F. Reviewed Before Issuance
      Orders should be reviewed before issuance:
      1. Test them by putting yourself in the position of the recipient
      2. If they involve new procedures, have the persons who are to do the work review them for suggestions.

   G. Reviewed After Issuance
      Persons who receive orders should be allowed to raise questions and to point out unforeseen consequences of orders.

H. Coordinated
Orders should be coordinated so that work runs smoothly.

I. Courteous
Make a request rather than a demand. There is no need to continually call attention to the fact that you are the boss.

J. Recognizable as an Order
Be sure that the order is recognizable as such.

K. Complete
Be sure recipient has knowledge and experience sufficient to carry out order. Give illustrations and examples.

A DEPARTMENTAL PERSONNEL OFFICE IS RESPONSIBLE FOR THE FOLLOWING FUNCTIONS

1. Policy
2. Personnel Programs
3. Recruitment and Placement
4. Position Classification
5. Salary and Wage Administration
6. Employee performance Standards and Evaluation
7. Employee Relations
8. Disciplinary Actions and Separations
9. Health and Safety
10. Staff Training and Development
11. Personnel Records, Procedures, and Reports
12. Employee Services
13. Personnel Research

SUPERVISION

I. LEADERSHIP

All leadership is based essentially on authority. This comes from two sources: It is received from higher management or it is earned by the supervisor through his methods of supervision. Although effective leadership has always depended upon the leader's using his authority in such a way as to appeal successfully to the motives of the people supervised, the conditions for making this appeal are continually changing. The key to today's problem of leadership is flexibility and resourcefulness on the part of the leader in meeting changes in conditions as they occur.

Three basic approaches to leadership are generally recognized:

A. The Authoritarian Approach
   1. The methods and techniques used in this approach emphasize the *I* in leadership and depend primarily on the formal authority of the leader. This authority is sometimes exercised in a hardboiled manner and sometimes in a benevolent

manner, but in either case the dominating role of the leader is reflected in the thinking, planning, and decisions of the group.
2. Group results are to a large degree dependent on close supervision by the leader. Usually, the individuals in the group will not show a high degree of initiative or acceptance of responsibility and their capacity to grow and develop probably will not be fully utilized. The group may react with resentment or submission, depending upon the manner and skill of the leader in using his authority.
3. This approach develops as a natural outgrowth of the authority that goes with the leader's job and his feeling of sole responsibility for getting the job done. It is relatively easy to use and does not require must resourcefulness.
4. The use of this approach is effective in times of emergencies, in meeting close deadline as a final resort, in settling some issues, in disciplinary matters, and with dependent individuals and groups.

B. The Laissez-Faire or Let 'em Alone Approach
1. This approach generally is characterized by an avoidance of leadership responsibility by the leader. The activities of the group depend largely on the choice of its members rather than the leader.
2. Group results probably will be poor. Generally, there will be disagreements over petty things, bickering, and confusion. Except for a few aggressive people, individuals will not show much initiative and growth and development will be retarded. There may be a tendency for informal leaders to take over leadership of the group.
3. This approach frequently results from the leader's dislike of responsibility, from his lack of confidence, from failure of other methods to work, from disappointment or criticism. It is usually the easiest of the three to use and requires both understanding and resourcefulness on the part of the leader.
4. This approach is occasionally useful and effective, particularly in forcing dependent individuals or groups to rely on themselves, to give someone a chance to save face by clearing his own difficulties, or when action should be delayed temporarily for good cause.

C. The Democratic Approach
1. The methods and techniques used in this approach emphasize the *we* in leadership and build up the responsibility of the group to attain its objectives. Reliance is placed largely on the earned authority of the leader.
2. Group results are likely to be good because most of the job motives of the people will be satisfied. Cooperation and teamwork, initiative, acceptance of responsibility, and the individual's capacity for growth probably will show a high degree of development.
3. This approach grows out of a desire or necessity of the leader to find ways to appeal effectively to the motivation of his group. It is the best approach to build up inside the person a strong desire to cooperate and apply himself to the job. It is the most difficult to develop, and requires both understanding and resourcefulness on the part of the leader.
4. The value of this approach increases over a long period where sustained efficiency and development of people are important. It may not be fully effective in all situations, however, particularly when there is not sufficient time to use it properly or where quick decisions must be made.

All three approaches are used by most leaders and have a place in supervising people. The extent of their use varies with individual leaders, with some using one approach predominantly. The leader who uses these three approaches, and varies their use with time and circumstance, is probably the most effective. Leadership which is used predominantly with a democratic approach requires more resourcefulness on the part of the leader but offers the greatest possibilities in terms of teamwork and cooperation.

The one best way of developing democratic leadership is to provide a real sense of participation on the part of the group, since this satisfies most of the chief job motives. Although there are many ways of providing participation, consulting as frequently as possible with individuals and groups on things that affect them seems to offer the most in building cooperation and responsibility. Consultation takes different forms, but it is most constructive when people feel they are actually helping in finding the answers to the problems on the job.

There are some requirements of leaders in respect to human relations which should be considered in their selection and development. Generally, the leader should be interested in working with other people, emotionally stable, self-confident, and sensitive to the reactions of others. In addition, his viewpoint should be one of getting the job done through people who work cooperatively in response to his leadership. He should have a knowledge of individual and group behavior, but, most important of all, he should work to combine all of these requirements into a definite, practical skill in leadership.

II. NINE POINTS OF CONTRAST BETWEEN *BOSS* AND *LEADER*

   A. The boss drives his men; the leader coaches them.
   B. The boss depends on authority; the leader on good will.
   C. The boss inspires fear; the leader inspires enthusiasm.
   D. The boss says I; the leader says *We*.
   E. The boss says *Get here on time*; the leader gets there ahead of time.
   F. The boss fixes the blame for the breakdown; the leader fixes the breakdown.
   G. The boss knows how it is done; the leader shows how.
   H. The boss makes work a drudgery; the leader makes work a game.
   I. The boss says *Go*; the leader says *Let's go*.

EMPLOYEE MORALE

Employee morale is the way employees feel about each other, the organization or unit in which they work, and the work they perform.

I. SOME WAYS TO DEVELOP AND MAINTAIN GOOD EMPLYEE MORALE

   A. Give adequate credit and praise when due.
   B. Recognize importance of all jobs and equalize load with proper assignments, always giving consideration to personality differences and abilities.
   C. Welcome suggestions and do not have an *all-wise* attitude. Request employees' assistance in solving problems and use assistants when conducting group meetings on certain subjects.
   D. Properly assign responsibilities and give adequate authority for fulfillment of such assignments.

E. Keep employees informed about matters that affect them.
F. Criticize and reprimand employees privately.
G. Be accessible and willing to listen.
H. Be fair.
I. Be alert to detect training possibilities so that you will not miss an opportunity to help each employee do a better job, and if possible with less effort on his part.
J. Set a good example.
K. Apply the golden rule.

II. SOME INDICATIONS OF GOOD MORALE

A. Good quality of work
B. Good quantity
C. Good attitude of employees
D. Good discipline
E. Teamwork
F. Good attendance
G. Employee participation

MOTIVATION

DRIVES

A drive, stated simply, is a desire or force which causes a person to do or say certain things. These are some of the most usual drives and some of their identifying characteristics recognizable in people motivated by such drives:

A. Security (desire to provide for the future)
Always on time for work
Works for the same employer for many years
Never takes unnecessary chances
Seldom resists doing what he is told

B. Recognition (desire to be rewarded for accomplishment)
Likes to be asked for his opinion
Becomes very disturbed when he makes a mistake
Does things to attract attention
Likes to see his name in print

C. Position (desire to hold certain status in relation to others)
Boasts about important people he knows
Wants to be known as a key man
Likes titles
Demands respect
Belongs to clubs, for prestige

D. Accomplishment (desire to get things done)
   Complains when things are held up
   Likes to do things that have tangible results
   Never lies down on the job
   Is proud of turning out good work

E. Companionship (desire to associate with other people)
   Likes to work with others
   Tells stories and jokes
   Indulges in horseplay
   Finds excuses to talk to others on the job

F. Possession (desire to collect and hoard objects)
   Likes to collect things
   Puts his name on things belonging to him
   Insists on the same location

Supervisors may find that identifying the drives of employees is a helpful step toward motivating them to self-improvement and better job performance. For example: An employee's job performance is below average. His supervisor, having previously determined that the employee is motivated by a drive for security, suggests that taking training courses will help the employee to improve, advance, and earn more money. Since earning more money can be a step toward greater security, the employee's drive for security would motivate him to take the training suggested by the supervisor. In essence, this is the process of charting an employee's future course by using his motivating drives to positive advantage.

EMPLOYEE PARTICIPATION

I. WHAT IS PARTICIPATION

Employee participation is the employee's giving freely of his time, skill, and knowledge to an extent which cannot be obtained by demand.

II. WHY IS IT IMPORTANT?

The supervisor's responsibility is to get the job done through people. A good supervisor gets the job done through people who work willingly and well. The participation of employees is important because:

A. Employees develop a greater sense of responsibility when they share in working out operating plans and goals.
B. Participation provides greater opportunity and stimulation for employees to learn, and to develop their ability.
C. Participation sometimes provides better solutions to problems because such solutions may combine the experience and knowledge of interested employees who want the solutions to work.
D. An employee or group may offer a solution which the supervisor might hesitate to make for fear of demanding too much.

E. Since the group wants to make the solution work, they exert pressure in a constructive way on each other.
F. Participation usually results in reducing the need for close supervision.

II. HOW MAY SUPERVISORS OBTAIN IT?

Participation is encouraged when employees feel that they share some responsibility for the work and that their ideas are sincerely wanted and valued. Some ways of obtaining employee participation are:

A. Conduct orientation programs for new employees to inform them about the organization and their rights and responsibilities as employees.
B. Explain the aims and objectives of the agency. On a continuing basis, be sure that the employees know what these aims and objectives are.
C. Share job successes and responsibilities and give credit for success.
D. Consult with employees, both as individuals and in groups, about things that affect them.
E. Encourage suggestions for job improvements. Help employees to develop good suggestions. The suggestions can bring them recognition. The city's suggestion program offers additional encouragement through cash awards.

The supervisor who encourages employee participation is not surrendering his authority. He must still make decisions and initiate action, and he must continue to be ultimately responsible for the work of those he supervises. But, through employee participation, he is helping his group to develop greater ability and a sense of responsibility while getting the job done faster and better.

STEPS IN HANDLING A GRIEVANCE

1. Get the Facts
   a. Listen sympathetically
   b. Let him talk himself out
   c. Get his story straight
   d. Get his point of view
   e. Don't argue with him
   f. Give him plenty of time
   g. Conduct the interview privately
   h. Don't try to shift the blame or pass the buck

2. Consider the Facts
   a. Consider the employee's viewpoint
   b. How will the decision affect similar cases
   c. Consider each decision as a possible precedent
   d. Avoid snap judgments—don't jump to conclusions

3. Make or Get a Decision
   a. Frame an effective counter-proposal
   b. Make sure it is fair to all
   c. Have confidence in your judgment
   d. Be sure you can substantiate your decision

4. Notify the Employee of Your Decision
Be sure he is told; try to convince him that the decision is fair and just.

5. Take Action When Needed and If Within Your Authority
Otherwise, tell employee that the matter will be called to the attention of the proper person or that nothing can be done, and why it cannot.

6. Follow through to see that the desired result is achieved.

7. Record key facts concerning the complaint and the action taken.

8. Leave the way open to him to appeal your decision to a higher authority.

9. Report all grievances to your superior, whether they are appealed or not.

DISCIPLINE

Discipline is training that develops self-control, orderly conduct, and efficiency.

To discipline does not necessarily mean to punish.

To discipline does mean to train, to regulate, and to govern conduct.

I. THE DISCIPLINARY INTERVIEW

Most employees sincerely want to do what is expected of them. In other words, they are self-disciplined. Some employees, however, fail to observe established rules and standards, and disciplinary action by the supervisor is required.

The primary purpose of disciplinary action is to improve conduct without creating dissatisfaction, bitterness, or resentment in the process.

Constructive disciplinary action is more concerned with causes and explanations of breaches of conduct than with punishment. The disciplinary interview is held to get at the causes of apparent misbehavior and to motivate better performance in the future.

It is important that the interview be kept on an impersonal a basis as possible. If the supervisor lets the interview descend to the plane of an argument, it loses its effectiveness.

II. PLANNING THE INTERVIEW

Get all pertinent facts concerning the situation so that you can talk in specific terms to the employee.

Review the employee's record, appraisal ratings, etc.

Consider what you know about the temperament of the employee. Consider your attitude toward the employee. Remember that the primary requisite of disciplinary action is fairness.

Don't enter upon the interview when angry.

Schedule the interview for a place which is private and out of hearing of others.

III. CONDUCTING THE INTERVIEW

   A. Make an effort to establish accord.
   B. Question the employee about the apparent breach of discipline. Be sure that the question is not so worded as to be itself an accusation.
   C. Give the employee a chance to tell his side of the story. Give him ample opportunity to talk.
   D. Use understanding—listening except where it is necessary to ask a question or to point out some details of which the employee may not be aware. If the employee misrepresents facts, make a plain, accurate statement of the facts, but don't argue and don't engage in personal controversy.
   E. Listen and try to understand the reasons for the employee's (mis)conduct. First of all, don't assume that there has been a breach of discipline. Evaluate the employee's reasons for his conduct in the light of his opinions and feelings concerning the consistency and reasonableness of the standards which he was expected to follow. Has the supervisor done his part in explaining the reasons for the rule? Was the employee's behavior unintentional or deliberate? Does he think he had real reasons for his actions? What new facts is he telling? Do the facts justify his actions? What causes, other than those mentioned, could have stimulated the behavior?
   F. After listening to the employee's version of the situation, and if censure of his actions is warranted, the supervisor should proceed with whatever criticism is justified. Emphasis should be placed on future improvement rather than exclusively on the employee's failure to measure up to expected standards of job conduct.
   G. Fit the criticism to the individual. With one employee, a word of correction may be all that is required.
   H. Attempt to distinguish between unintentional error and deliberate misbehavior. An error due to ignorance requires training and not censure.
   I. Administer criticism in a controlled, even tone of voice, never in anger. Make it clear that you are acting as an agent of the department. In general, criticism should refer to the job or the employee's actions and not to the person. Criticism of the employee's work is not an attack on the individual.
   J. Be sure the interview does not destroy the employee's self-confidence. Mention his good qualities and assure him that you feel confident that he can improve his performance.
   K. Wherever possible, before the employee leaves the interview, satisfy him that the incident is closed, that nothing more will be said on the subject unless the offense is repeated.

www.ingramcontent.com/pod-product-compliance
Lightning Source LLC
Chambersburg PA
CBHW081800300426
44116CB00014B/2193